50 Hikes in the Lower Hudson Valley

Near Anthony's Nose on the Camp Smith Trail

50 *Hikes*

In the Lower Hudson Valley

Hikes and Walks from Westchester County to Albany

STELLA J. GREEN AND H. NEIL ZIMMERMAN

Backcountry Guides

Woodstock, Vermont

AN INVITATION TO THE READER
With time, access points may change, and trails, signs, and landmarks referred to in this book may be altered. If you find that such changes have occurred, please let the authors and publisher know so that corrections can be made in future editions. Other comments and suggestions are also welcome. Address all correspondence to:

Editor, 50 Hikes™ Series
Backcountry Guides
P.O. Box 748
Woodstock, VT 05091

LIBRARY OF CONGRESS CATALOGING-IN-PUBLICATION DATA

Green, Stella J., 1926–
  50 Hikes in the lower Hudson Valley : hikes and walks from Westchester County to Albany / Stella Green and H. Neil Zimmerman.
  p. cm.–(Fifty hikes series)
  Includes index.
  ISBN 0-88150-557-9
  1. Hiking–Hudson River Valley (N.Y. and N.J.)–Guidebooks. 2. Hudson River Valley (N.Y. and N.J.)–Guidebooks. I. Title: Fifty hikes in the lower Hudson Valley. II. Zimmerman, H. Neil. III. Title. IV. Series.

GV199.42.H83 G74 2002
796.51'09747'3–dc21   2001058981

Maps on pages 91, 113, 145, 178, 187, 192, 236, 248, 257, 271, and 275 by Richard Widhu; all other maps by Mapping Specialists Ltd., Madison, Wisconsin

Cover photograph of the Hudson River Valley by James Bleecker

Published by Backcountry Guides, a division of The Countryman Press, P.O. Box 748, Woodstock, Vermont 05091

Distributed by W.W. Norton & Company, Inc., 500 Fifth Avenue, New York, NY 10110

Printed in the United States of America

10 9 8 7 6 5 4 3 2

This book is dedicated those who work so tirelessly to protect and preserve the Hudson Valley.

Thanks go to the Harriman, Rockefeller, Osborn, Perkins, Ogden, Smiley and Fahnestock families who assembled, preserved and often donated great tracts of land to the public, forming the core of our hiking areas. In the most recent two decades, these public open spaces have been significantly augmented by land purchases and easements coordinated by Scenic Hudson and The Open Space Institute. These two organizations, funded by The Lila Acheson and DeWitt Wallace Fund for the Hudson Highlands, have helped preserve at least 60,000 acres. Support from the Wallace Fund, established by the founders of Reader's Digest, continues to insure that our beloved Hudson Valley will long remain a prime destination for those of us who treasure and enjoy the great outdoors.

50 Hikes at a Glance

HIKE	COUNTY
1. Mianus River Gorge	Westchester
2. Ward Pound Ridge/Leatherman's Cave	Westchester
3. Rockefeller State Park Preserve	Westchester
4. Teatown Lake Reservation	Westchester
5. Old Croton Aqueduct State Historic Park	Westchester
6. Blue Mountain Reservation	Westchester
7. Anthony's Nose and the Camp Smith Trail	Westchester
8. The Osborn Loop	Putnam
9. Breakneck-Undercliff Loop	Putnam
10. Fishkill Ridge Conservation Area	Dutchess
11. Hubbard-Perkins: Round Hill	Putnam
12. Hubbard-Perkins: Jordan Pond	Putnam
13. Hidden Lake Loop	Putnam
14. Pawling Nature Reserve	Dutchess
15. Dutchess County Backpack	Dutchess
16. Hook Mountain	Rockland
17. The Tors, High and Low	Rockland
18. Southern Ledges of Harriman	Rockland
19. Ladentown Ramble (or Breakneck Mountain Loop)	Rockland
20. Kerson Nurian Revisited	Orange
21. Rockhouse Loop	Rockland/Orange
22. Iron Mine Walk	Orange
23. Black Mountain	Orange
24. Anthony Wayne Loop	Orange
25. Dunderberg and the Timp	Orange
26. Bear Mountain	Orange

DISTANCE (miles)	DIFFICULTY	RISE (feet)	TIME (hours)	VIEWS	KIDS	CAMP	X-C SKI	FALLS	SHUTTLE	NOTES
.00	E	1,500	2.00	Y			Y			Closed in winter, old mine
.50	E	700	2.25	Y	Y	Y				Historic attraction, nature center
.00	E	300	3.00	Y		Y				Carriage roads, lake, exhibits
.40	M	750	4.00	Y	Y	Y				Nature center, wildflower sanctuary
.50	E	Min.	3.00	Y		Y		Y		Level, bikes okay, museum
.00	E/M	750	3.00	Y	Y	Y				Major biking area
.20	M	1,000	2.50	Y	Y				O	Some steep sections
.50	M	1,000	3.50	Y	Y					Steep at start, carriage roads
.70	S	2,000	5.50	Y						Craggy trails, views, history
.00	M/S	1,700	3.00	Y						Newly opened area
.50	M	1,100	4.00	Y						Newly opened area
.60	M/E	300	3.00							Farm fields, stream side walk, lake
.50/.30	M/E	500	3.00/1.50	Y		Y				Historic, mining, railbed
.20	M	700	4.00	Y			Y			Appalachian Trail, lightly used area
.60	S	2,300	Days	Y	Y			Y		Swimming
.00/.00+	M/S	1,200	6.00	Y					O	Spectacular ridge
.50	M	850	3.00	Y	Y					Rock scramble
.00	M/S	1,000	7.00	Y			Y			Varied terrain
.75	M	900	3.75							Deep woods
.25	M	1,000	4.50	Y		P				Massive boulders, open slabs, mines
.30/.80	M	1,000/800	4.00/3.00	Y	Y					Historic mines
.00	M	1,050	5.00							Historic mines, varied terrain
.75	M	900	2.50	Y	Y	P				Open summit, varied terrain
.80	M	1,000	4.00	Y		P				Ridge walk
.00	M/S	1,200	6.00	Y						Open summit
.75	M/S	1,127	2.50	Y	Y					Major destination, historic inn, carousel, major activity center

50 Hikes at a Glance

HIKE	COUNTY
27. Sterling Ridge to the Fire Tower	Orange
28. Mount Peter to Arden on the AT	Orange
29. Indian Hill Loop	Orange
30. Summit of Schunemunk	Orange
31. Schunemunk Loop	Orange
32. Mighty Storm King	Orange
33. Black Rock Forest–Northern Loop	Orange
34. Black Rock Forest–Southern Ledges	Orange
35. Shawaungunk Ridge	Ulster
36. Verkeerder Kill Falls Loop	Ulster
37. Minnewaska Loop	Ulster
38. The Trapps to Gertrude's Nose	Ulster
39. Trapps Gateway Center Loop	Ulster
40. Duck Pond Scramble in Mohonk	Ulster
41. Mills-Norrie State Parks	Dutchess
42. Black Creek Forest Preserve	Ulster
43. Shaupeneak Ridge	Ulster
44. Stissing Mountain	Dutchess
45. An Ascent of Slide Mountain	Ulster
46. Olana	Columbia
47. Huntersfield State Forest	Green/Schoharie
48. South Taconic Trail	Columbia/Dutchess/Mass.
49. Vroman's Nose	Schoharie
50. Thatcher Park and Indian Ladder	Albany

DISTANCE (miles)	DIFFICULTY	RISE (feet)	TIME (hours)	VIEWS	KIDS	CAMP	X-C SKI	FALLS	SHUTTLE	NOTES
60/60	M	500/800	3.00/4.50	Y	Y				O	Fire tower
30/70	S	3,500/1,000	6.50/5.00	Y		P		Y	Y	Cross-ridges walk
25	M	900	3.00	Y	Y					Historic furnace
50	S	1300	5.00	Y					O	Attractive slabs, open summit
30	S	2,200	5.50	Y			Y			Open summit, megaliths
00	M/S	1,200	5.50	Y	Y					Open summit, major destination
50	M	600	3.50	Y	Y					Lightly used area
00	S	1,300	6.50	Y						Varied terrain, peaceful
15	M	1,100	3.25	Y			Y	Y		Cascade, interesting rock outcrops
00	S	900	4.50	Y				Y		Major falls, open slabs & summit, views
75	S	1,000	5.00	Y			Y			Streamside walk, open slabs
15	S	800	6.00	Y						Open slabs, old homestead & spring
75	E	500	2.50	Y	Y		Y			Carriage roads, visitor center, cliffs with climbers
00	S	1,000	4.00	Y						Rock scrambles, Mohonk Mountain House and Lake
00	E	Min.	3.00	Y	Y		Y			Formal estate, environmental center
50	E	300	1.00	Y	Y		Y			Hudson River, streamside walk, vernal pools, peaceful
25	M	1,350	2.50	Y	Y		Y			Varied terrain, falls, lake
00	M	950	4.00	Y	Y					Fire tower
50	S	1,800	5.00	Y	Y	P	Y			Catskill high point 4,180 feet
00	E	300	3.00	Y	Y		Y			Leisurely, historic castle
00	M	1,000	2.50	Y	Y	P				Remote
40	S	2,000	7.00	Y				Y	Y	Ridge walk, major falls
00	E	760	1.00	Y	Y					Interesting geological feature
50	E	Min.	0.75		Y		Y	Y		Spectacular gorge

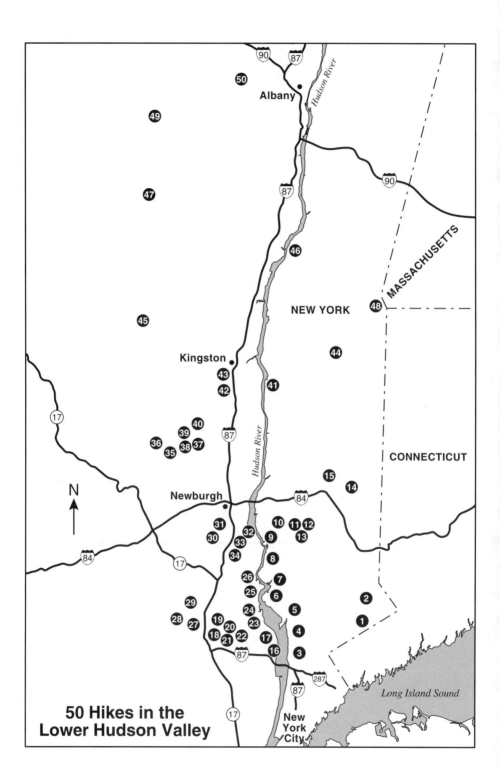

**50 Hikes in the
Lower Hudson Valley**

CONTENTS

Acknowledgments

Creating this new guide has been a joy. Although we have been hiking in this area for several decades, writing the book and pumping our friends for ideas and suggestions has led us to some lovely places we had overlooked previously. Now we invite you, the reader, to explore with us an area of exceptional beauty, peace, and diversity.

Helping us with our task in bringing this guide to life were friends, associates, and park officials. Thank you Todd Baldwin, Roderick Christie, Jane and Walter Daniels, Jakob Franke, Robert Green, Brian Good-man, Peter Heckler, Beth Herr, Ed Hicks, Joan James, John Jurasek, Seth McKee, Rachel Madison, Stephen Nickerson, Michael Pogue, Ron Samuelson, Malcolm Spector, and Edward Walsh.

We are especially indebted to our friend Barbara McMartin, who coauthored *50 Hikes in the Hudson Valley* (now out of print). Barbara, who has now moved full-time to the Adirondacks, offered sound advice, much encouragement, and kind permission to use some of her writings on this area. Without you, Barbara, this book would not have come to fruition.

Introduction

The Hudson River is a 350-mile-long corridor of history and a monument to our natural heritage. For half its length the Hudson is an estuary—a place where seawater blends with fresh water, creating one of the most productive ecosystems on earth. This territory is the spawning ground and nursery for 207 species of fish, and it supports thousands of acres of tidal wetlands.

Settled by Europeans more than 350 years ago, and much earlier by native peoples, the Hudson Valley has provided generations of Americans with rich farmland and been a vital source of strength and inspiration for artistic expression in painting, poetry, and literature.

Southeastern New York State is dominated by the Hudson River, which flows past the wonders of its cities and industries. At the same time, the river touches some of the state's wilder lands, where the hiker can quickly escape the centers of civilization that dot the Hudson's banks. The wilderness at the Hudson's Adirondack headwaters needs no introduction. Some of the wild lands near the Hudson's southern cities are well known, whereas others are almost undiscovered. This guide includes a variety of day hikes that will introduce you to the best of southeastern New York's wild lands not far removed from the Hudson.

The first visitors to the Hudson were mightily impressed by the fortresslike rocks of the Palisades, the rugged Hudson Highlands, and the mysteries of the distant blue Catskills. It is in these rocky hills and mountains bordering the Hudson that most of the hikes described in this guide take place. The book leads you to the northern Palisades, the Ramapos, the Highlands, the isolated lump of Schunemunk, the white cliffs of the Shawangunks, and the high point of the Catskills. It reaches east to the Taconics and north to the fortress of the Helderbergs. It takes you to the tops of this series of ranges, which stand as if designed to give the best possible views of their succession and of the Hudson and Mohawk Valleys.

THE HISTORY OF THE ROCKS AND MOUNTAINS

The drama of the southeastern New York landscape has a second story in the very rocks themselves. From the resistant limestone of the Helderberg Escarpment to the dissected plateau of the Catskills and into the crystalline Hudson Highlands that lie beside the younger folded rocks of the Appalachians, you can see the parts of the puzzle that make up the region's geological history.

The Shawangunks are close to the Taconics in age, although their evolution is more related to the Catskills. Extensive sands and quartz-rich gravels were deposited in a shallow sea during the Silurian period, about 450 million years ago. Much later the resulting sandstones and conglomerates were uplifted and differentially eroded.

The Hudson Highlands to the south are

The Alpine boat basin on the Hudson

a series of granitic and metamorphic rocks. They were intruded and metamorphosed at great depth more than a billion years ago. Later, during the Taconic orogeny, the rocks were folded, faulted, and uplifted to their present form.

HIKING IN SOUTHEASTERN NEW YORK

This guide offers the hiker an excellent range of opportunities. For residents of southern New York State, the special appeal of most of these trails is their proximity to New York City. The majority of the trailheads lie within two hours of the city.

The area offers many more walks than are described in this book, and references to some of the best of the other hiking guides are given in the bibliography. Social hikers can find many walking groups that offer regularly scheduled trips to help them discover other hikes and prepare for outdoor adventures. A list from the New York–New Jersey Trail Conference (NY–NJTC) can put you in touch with many of these groups. Organizations such as the Catskill 3500 Club, the Appalachian Mountain Club, the Sierra Club, and chapters of the Adirondack Mountain Club all offer outing schedules for a variety of hikes. Each organization, coordinated by NY–NJTC, also fills a secondary role by providing mechanisms for the hiker to return something to the land. With programs of trail maintenance, conservation, planning to prevent overuse, and education to promote wise use, these organizations help protect our wild lands.

Some routes are never heavily used. Others are, but even here, early-spring, winter, and late-fall trips will mix solitude with expanded vistas in ways sure to please any wilderness seeker.

The gentler hills on the east side of the

Hudson were settled early. The farms are shrinking today, because of development that has grown to fill much of the open land. In contrast, some forests on the west side of the Hudson have been preserved as the valley's water source and as part of the New York State Forest Preserve, whose unique state constitutional protection ensures they will remain "forever wild."

Almost all the lands traversed by today's trails were once settled and used by farmers, miners, loggers, and romantics. Their presence inevitably is reflected in the lore that surrounds the trails, and we explore that history as well as the natural scene. Although this guide serves as an invitation to the mountain ranges and valleys of the southern part of the state, it cannot even begin to probe the vast history that enlivens each route. For further information, consult the bibliography at the end of this book.

BEFORE YOU START

There is an enormous range of hikes in this guide, from easy strolls to strenuous climbs. The information given about distance, time, and elevation change should help you gauge the difficulty of each hike and your preparedness. Almost all hikes follow clearly marked trails, although this changes occasionally. The greatest source of confusion seems to be the constant revisions in trail designation for the more southerly trails, where interconnecting routes and color changes in the markings can be confusing.

Preparedness is key to your enjoyment, and you should be suitably equipped before you start. Knowledge should include understanding the use of map and compass to complement the information in this guide. If you are new to hiking, it is definitely a good idea to join a hiking group

and learn from those with experience. The more background you have in the woods, the greater your safety as well as your enjoyment. Do not count on the following summary of what you need to know to prepare you for every situation you're likely to encounter. This guide includes excursions for all ranges of experience, but this introduction is not a primer for beginning hikers. Treat it instead as a checklist and a set of reminders.

THE WEATHER

Whenever possible, wait for a sunny day, as the hiking pleasures are much greater and the problems more predictable. But even on sunny days you should be prepared for changes and extremes. It can be 20 or more degrees colder on the mountaintops of the Catskills than in the nearby Hudson Valley, 30 degrees colder than in the city. Storms can and do appear with little warning.

The weather can often be too hot in summer for strenuous hikes. Many people prefer walking in southern New York State in late fall and early spring, but these are the most changeable times. Extremes from heat waves to snowstorms can occur. But the rewards of fewer people and expanded distant vistas in the leafless season make it worthwhile.

Walking in the winter months and colder weather at any time of the year is wonderful and brings its own rewards. Vistas are more easily seen when leaves are down from the trees, those annoying blackflies and mosquitoes are missing, and other walkers in the woods are fewer. However, the winter hiker needs to take additional precautions. Always remember to file a "flight plan" with a stay-at-home friend, be prepared to shorten your planned hike if necessary, and carry additional clothing and emergency supplies. In extreme weather conditions when snow is on the ground, it is recommended to walk out and back on the same route because the way ahead may contain unexpected challenges and surprises. In colder weather, hike with a group of four or more—one person to stay with anyone injured on the trail and two to seek help. In extreme cold or in windy conditions, watch your companions for signs of hypothermia and/or frostbite. If the snow is more than 8 inches deep, you may need snowshoes; if the trail is icy, crampons. There may be little or no snow in the city when places like Harriman Park could easily still have a foot or more of the white stuff on the ground.

PREPARATIONS

Even with the best of forecasts, plan for the unexpected. Possible changes in temperature require that you should take extra clothing, especially rain gear. Experiment with layers of light, waterproof gear. In the mountains you will want a layer of wool, even if, in summer, it is only a sweater in your day pack. Places to swim are noted on these hikes, so take along a bathing suit.

Many of the trails are as smooth as a sidewalk; some are as rubble-filled as a rock pile. For most of these hikes a sturdy pair of well-broken-in, over-the-ankle boots is essential. Lightweight boots lined with Gore-Tex® or similar material are wonderful; they give good traction and support, and they are all you need, except when hiking on the higher mountain trails in winter or early spring. Wear two pairs of socks, an inner lightweight pair and a heavy outer pair that's at least partly wool.

Carry a sturdy day pack large enough to hold your lunch, plenty of water, and a few necessities. The separate pouches along the sides of our packs always contain a whistle, a waterproof case with dry matches, a jackknife, lip balm, and a space blanket. We have used them all.

Carry a map of the trail and a compass, a flashlight in case you are delayed beyond dusk, and a watch so you don't panic if that happens. You also need a small first-aid kit containing a few bandages, first-aid cream, and moleskin for the unexpected blister.

Take along a small bottle of insect repellent. Some hikers prefer one that contains DEET (N-diethylmetatoluamide), but others prefer a natural repellent. There are blackflies in early spring, although not the legions that endure so long in the Adirondacks. Fill a plastic bag with toilet paper, and throw in a few moist towelettes or a liquid sanitizer to use before lunch on those dry mountaintops.

It is strongly recommended that you wear a pair of unbreakable sunglasses even if you require no prescription. It's all too easy to run into an overhanging branch or twig. If you're helpless without your glasses, carry an extra pair.

You'll enjoy the hikes more if you carry binoculars and watch for birds. Besides, binoculars are essential for identifying distant sights. A small magnifying glass can add to your discoveries of nature. You may even enjoy carrying a small, lightweight altimeter that works according to barometric pressure. On relatively steady days it's a good clue to progress on a mountain; on unstable days it can alert you to sudden changes in the weather.

Of course, you should always carry water when you hike—even more than your anticipated needs. Dehydration on summer days is quite possible, and it can even happen on a sunny, leafless early-spring or winter day. These mountains are dry much of the year, and there are few springs. It's becoming increasingly dangerous to trust open water sources because of the spread of *Giardia lamblia*, so don't drink from a stream, no matter how lovely it looks.

Remember, hiking should be fun. If you are tired or uncomfortable with the weather, turn back and complete the hike another day. Do not create a situation in which you risk your safety or that of your companions.

Never walk alone. Be sure someone knows your intended route and expected return time. Always sign in at trailhead registers where available. The unexpected can occur. Weather can change, trail markings can be obscured, you can fall, and you can get lost. But you won't be in real danger if you have anticipated the unexpected. Use a cell phone for emergencies only—to others around you in the woods, conversation on a cell phone is no better than listening to a loud radio.

Timber rattlesnakes are a state-threatened species. Be cautious when hiking, and on no account interfere with individual snakes or their dens.

Mountain bikers and/or equestrians may be encountered in some areas. User conflicts continue to occur. Hikers often resent the silent approach from behind, the encroachment and possible trail destruction from knobby wheels. Equestrians dislike the speed at which some bikers travel the trails that often scares horses. Cyclists must always yield the trail, but it is still a good idea for hikers to remain alert. Unleashed dogs can also be a hazard. If sharing the trail is of concern to you, then call ahead for information on the park's policy.

Hunting is allowed in the Catskills, Storm King, most of Sterling Forest, Huntersfield Ridge, the tristate South Taconics, and some other areas used in this guide. Bow hunting is allowed in other areas such as Fahnestock Memorial State Park. No-hunting zones include Harriman–Bear Mountain, Westchester County, and most of Minnewaska State Park Preserve. Deer season usually runs from late November into mid-December, and specific dates are available from the New York State Department of Environmental Conservation and NY–NJTC. We do not recommend hiking in hunting areas during deer or bear season. However, should you decide to do so, be sure to wear a blaze-orange hat and/or vest.

LYME DISEASE

Lyme disease is caused by a tick-borne spirochete that may produce a rash, flulike symptoms, and pain in joints. If untreated it may cause chronic arthritis and nervous-system disorders. It is difficult to diagnose but treatable if diagnosed early.

The deer ticks that transmit Lyme disease are now found north and west of Westchester County, where the problem has reached epidemic proportions. Their range is expanding rapidly, and users of this guide should take preventive measures.

There is no foolproof way to protect yourself from these minute ticks, so make sure to check yourself frequently; tuck pants into socks and boots; put insect repellent containing DEET on your pants, shoes, and socks (note that DEET does weaken elastics); and wear tightly woven and light-colored clothing (making it easier to see the ticks). Staying on the trail and avoiding tall grass is also a good preventive measure. Above all else, we strongly recommend that you shower and change clothes at the end of your hike because this is the best time to make a complete body check. Change out of your hiking clothes to prevent any ticks that are present from attaching themselves to you. If you suspect that you have contracted Lyme disease, call your physician right away. A vaccine is now available, but its safety and efficacy is still controversial.

BEHAVIOR IN THE WOODS

So, now *you* are safe in the woods, but what about the woods themselves? The environment that may threaten you can be just as fragile as you are, and you are the only one who can protect it.

Trail erosion is becoming a serious problem in many areas. Please stay on main trails at all times to minimize damage to soils, tree roots, and vegetation. Never cut across switchbacks, and use stepping-stones whenever possible to cross wet areas of the trail. Do not pick wildflowers or dig up woodland plants.

Leave no sign of your presence. Use pit privies if available. If not, bury your personal waste at least 200 feet from water or from a trail or path, and carry out used toilet paper—doubled plastic bags work well. When you camp, do not bathe with soap in lakes or streams; when picnicking or camping, carry wash water and dishwater back from the shore. If you're camping, carry a stove for cooking, and do not build fires. In most parks fires are prohibited because these areas are very prone to wildfire.

Respect the rights of others, and help preserve natural areas for future hikers.

The hemlock woolly adelgid has been active in the Hudson Valley for the last few years. Many trees are dying as a result of its depredations, and large stands of once magnificent hemlocks have already succumbed in our hiking areas. The loss of hemlock groves with their deep shade changes the character of our woodlands. When deciduous hardwoods replace hemlocks, more light filters through, dries the forest floor, and shrivels the vernal pools used by frogs and salamanders for breeding. The aphidlike insect was introduced inadvertently to the United States from Asia in 1924. Originally discovered in Oregon, the infestation has now spread to the eastern states. The insect feeds on new twig growth and can be seen at maturity between late winter and early spring at the base of individual hemlock needles when they cover themselves with easily seen white, cottony wax that remains attached to the branches even after the insect has left. Individual trees can sometimes be saved by spraying. A natural predator of the insect does exist, and some encouraging results are being seen in areas where the imported ladybird beetle has been introduced.

NOTES FOR USING THIS GUIDE

The hike description tells you how to reach the trailhead itself, but getting to the nearby town is up to you. Consulting a road map will help (see Bibliography).

Summaries at the beginning of each hike list hiking distance, vertical rise, time on the trail, and United States Geological Survey (USGS) topographic map (or maps) and/or the NY–NJTC trail map for the area the hike traverses. Unless otherwise noted, distances are for the round trip or circuit. Where measured mileage information has not been available, distances have been estimated and are usually correct to within 10 percent.

Vertical rise refers to the total change in cumulative elevation for the hike. Where the terrain is relatively level, no numerical figure has been used. Hiking time is given for the total time at a leisurely pace and is simply the minimum needed to walk the trail as described, without prolonged stops. The text often tells you to allow more time for sightseeing.

Most of the hikes in this book are accompanied by sections taken from the topographic map (or maps) mentioned at the beginning of each hike description. Carrying the complete map gives a larger picture, and your enjoyment will be increased on high ground if you can identify the surrounding countryside. A cautionary note on the USGS maps: Although contours and elevations are mostly reliable, some of the man-made features, including trails, are seriously out of date. The New York State Department of Transportation (NYDOT) 7.5' quadrangles, which correspond in area and name to the USGS quads, tend to have more recent planimetric information, but they have the disadvantage of being printed in only two colors (USGS maps are in four colors.) We recommend using the trail map sets published by the NY–NJTC (see page 281), which are more convenient and up-to-date than either the USGS or NYDOT quads. With the exception of Mohonk (Hike 40), all hikes using a topographic base map have a trail overlay and, for loop hikes, arrows showing the direction of travel. A few of the hikes are in state parks, and for reasons of scale a sketch map instead of a topographic map has been provided for Olana (Hike 46).

If you don't know how to read a map, you should learn to do so before hiking. Spend time, if you can, walking with someone who does know how to read a map. The same instructions are appropriate for the use of a compass. You may not need either on the easiest of this guide's trails, but walking these routes with map and compass will allow you to become comfortable with their use so that you can extend your hikes beyond the ones described or to more difficult hikes.

Most trails are blazed with paint according to the designated trail color, either on trees adjacent to the trail or on rock underfoot, but in some locations, plastic or metal disks are nailed to trees. Two blazes, one above the other, indicate an abrupt turn in the trail, the direction of the turn being indicated by the offset of the upper blaze. Standing at one blaze, the hiker can normally expect to see the next one ahead, though where the footway is clear—such as on a woods road—blazes may be less frequent. Three blazes indicate either the beginning or the end of a trail. Frequently new trails are cut, and existing trails are rerouted from time to time. The original blazes are then obscured with gray or brown paint, though they may still be visible for many years.

Some trails border on or cross private property, so please honor any NO TRESPASSING or KEEP OUT signs, close any gates you may walk through on your hike, and generally be respectful of the landowner.

Keep in mind those two familiar mottos: *Take only photographs, leave only footprints* and *Carry in, carry out.* We routinely carry a plastic shopping bag to take out any litter left by others.

LONG-DISTANCE TRAILS

Three long-distance trails can be found in the Hudson Valley.

The **Appalachian Trail (AT),** a National Scenic Trail, passes through on its 2,152-mile journey from Georgia to Maine. Through-hikers are those completing the AT's entire length on one trip, most taking about six months on the trail and adopting trail names for the journey. Other hikers tackle the project by hiking separate sections, one or more at a time, and still others walk the trail as day hikers. The first section of the AT from the Bear Mountain Bridge to the Ramapo River south of Arden in Bear Mountain–Harriman State Parks was built by volunteers from NY–NJTC in 1922–23. Marked with white rectangles, the AT is administered by the Appalachian Trail Conference in Harpers Ferry, West Virginia.

The **Long Path (LP),** marked in turquoise, begins its northward journey at the George Washington Bridge. For years the trail's northern terminus was at Windham in the Catskills, but the trail has now been extended as far north as the Mohawk Valley, and there are plans to extend the trail into the Adirondacks and perhaps beyond to the Canadian border. Administered by the NY–NJTC, the length of the LP is approximately 300 miles, and it is ever lengthening.

Joining the other two traditional long-distance trails is the **Highlands Trail (HT),** designated with diamond-shaped teal-colored markers. This comparatively new trail of about 150 miles links the Delaware and Hudson Rivers. The not-yet-complete route uses established trails, with some new footway construction where necessary and connections made by short sections of paved road. The system links 26 county, state, and federal parks, forests, and open spaces and is the result of cooperation among the NY–NJTC, conservation organizations, state and local governments, and local businesses.

These three trails are all maintained by volunteers, as are most trails in this book.

OTHER HELPFUL INFORMATION

New York–New Jersey Trail Conference (NY–NJTC)
156 Ramapo Valley Road
Mahwah, NJ 07430
201-512-9348
email: info@nynjtc.org
www.nynjtc.org/clubs (to obtain a list of local hiking clubs)
www.nynjtc.org/pubs (to obtain a complete list of–and to order–their maps and guides)

The NY–NJTC coordinates the construction and maintenance of some 1,500 miles of hiking trails, including the Appalachian Trail in New York and New Jersey; the Long Path, which connects the metropolitan area with the Catskills and beyond; and other hiking areas. The organization publishes books and regional maps of the Catskills, Northern New Jersey, and the Hudson Valley, and these items may be purchased from the conference, with significant discounts for members (see Bibliography).

Some 85 hiking clubs and conservation organizations belong to the conference, along with 10,000 individual members. Applications for membership are invited, and the annual fee includes, among other things, a subscription to the *Trail Walker.* This bimonthly publication describes the activities of the member clubs and features timely articles, book reviews, and trail updates. It is a reliable source of information on trail closings, relocations, and other potential problems associated with the hikes described in this book.

For a list of local hiking clubs, a complete list of publications, and to order books and maps, either call them or use their web site above.

FOR THE CATSKILLS:

Department of Environmental Conservation Region 3 Headquarters
21 South Putt Corners Road
New Paltz, NY 12561-1696
845-256-3000, x4182 (for recorded trail conditions)
www.dec.state.ny.us/website/reg3

Department of Environmental Conservation Region 4–Lands and Forests Sub Office
Route 10
Stamford, NY 12167
518-357-2234
www.dec.state.ny.us/website/reg4

FOR THE SHAWANGUNKS:

Mohonk Preserve, Inc.
P.O. Box 715
New Paltz, NY 12561
845-255-0919
email: mohonk@idsi.net
www.mohonkpreserve.org

The Mohonk Preserve manages this unique natural resource and supervises access to preserve lands. An admission fee is required from nonmembers.

Mohonk Mountain House
1000 Mountain Rest Road
New Paltz, NY 12561
845-255-1000
www.mohonk.com

Admission fee required except for overnight guests and Mohonk Preserve members.

OTHER:

Scenic Hudson, Inc.
One Civic Center Plaza, #200
Poughkeepsie, NY 12601
845-473-4440
email: info@scenichudson.org
www.scenichudson.org

Founded in 1963, Scenic Hudson is a nonprofit environmental organization and separately incorporated land trust. They are "dedicated to protecting and enhancing the scenic, natural, historic, agricultural and recreational treasures of the majestic 315-mile-long Hudson River and its valley."

The Nature Conservancy, Eastern New York Chapter
200 Broadway, 3rd Floor
Troy, NY 12180
518-272-0195
www.nature.org/states/newyork

Founded in 1951, The Nature Conservancy is the world's largest private, international conservation group. The organization manages and protects natural areas, and some hikes in this guide are in conservancy preserves. Threats to remaining wild places are escalating, and The Nature Conservancy is working in New York to counter and preempt these threats.

The Open Space Institute
1350 Broadway, #201
New York, NY 10018
212-629-3981
www.osiny.org (in development)

Responsible for preserving many thousands of acres in the Hudson Valley.

New York State Office of Parks, Recreation, and Historic Preservation
Albany, NY 12238
518-474-0456
www.nysparks.state.ny.us

The New York State OPRHP welcomes 65 million visitors a year to its parks, historic sites, and recreation areas from Jones Beach to Niagara Falls. Regional offices, or Commissions, administer the specific sites.

Taconic State Park Commission
Staatsburg, NY 12580
845-889-4100

The Taconic State Park Commission manages the lands of the OPRHP on the east side of the Hudson. It is responsible for state parks and historic sites there, including Hudson Highlands, South Taconic, and Fahnestock Memorial State Parks.

Palisades Interstate Park Commission (PIPC)
Bear Mountain, NY 10911-0427
845-786-2701
www.pipc.org

The PIPC manages the lands of the OPRHP on the western side of the Hudson River and supervises Harriman and Bear Mountain State Parks, Storm King, Sterling Forest, and the state lands of the Shawangunks. Responsibility for a new Schunemunk State Park will soon be added to PIPC jurisdiction.

Map Information Unit, New York State Department of Transportation
State Campus, Building 4, Room 105
Albany, NY 12232
518-457-3555
www.dot.state.ny.us/magis/paper/paper/html

NYSDOT publishes and sells a variety of maps, including topographic maps based on the USGS quadrangles.

Map Distribution Branch
U.S. Geological Survey, Box 25286
Federal Center
Denver, CO 80225
800-USA-MAPS
www.usgs.gov

Many sporting-goods stores sell USGS maps, but for the occasional one that is unavailable, it's good to be able to order from the source.

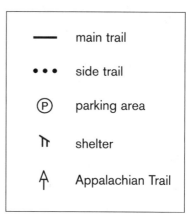

main trail

side trail

parking area

shelter

Appalachian Trail

I. Westchester County

Introducing Westchester

Extending some 35 miles from the New York City border north to the Hudson Highlands, Westchester is a complex region. A mix of wealthy suburbs and corporate office headquarters, it is certainly one of the Hudson's most developed regions. Still, the county has made a major effort to protect natural and historic areas. Small parks in the south and especially the larger ones in the north provide worthwhile outings. Private preserves like Teatown and Mianus, as well as a few New York State parks, round out the offerings.

Some 400 years ago Henry Hudson, thinking he had found a route to China, sailed up the river that would bear his name, passing native villages on the Westchester shore. His ship, the *Half Moon*, was 58 feet long and armed with cannons.

Just a hundred years later, the native peoples had all but disappeared—but their memory lives on. Towns, villages, rivers, and roads still carry the Indian names. They had bright descriptive meanings—Katonah was "principal hill"; Ossining, "place of stone"; Chappaqua, "rustling land"; and Kisco "muddy place."

The railroads arrived in the 1840s and the development rush began eating up land that might have been preserved as open space. This was somewhat countered by New York City, which at the same time began acquiring land and building its reservoir system.

Hiking in Westchester is generally not as strenuous as in other areas, but many of the paths allow you to stride out without the usual necessity of watching your feet. Numerous wandering woods roads were first laid down by the owners of great estates that are now open to public visits. The rolling hills remain replete with streams, forests, fields, old stone walls, fantastic piles of boulders, and rock outcroppings.

Westchester County is actively constructing longer recreation trails. Often paved, they are open to bicyclists and equestrians as well as walkers. The Old Croton Aqueduct, Briarcliff-Peekskill Trail, and trailways along some of the county's parkways allow for full-day outings. Trailway maps and brochures are available from the Westchester Parks Department (914-242-PARK; www.co.westchester.ny.us/parks). Westchester residents can purchase an annual pass that reduces entry fees.

1

Mianus River Gorge

Total distance: 5 miles

Walking time: 2 hours

Vertical rise: 1,200 feet

Maps: USGS 7.5' Pound Ridge; the Mianus River Gorge Wildlife Refuge and Botanical Reserve Trail Map

Protection of this stretch of the Mianus River was The Nature Conservancy's first project when, in 1953, the infant organization became involved with a group of local citizens to preserve this unique area. More history was made in 1964 when the Mianus River Gorge was registered as a National Historic Landmark and became the first natural area to be granted this designation. The Mianus River begins in Greenwich, Connecticut, and flows north through New York before reversing its direction and turning south through the gorge and on into Long Island Sound. The Mianus River was named after Chief (or Sachem) Mayano of the Wappinger tribe, whose name in the Wappinger language means "he who gathers together" and who was killed near the gorge in 1664. In 1600 the seven Wappinger tribes probably numbered about 8,000 in 30 villages, but epidemics, such as smallpox and malaria, and the Wappinger War of 1643–45 seriously depleted their numbers. Only a few hundred remained in the lower Hudson after 1700, and almost all were gone by 1758.

Three trails have been laid out through the property: the Brink of Gorge Trail (red), the Fringe of Forest Trail (blue), and the Bank of River Trail (green). This hike uses the red trail for the outgoing trip, with a possible side trip on the green, and returns on the blue. The trails are particularly well marked so that navigation is easy; the footway is mostly wide and gentle on the feet, passing quiet waterways through tranquil woods. Side trips take the walker to various

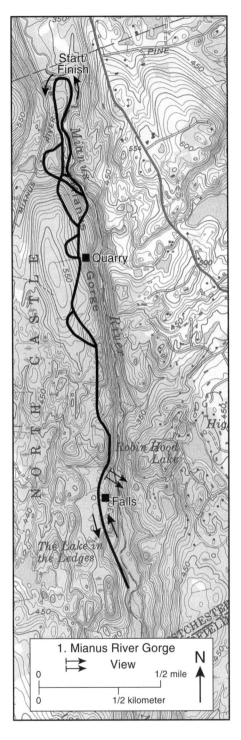

1. Mianus River Gorge
View
N
0   1/2 mile
0   1/2 kilometer

landmarks such as an old mine, an overlook, a cascade, and a hemlock grove, where some trees are estimated to be more than 325 years old. The hardwood trees are immensely tall and straight, and the aura of peacefulness is striking throughout the gorge. Along the way walls divide the once-farmed uplands from the steep slopes of the gorge, which are largely old-growth forest. The climbs are easy and short as the trail meanders along.

There are restrictions. No bicycles are admitted; no dogs are allowed, even if leashed; and picnicking is only permitted in the Map Shelter area. There is no entry fee, though as the preserve relies on donations to continue its work, a contribution box is provided. The preserve is open daily between April 1 and November 30 from 8:30–5, and we suggest you call 914-234-3455 beforehand to confirm that the preserve is open. Most damage occurs underfoot during freeze/thaw and mud periods, so all trails are closed for a "winter rest."

The preserve is located in Bedford, Westchester County. From exit 4 on I-684, drive east on NY 172 for approximately 1.5 miles before turning left onto NY 22 north. NY 172 and NY 22 run together for a mile into Bedford, where the triangular village green is reached, and NY 22 leaves to the left. Bear right to stay on NY 172 (Pound Ridge Road) toward Pound Ridge and Stamford. After approximately 1 mile you come to a traffic light (and gas station), where you turn right (south) onto CT 104 (Long Ridge Road). Turn right again onto Millers Mill Road (first right) after another 0.5 mile. Proceed 0.1 mile over the bridge, and immediately turn left onto Mianus River Road. The entrance to the preserve is on the left, 0.6 mile farther on.

Alternatively, from Connecticut's Merritt Parkway, exit 34, take CT 104 (Long Ridge

Samuel J. Bargh Reservoir

Stella Green

Road) into New York State, where it becomes NY 104 for 7.7 miles. Turn left onto Millers Mill Road, and thence to the preserve on the left.

There is a water pump provided at the Trail Map and Shelter, and composting rest rooms are discreetly located a short distance away to the right. Study the large-scale map at the board, pick up a trail map to carry with you, and enter the trail system by walking left from the board. Note the red-painted circle on a light-colored wooden arrow. This marker style is the one you will follow for the entire outward trip to Point C. The trail at the beginning is handicapped accessible and leads gently downhill to a thoughtfully placed bench named for Lucy Adams, a local educator and preservationist. The trail follows the route of the Mianus River for a short distance, sometimes high above the water, before it turns away and dips down to the Edith Faile Footbridge, a

wonderful example of natural-looking trail work, named after an ardent conservationist.

Your outgoing route is on the red-marked trail, though the blue-marked trail to be used on the return trip enters and leaves the outgoing route several times. If you decide to take the green loop for a closer look at the Mianus River, turn left when you see the first green marker. Simply keep left along all the river trails until the route ascends stairs back to Monte Gloria and the so-called Hemlock Cathedral. This hilltop is named after Gloria Hollister Anable, one of the five conservationists who originated the preserve in 1953.

If you have remained on the red trail, Point A is reached with its excellent signing, and the Hemlock Cathedral is close. Most of the hemlocks surrounding the Mianus Gorge Preserve have already been attacked and lost to the woolly adelgid. In an attempt to halt this destruction within the preserve in general and this impressive stand in particular, an imported ladybird beetle from Japan was released during May 2000. Hemlocks thrive in the cool, moist microclimate of the gorge, and it has been confirmed that some of these trees are more than 325 years old. If hemlocks are lost, the whole environment changes. These deep-shade trees will give place to deciduous trees, resulting in drying up of the moist areas critical to breeding of certain species, such as salamanders and frogs.

At about 45 minutes into the hike you arrive at the junction with the short spur trail to the Hobby Hill Quarry. This trail makes a small circle at the quarry, which still contains boulders gleaming with mica. Mica, quartz, and feldspar were mined from here during the 18th century, and the trail itself still sparkles with mica. Please honor the preserve's request not to take away any samples from the quarry.

Almost a mile from the quarry trail, a vernal pool is skirted on its left-hand side. The trail then reaches the junction with the short side trail offering a view of the Samuel J. Bargh Reservoir, which supplies water to several localities, including Greenwich. Bargh was the president of Connecticut American Water Company at the time the reservoir and dam were constructed.

Back on the main trail, follow the red markers the short distance down to the shores of the reservoir to enjoy the ambience at Point C, the end of the outgoing hike. Return to the main trail, where you have recently been following both red and blue markers, and retrace your footsteps, concentrating now on following blue markers. The blue trail shows greater evidence of the previous use of the area as farmland. Many old stone walls are still in place from a time when farmlands were fenced with native stone and wood gates; some of them have barways—a gap in the wall giving access from one field to another.

The blue markers return you to the parking lot and your car.

SJG

2

Ward Pound Ridge/Leatherman's Cave

Total distance: 4.5 miles

Walking time: 2.25 hours

Vertical rise: 600 to 700 feet

Maps: USGS 7.5' Pound Ridge; Westchester Parks Ward Pound map

At 4,700 acres (about 6 square miles), the Ward Pound Ridge Reservation is the largest park in Westchester County. The basic tract was assembled and acquired in 1925–1926 and is named for the nearby town of Pound Ridge. Originally the Indians had a "pound" in the area where they kept live game until needed for food. The "Ward" was added later to honor William Lukens Ward, Westchester's Republican county leader from 1896 until 1933. In addition to the trails, picnic areas, and camping areas, the park is home to the Trailside Museum (914-864-7322). It's well worth a visit and is especially welcoming to children. The park office can be reached at 914-864-7317.

To get to the park, take exit 6 off I-684 (at the merge between I-684 and the northern end of the Saw Mill River Parkway), and proceed east on NY 35 for 3.6 miles to NY 121. Turn right onto NY 121. The park entrance is almost immediately on your left. After going through the tollbooth ($7 per car, park map included), turn right onto the first paved road, Michigan Road. Pass the side road to a camping area, and park at the end of the road near a circular turnaround.

Head right, across a field, to a cable gate flanked by two large, white posts. The hike, a circular one, begins at the signboard just beyond the gate. Bear right where the trail forks, almost immediately. Follow the metal trail markers with red and green arrows. Throughout this hike the trails are mostly wide with good footing. Many of the junctions are posted with brown numbers, a proj-

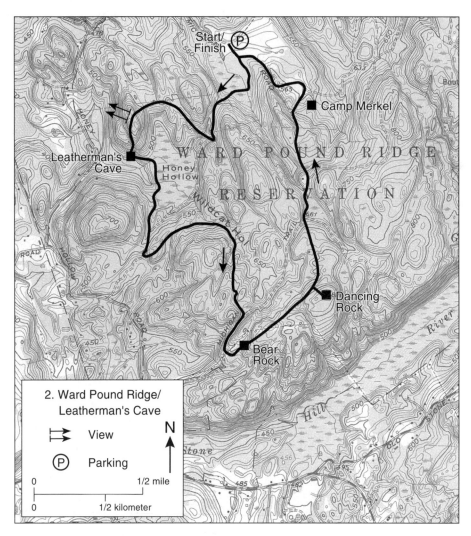

2. Ward Pound Ridge/
Leatherman's Cave

View

N

Parking

0   1/2 mile

0   1/2 kilometer

ect completed by park personnel in 1999, and these are the numbers referred to in this text and on the park's map; ignore the white-on-blue numbered signs occasionally seen. Most trails are used for cross-country skiing, and some are marked only in one direction.

This first section of trail is built higher than the surrounding ground. Constructed by the Civilian Conservation Corps (CCC) in the 1930s, the path goes through an engrossing swamp area. Most of the park was heavily farmed, and evidence of that bygone era abounds in the many stone walls and foundations.

After 5 minutes you reach an unnumbered junction with a green-marked trail continuing straight ahead. Bear right, staying with the main trail marked by red-and-green metal arrows. At 10 minutes into the hike, pass a pink trail, and stay on the red-green. Soon you encounter #25, the first of the numbered junctions. In another minute you come to a signed-posted intersection (#31) with a white-marked trail to Leatherman's Cave.

Make a right turn here, but just past this turnoff, on the main trail, is one of a dozen or so informational signs placed throughout the park as an Eagle Scout project. This one gives a brief history of mining in the area.

Return to junction #31, and follow the white markers. Another 5 minutes brings you to #26. Here the white trail makes a sharp left, steeply downhill. Do not follow it, but go straight ahead, slightly uphill, on what appears to be a wide unmarked trail. In fact, you soon begin to see white markers not apparent from junction #26. Using this alternate route allows you to make a loop to the lookout and then the cave.

About 3 or 4 more minutes brings you to a T junction (#27). Stay on the white trail, which turns left and begins to wind and climb slowly up to a fine overlook. The footway thins as it gets higher and passes some rock outcroppings. You are now about 30 minutes into the hike.

At an elevation of 665 feet, the viewpoint, complete with wooden bench, has an expansive western view across to the Cross River Reservoir, built in the early 1900s. On a clear day, you can see the Hudson Highlands.

After your "view break," continue following the white markers as the trail descends, turns right near a stone wall, and passes a massive rock outcrop and overhang. Ward Pound Ridge has many truly magnificent rock outcroppings, and this specimen is one of the best.

Soon, less than 10 minutes from the view, junction #29 is reached. Turn around and go back a few feet the way you came, and you'll see two small wooden signs. One points left for the short 1-minute walk up to

Leatherman's Cave. The cave itself is not very large—more of a rock shelter than a true cave. It's the story that makes it interesting.

Leatherman's Cave is named after a mysterious homeless man who wandered through the area from 1858 to 1889. He traveled a 365-mile circuit, stopping at the same 34 campsites on a regular schedule. His loop went from Danbury (Connecticut) to Waterbury, then to Saybrook and along the Connecticut River. Then he headed toward Long Island Sound, New Canaan, Wilton, White Plains, and back here. He was clad in scraps of leather and mostly communicated using crude signs. People often left food for this gentle soul or invited him in for a meal. Another one of his camps is preserved on the Mattatuck Trail near Route 6 in Connecticut. According to one of the Eagle Scout signs, the Leatherman was a Frenchman, Jules Bourglay, employed in his home country by a leather merchant. He wanted to win the affection of the merchant's daughter but ruined the business instead. He migrated to America in 1857 in disgrace and soon began his treks. We find him a fascinating historical personality. His photograph, a printed handout, and other information about him are available at the museum.

After your visit to the cave, return to #29 and turn left, following the white trail for 2 minutes to #28, where the trail makes a distinct left turn. However, turn right, leaving the white trail, and walk on a wide, unmarked trail along Honey Hollow (a farmer kept bees there in the 1800s).

Ten minutes along the unmarked trail brings you to a Y junction. Bear left, and immediately approach #30 and a red-green trail. Take the right fork of this trail (level, not down). The trail climbs along this stretch, but the route is wide with good footing, meandering through mature hardwoods rich with

Peering into Leatherman's Cave

bird life and signs of settlers long since gone.

Keep your eyes open for junction signs. Pass #32 and then an unmarked junction, but you're looking for junction #38, which will take 15 to 20 minutes to reach. Here you leave the main trail, making a sharp right turn onto a woods road with occasional white-and-red blazes.

Cross under the power line to junction #39 (you probably won't see the actual sign, which is a bit downhill) where the trail turns left at first parallel to the line, and then quickly bears right uphill, then left. Only a minute from the power line, Bear Rock is to the left of the trail (a red-white sign on the tree above indicates M6).

Bear Rock is noted for its perhaps historic carving that looks like a bear's head, carved on a boulder identified as Pound Ridge leuco-granite. According to the July 1972 *Bulletin of the NY State Archeological Association*, 12 designs are distinguishable, measuring up to a half-inch deep. The investigator made out the contour of a bear, a twin deer-bear profile, and a wild turkey, with the rest being unclear. However, Jim Swager, who wrote the book *Petroglyphs in America*, called it "questionable" and was not willing to stake his reputation on this positively being a petroglyph.

Continue ahead on the trail. Note the vegetation change at the top of this ridge. It's a little higher, and plants must exist on direct rain with no runoff from the surrounding land. The trail recrosses the power line and in another 5 minutes comes to junction #37, a side trail on the right up to Dancing Rock. Proceed up the trail until it levels off, with rocks rising to the left. Bushwhack a few yards left to a large flat rock surface that was used for social dancing by local farm-

ers, perhaps at harvest time. Imagine it devoid of trees and packed with rejoicing farmers. Note some of the stone constructions nearby—platforms and fire rings, probably more than a hundred years old. Notice, too, the moss along the access trail—some of the most brilliant green vegetation you'll ever see.

Return to the main trail, and continue on for around 10 minutes until it joins a larger trail and quickly comes to sign #36. Continue straight (not right), crossing a stream, passing #22, and continuing downhill on a trail blazed yellow. In another 10 minutes reach junction #23, the former site of the parks main CCC camp. Known as Camp Merkel, it was in operation from 1933 to 1941, when America's entry into World War II ended the CCC program. Turn right at #23 (sign to Pell Hill), passing the steps and foundations that are all the remains of CCC Camp CO210 Camp SP Katona. The CCC camp may be gone, but the work remains for us to enjoy—trails, bridges, shelters, even the Trailside Museum.

A minute past the CCC camp brings you to a T junction. Turn left onto a yellow-arrow trail, soon passing through an open field and followed by a bend to the left. The cable gate and parking lot will shortly be in sight.

OPTIONS

To complete the day, consider a trip to the nearby John Jay State Historic Site, home of the first chief justice of the U.S. Supreme Court. Return on NY 35 west (toward I-687) about 3.5 miles. Turn left (south) onto NY 22 for 1.6 miles to the entrance on the left. There is no admission charge for the grounds and a self-guided walk, but the house tour costs $3 (914-232-5651). HNZ

3

Rockefeller State Park Preserve

Total distance: 6 miles

Walking time: 3 hours

Vertical rise: 300 feet

Maps: USGS 7.5' White Plains; park brochure map

The Rockefeller State Park Preserve was created in 1983 when the Rockefeller family deeded 715 acres to New York along with an endowment fund for its upkeep. Subsequent donations have increased the preserve's size to 859 acres, with more promised for the future. A beautiful visitors center, opened in 1994, contains exhibits on the historical and natural features of the park. A pleasant place for a walk or a stroll, the preserve is open for public use during daylight hours. The office phone is 914-631-1470.

Attracted by the commanding views of the Hudson Valley, oil magnate and philanthropist John D. Rockefeller Sr. began buying land in the Pocantico Hills area in 1893. His estate would eventually reach 4,000 acres. A 40-room Georgian mansion, Kykuit (Dutch for "lookout"), was built as the family home.

During the 1900s, the Rockefellers restored much of the land to a natural state. An earthen dam created Swan Lake in 1932, and to this day some family land is still used for growing corn and breeding cattle.

The Rockefellers built 55 miles of carriage roads during the 1920s and 1930s. Designed to highlight the beauty of the area, they have been traditionally (but informally) open for public use. A similar network was built at the family's summer estate on Mount Desert Island, Maine, which now forms the core of Acadia National Park—also a Rockefeller gift to the public.

The carriageways, as they are now often called, are used by walkers and equestrians alike, though bicycles are not allowed. This

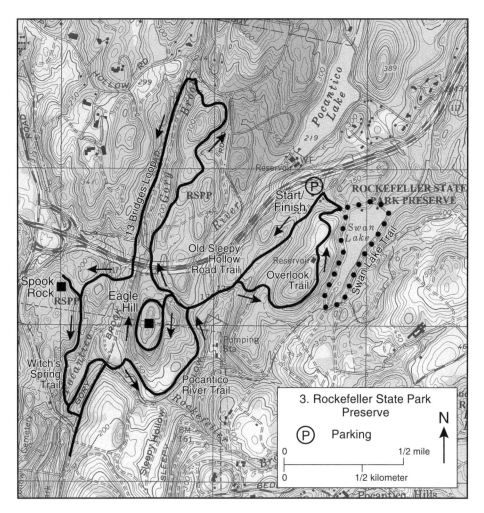

3. Rockefeller State Park
Preserve

N

(P) Parking

0   1/2 mile

0   1/2 kilometer

hike, entirely within the park, uses these carriageways. Almost all the junctions are well marked with concrete or fiberglass posts. Triangular arrows on the posts indicate the shortest route back to the parking area. As the carriageways are smooth and have been well maintained, any good walking shoe or sneaker will suffice.

To get to the park, leave the New York State Thruway (I-87) at exit 9 (at the eastern end of the Tappan Zee Bridge). Proceed north 3 miles on US 9 through Tarrytown and Sleepy Hollow to a junction with NY 117. Turn right onto NY 117 for 1.4 miles to the park entrance. There is a parking fee, currently $5, which includes a trail map.

The hike begins at the tollbooth. Follow a paved road parallel to the parking area for a short distance past a DO NOT ENTER sign (meant for cars) to a dirt road and to a metal gate. This marks the beginning of the Sleepy Hollow Road Trail.

The trail, which heads downhill, passes the Ash Tree Loop and Nature's Way and then crosses the paved Sleepy Hollow Road and a map signboard. In a few minutes you'll cross a bridge and come to a T junction with the Pocantico River Trail. Turn left and then almost immediately right onto the Eagle Hill Trail. After a short climb you will reach a junction with the Eagle Hill Loop. Make a left onto the loop for a five-minute walk on a spur to a fork in the trail. Here begins the loop. Take it either way.

There is a modest viewpoint along the way that has, unfortunately, grown in somewhat over the years. We hope park authorities will restore the viewpoint before your hike.

After completing the loop, take the spur back down to the junction. Continue straight, crossing a large metal bridge over NY 117. As you drove in, did you wonder why such a substantial, limited-access road was built here? It is certainly out of character for the area. Interestingly, this section of highway was part of a major controversy in the mid-1960s. NY 117 was to be upgraded to connect with the planned Hudson River Expressway, I-487. A major interchange was to be built on landfill in the river. When I-487 plans were finally abandoned, this upgraded section of NY 117 had already been constructed.

After crossing the long bridge, you begin walking the 2-mile Thirteen Bridges Loop. There are a few junctions, but this trail is well signed and easy to follow. The "13 bridges," of standard design, are primarily on the last part of the loop as it crosses and recrosses meandering Gory Brook.

This part of the preserve, somewhat distant from the parking area, is less traveled and usually quite peaceful. But it was not always so. Gory Brook got its name after a Revolutionary War skirmish left the stream red with the blood of British troops. Some fine rock outcroppings rise along the edges of the trail.

Have you noticed the large stones that often mark the edge of the carriageways?

Road workers, especially those employed on Rockefellers' Maine estate, often fondly referred to these as "Mr. Rockefeller's teeth."

The loop ends just after going under NY 117. Take the first right, downhill, onto the Witch's Spring Trail. You'll quickly pass two junctions to Spook Rock, and you can take a quick five-minute side trip to this "Indian Legend" rock. It's just off to your left as the trail makes a sharp turn. No reliable historic information on this rock or the legend is available—but it's a nice place to sit and have a snack.

Return to the Witch's Spring Trail, and continue a few minutes to a T junction. Take the left following the sign TO POCANTICO RIVER TRAIL (PRT). Here you'll cross one of the many truly fine stone bridges built by the Rockefellers. The nicest one, Three Arches, is a short detour away. Take a right onto the Pocantico River Trail after crossing the bridge. In a few minutes you'll spot Triple Arches Bridge off to the right. The massive structure just downstream is the Pocantico River Viaduct, part of the Old Croton Aqueduct (see Hike 5). Retrace your route back, passing the first stone bridge, and bear right, continuing on the Pocantico River Trail past an unsigned junction.

Now comes the only poorly signed part of the hike. You want the second left over the river. After crossing the bridge, you'll come to a concrete signpost marking the junction of the Pocantico River Trail and Gory Brook Road Trail. Look on the far side of the post to be sure you're at this specific junction, and then turn right, staying on the Pocantico River Trail. The river should be on your right, and the route should soon take you through some open fields.

You'll pass two close-together junctions (both with nice bridges) as the trail bends left and comes nearer to the river. A section

One of many fine stone bridges in Rockefeller State Park Preserve

with a smooth-topped stone wall is shortly reached. Here the Pocantico River has some small cascades that are especially lovely if the water level is high.

Continuing, you'll pass by the junction with the Eagle Hill Trail taken earlier in the hike. A few more steps brings you to a right turn onto the Old Sleepy Hollow Trail heading back toward the parking lot. Proceed across the paved road, pass by the Nature's Way junction, and continue to the Ash Tree Loop on the left. If time and/or energy are waning, you can continue straight ahead to the tollbooth and parking lot.

To complete the full hike, turn right onto Ash Tree Loop, and head to the Overlook Trail. From here for the rest of the hike, you should take all significant left junctions, ignoring only grass-covered (abandoned) trails. The Overlook Trail wanders high above Swan Lake as it heads back toward the visitors center. The strange-looking low concrete building you pass is, surprisingly, an emergency water-supply system for the village of Sleepy Hollow.

When you reach a major five-way junction with a signboard, a sharp left will take you back to the visitors center. For the more energetic, end the day by walking the pleasant 1.3-mile loop around Swan Lake. It's called Swan Lake Loop on most maps but was recently renamed Brother's Path.

HNZ

4

Teatown Lake Reservation

Total distance: 6.4 miles

Walking time: 4 hours

Vertical rise: 750 feet

Maps: USGS 7.5' Ossining; Teatown Lake Reservation Map

Teatown Lake Reservation has much to interest its visitors. In addition to the 14 miles of marked hiking trails, the Nature Center boasts a small store focused on nature items and a museum with indoor and outdoor displays, including live exhibits. The 730-acre preserve offers a lake, interesting scenery, and a 2-acre wildflower sanctuary, home to 200 native and endangered species of wildflowers. Guided tours of Wildflower Island by experienced volunteer guides are offered mid-April through September. To preregister, call 914-762-2912, ext. 10. A small per-person fee is charged.

This reservation of 730 acres is Westchester County's largest private nature preserve. The Briarcliff-Peekskill Trailway (BP), a 12-mile linear park, uses one of the Teatown Reservation Trails, and there are plans to connect this path with others, such as the Old Croton Aqueduct State Historic Park, to form a linked trail. This hike uses the Hidden Valley, Overlook, Hilltop, Northwest, and Lakeside Trails in a series of loops, all walked in a counter-clockwise direction. Any one of these loops could be omitted to make a shorter hike. Along the way you walk through an unspoiled gorge, swamps, mixed forests, meadows, and by the side of Teatown Lake.

To reach the preserve from the Taconic Parkway, exit at NY 134 for Ossining, and drive west 0.2 mile to turn right onto Spring Valley Road—a curving country road. After 1 mile, turn left at the fork (at the sign for the preserve) and then right into the preserve

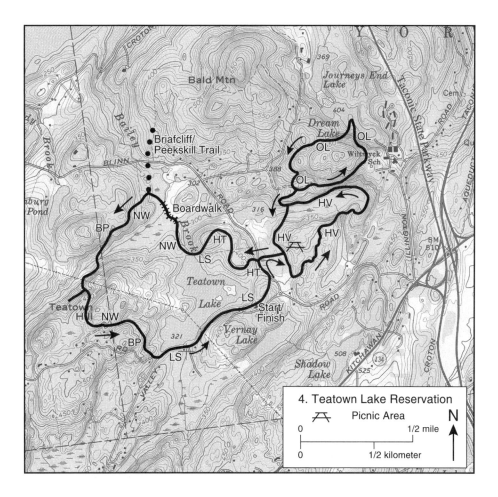

4. Teatown Lake Reservation

△ Picnic Area

0   1/2 mile

0   1/2 kilometer

N

after another 0.2 mile. Alternatively, from NY 9, turn right onto NY 133 in Ossining and immediately left onto NY 134. After 2.5 miles turn left onto Spring Valley Road, then left again for the preserve at the fork mentioned above. Ignore the several smaller roads that join Spring Valley Road.

No entry fee is charged, and the trails are open from dawn to dusk. The Nature Center is open from 9–5 Tuesday through Saturday, and 1–5 Sunday. Dogs must be leashed; no hunting is permitted; bicycles or wheeled vehicles are allowed; but permits are required to camp, fish, or swim. For more information call 914-762-2912. The reservation is a private, nonprofit organization that depends on contributions to support its educational and land preservation efforts, so donations are welcomed. Teatown Reservation offers educational programs and volunteer opportunities.

Walk from the parking lot along the right-hand side of the building on a paved path, and bear left through a gateway labeled TEATOWN NATURE CENTER. Enter the building on the left to obtain a trail map. Proceed down the paved ramp toward the bulletin board and the Hidden Valley Trailhead, marked in red, that leaves on the right. The Hidden Valley Trail is described on the sign as a moderate 1.6-mile loop blazed in red, though the park map lists the distance as 2.4 miles. Uphill on the right of the trail are animal cages. To the left are a children's playground and a sugarhouse that is still operational. Maple trees are tapped for their sap early each year, and the sweet liquid is boiled down into syrup.

The blazing throughout the preserve is sometimes unclear, though supplemented by Teatown Reservation disks and signs, and on the Hidden Valley Trail the blazes are occasionally white instead of the expected red. Follow blazes downhill, curving left and right to reach the lakeside parking lot on Blinn Road, where there is another bulletin board. Here you need to be aware of occasional traffic. Turn left, and be alert to traffic as you walk down Blinn Road for 20 yards before turning right into the woods. Walk straight ahead through the remnants of a stone wall onto a boardwalk to reach a T junction at a grassy meadow. Notice the picnic table straight ahead, and turn right. Here the Hidden Valley Trail goes in both directions. Turn right to begin the first loop of the hike. Nesting boxes and bird feeders are installed throughout the preserve, and you may notice them here. Pass by the bird blind and the disintegrating old tree, dubbed "Mowers' Maple," which has been left as shade for workers and animals by farmers.

The trail continues for a couple of minutes through a flat, sometimes swampy area before turning left uphill. While blazes are faded, good signage keeps you on the correct route as the trail undulates and takes you across another swampy area on a boardwalk. The trail passes by a ravine before crossing yet another swampy area and entering Hidden Valley, a serene and peaceful region. The route is now between a swamp on the left and a rocky hill above you on the right.

Turn right at the junction with the Overlook Trail, blazed in yellow, where there is a signboard giving information on Teatown Lake Cooperative Land Preservation efforts. The Overlook Trail climbs above the sign and follows a route now marked with yellow circular Teatown Reservation disks that are a great improvement on the previous paint blazing.

A 60-foot climb on the hill above Hidden Valley brings you to a T-junction opposite a small pond and a private house right in the center of the reservation. Turn right, again to walk counterclockwise, around the Overlook Trail loop. Quite soon the trail crosses a gorge over an artificial wood bridge and climbs by its side with assistance provided by ropes and wooden posts. After a short descent on stone steps, the trail approaches a stone wall. Turn left, and after a short climb, walk across an open area and downhill to turn right at another sign for the Overlook Trail. The Overlook Trail seems not to have any particular overlook, but the terrain is high, and in winter the rolling countryside and private homes of Westchester County can be glimpsed through the trees. The trail now bears to the left, still descending, crosses beneath a telephone wire, and emerges to turn left onto a paved private road. Twenty yards along the road the trail turns right and reenters the woods.

Just over the crest of the next little climb you may notice a spur trail to the left (there is a sign here) leading to a bench overlooking the field containing the picnic table and the junction with the Hidden Valley Trail. We recommend a rest stop in this delightful place before walking across the meadow, downhill, to the junction. If you miss this shortcut, the Overlook Trail still takes you to the junction with the Hidden Valley Trail.

Warren's Sugar House at Teatown Lake Reservation

Turn right, and retrace your footsteps back to Blinn Road.

Walk straight across Blinn Road, and climb to the ridge to the junction with the Hilltop Trail. (The alternative is to return to Blinn Road, walk through the lakeside parking lot a short distance into the back lot, and turn right uphill back into the woods.)

Orange blazes are faded, but along the Hilltop Trail the plastic disks used for orienteering are visible with numbers, degrees, and paces recorded.

Five minutes along the way a bench has been placed in honor of Evelyn Harris, and this memorial is followed soon afterward by a trail leading left to the boathouse. Teatown Lake can be glimpsed through the trees, and a sign directs the walker straight ahead to the dam.

At the base of a small descent signs show that Lakeside Trail (blue), Cliffdale/ Teatown (white), and Northwest Trail (yellow), continue straight ahead. The dam is another good spot for a break. Bailey Brook is the outlet for Teatown Lake. The stream was dammed in 1923 by Gerard Swope to form Teatown Lake, and the original 190 acres surrounding the lake was donated by the family in 1963.

Just before crossing Bailey Brook, and about two-thirds of the way across the boardwalk, look closely for the sign for the Northwest Trail, and turn right onto that trail following yellow blazes, leaving other trails to continue ahead. Pretty Bailey Brook on the left is soon crossed on a bridge.

Within a few minutes the trail crosses Griffin Swamp, with its distinctive swampy smell, on a boardwalk and makes a 90-degree left turn, still with yellow blazes. Briarcliff-Peekskill Trailway with its green diamonds enters here, and for a while the

Hilltop Trail and Briarcliff-Peekskill Trailway use the same footway. Trail maps for the Briarcliff-Peekskill Trailway may be obtained by calling the Westchester County Parks Department at 914-242-7275.

Within 5 minutes on this joint trail a conglomerate of boardwalks and a bridge follow, navigating across another section of Griffin Swamp. Just before the longest boardwalk Cliffdale/Teatown (also leading to the Lakeside Trail) joins the Northwest Trail and Briarcliff-Peekskill Trailway. Continue across the boardwalk on Northwest, now following white, yellow, and green blazes. Walk gently uphill; then Cliffdale/Teatown leaves to the left and the Northwest Trail/Briarcliff-Peekskill Trailway turns right, proceeding through a thicket of mountain laurel. The continuing uphill gradient leads out to the power line immediately beneath Teatown Hill. The climb by the side of the power line is steep and rocky, and at the top of the first ascent a jog to the left of the trail leads to the summit of Teatown Hill, unfortunately with a stanchion placed on the high point. The view is extensive but marred by the power lines marching across the countryside.

The trail descends and makes a 90-degree turn to the right immediately underneath one of the towers. It then continues its downward gradient and moves away from the power line. Passing to the right of a bundle of rocks, you may notice a faded yellow marker and the remnants of an old boardwalk, probably leftovers from an old trail route. Teatown Lake is visible as you continue 15 minutes downhill to a gap in an old stone wall. The area was farmland 100 years ago, but cultivation slowly died out, leaving the forest to move back in. The Lakeside Trail enters here from the left, but unless you wish to add more than 2 miles to your outing by walking around the lake, continue ahead toward Teatown Road and the Bergmann Boardwalk, which has been out of commission for some time. It is anticipated that repairs will be complete and the boardwalk usable again during the spring of 2001. Should the boardwalk not be repaired, walk the short distance down Teatown Road, and re-enter the woods farther along. The Lakeside Trail is rocky and routed close to the lakeshore, but benches are provided at intervals—very suitable locations to catch your breath.

Boardwalks toward the end of the Lakeside Trail offer interpretive signs and you then pass the gatehouse entry to the bridge, originally built in 1982, leading to Wildflower Island.

The Lakeside Trail leaves the island gatehouse on the left and passes through a large grove of Norway spruce, probably planted when this area was farmed. Farmers seemed to prefer this European species for windbreaks and decoration because of its dense hanging branches.

Bear right and walk uphill to your car. A visit to the Nature Center is highly recommended.

SJG

5

Old Croton Aqueduct State Historic Park

Total distance: 5.5 miles

Walking time: 3 hours

Vertical rise: Minimal

Maps: USGS 7.5' Ossining; Old Croton Trailway State Park Map available free of charge from the park manager: 914-693-5259. A more detailed map in color and containing historical comments on the aqueduct and its neighbors can be purchased for $5.25.

Once called the Old Croton Trailway State Park, the Old Croton Aqueduct State Historic Park extends over a total of 26.3 miles but covers only a portion of the 41-mile aqueduct route that originally carried water into New York City. Its purchase in 1968 by New York State enabled one of the great engineering feats of the 19th century to be converted into a linear park. Construction of the old aqueduct and the first dam began in 1837 and was carried out largely by Irish immigrant labor. It seems incredible that this gravity-fed tube maintains its steady gradient of 13 inches per mile over its entire length, modeled on principles used by the Romans.

Water first flowed through the tube in 1842 and continued to supply New York City until 1955. Plentiful water encouraged the growth of the city, but increased demands by new industries and the need for flush toilets and baths rendered the old aqueduct inadequate to supply the city's inhabitants. Construction of the New Croton Aqueduct, three times the size and a few miles to the east, began in 1885, and service started in 1890. The northernmost portion of the Old Croton Aqueduct was brought back into service in 1989 to supply the town of Ossining with water.

This particular hike begins at the New Croton Dam above Croton Gorge Park and ends in Ossining, close to the unique double arch across the Sing Sing Gorge. The conduit tends to be only a few feet under the surface, so no buildings can be constructed over the masonry tunnel, thus making this

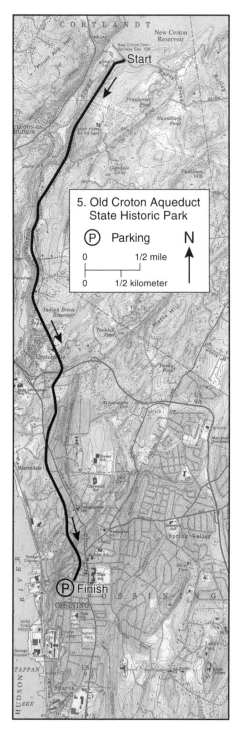

5. Old Croton Aqueduct
State Historic Park

Ⓟ Parking   N

0   1/2 mile

0   1/2 kilometer

unobstructed path ideal for nonmotorized recreation. The flat, grassy mound, often with a dirt path in the center, is easy to follow, sometimes passing close to homes and often over streams running from left to right down to the river. Mountain bikes are permitted on the trail, and dogs must be leashed. Please be considerate as you walk by backyards. Most of the route is unmarked, though round yellow-disk markers may be seen periodically, and care must be taken when the trail crosses or uses public streets. The traveler is alerted at the northernmost road crossings by single metal bar gates with concrete posts. The aqueduct at first parallels the Croton River, east of the Hudson. Along the way the route passes several attractive stone towers called ventilators. Their purpose, before the introduction of chlorination, was to freshen the water.

A car shuttle is needed unless you wish to retrace your steps. Park one car where your hike will end in Ossining at the Ossining Heritage Area Visitor Center on Broadway, just west of the junction of US 9 and US 133 in Ossining. The two-hour parking rule is usually not enforced on weekends, though as a safeguard you should confirm this fact at the visitors center. There are rest rooms here and a museum (914-941-3189) with exhibits relating to the construction of the aqueduct. The facility is normally open from 10–4 daily but is closed on Sundays during the colder months.

Use a second car to reach the beginning of the hike by turning left out of the Ossining Heritage Area Visitor Center parking lot, and make an immediate right onto US 9 at the light. (Only right turns are permitted here.) Almost immediately turn right again onto Main Street, and quickly bear left onto Church Street (do not go down the hill on the right into town) and left (north) again at the traffic light back onto US 9. Drive north on US 9 for just more than 3 miles, and immediately after the open water crossing, exit on NY 129. Turn right at the bottom of the ramp and left onto Riverside Avenue at the T junction. Continue for 0.5 mile, and then bear right, continuing on NY 129 at the Croton Diner. Continue in a northeasterly direction for 2.3 miles, and watch for, but do not turn into, an entry road on the right that leads down to the Croton Gorge Park. (The park is attractive, gives a wonderful view of the water pouring over the spillway, and is a pleasant place to picnic.) Take the first right (a sharp turn) after the park entry onto Croton Dam Road. After crossing the dam, find parking either on the shoulder or in the small space on the right.

Without a car the aqueduct is accessible by train at several places between Yonkers and Ossining from any of the stations on Metro-North Railroad's Hudson Line. Call 1-800-638-7646 for information on stops close to the aqueduct. For bus information call Westchester County's Beeline Bus System at 914-682-2020.

Before starting the walk, take time to admire the New Croton Dam, also known as the Cornell Dam, and to look down into the Croton Gorge Park. More than 200 feet high, the dam was completed in 1907 and resulted in the original dam being submerged.

From the parking area, walk south through the gate. The green diamond on the metal post to the right is a marker for the Briarcliff-Peekskill Trail, a 13-mile path through Westchester County. The wide white-stone road is the access road to the aqueduct, which is down to the right at this point. The water is turned off periodically so that the tube can be inspected. After 5 minutes' walking, ignore the road that continues down to Croton Gorge Park and rest rooms, and bear left past a sign: OLD CRO-TON AQUEDUCT TRAILWAY STATE HISTORIC PARK. The tube is now immediately below.

After passing between concrete posts that once supported a metal bar blocking the route to vehicles, the first ventilator comes into view. The canopy continues, and the path becomes sandy, passing beneath power lines. The building down to the right has recently been bought by Westchester County, and there is some possibility that an interpretive center might be established here. No vehicles are permitted on the aqueduct, so access would be by foot only. The trail is now wide, with evidence of an old stone wall up to the left and glimpses through the trees of the river below and the ridge on the other side to the right. At about 25 minutes into the hike you pass through a rock cut. This feature is one of only three such cuts in Westchester County.

Quaker Bridge Road East, reached in about a mile, is the first road crossing. Walk straight across and through another gate to arrive at the second ventilator. After passing gates at a crossing of Quaker Bridge Road, the aqueduct parallels that road, which is below on the right. Very soon the second ventilator is reached, followed quite quickly by a second crossing of Quaker Bridge Road. Three-quarters of an hour from the start, the Croton Gorge Unique Area is reached, advertised by a Department of Environmental Conservation sign and a small parking lot to the left.

Farther down it may be seen that Hurricane Floyd washed out part of the trail, exposing the roots of a large tulip tree. There are plans to restore this section, and in raspberry season you might want to stop to gather some fruit. In quick succession you pass an old wall to the right, probably 100 years old; the third ventilator; and another crossing of Quaker Bridge Road.

Now walking on a "hog's back," you reach the end of the section of the aqueduct carrying water and see a small building on the left that houses a pump to move the water up to a filtration system. Turn right onto Quaker Bridge Road, ignoring the paved road coming in on the right, and walk to the left, back onto the trail. The route leaves the aqueduct here to skirt the General Electric Management Institute. Cross in front of the gate, and keep to the right-hand side of a wire-mesh fence protecting a parking lot. Continue to follow the chain-link fence as it turns left, right, and left again to lead you out onto paved Shady Lane Farm Road. Turn right on this road, walk down to Old Albany Post Road, and turn immediately left under a bridge carrying County 9A. On the west side of Old Albany Post Road note the face carved on a tree stump. The two old buildings close by are the old Crotonville one-room schoolhouse and an ancient church. The letters carved into the stonework: F.O.E. OSSINING AERIE 1545 stand for "Fraternal Order of the Eagles"; the number 1545 is assigned to Ossining; and an aerie is the nest of a raptor. Below is also carved AD 1897.

Turn left onto Ogden Road, and march straight uphill almost to the crest. Turn right opposite house #9 back onto the aqueduct. By now you have walked almost 4 miles and are approaching the fourth ventilator. The brown building on the left bears a trail marker and is now in use as a maintenance barn. Look down to the left to see a stream that is neatly channeled into a culvert.

Immediately behind the fourth ventilator is a rough, steep path. This location was used to store fill for the construction of the road crossing. At the top, cross Piping Rock Road, and proceed steeply down the other side to a delightful grassy section,

slightly on a hog's back, that is mowed by the property owners adjacent to the trail. Users of the trail owe these volunteers a debt of gratitude.

Moving out on to US 9, you pass a sign on the left: OLD CROTON AQUEDUCT. Cross this busy road using the pedestrian crossing, and walk down a paved trail toward a chain-link fence. Turn left through three wooden posts, and pass through the grounds of the Kane Mansion, a Gothic Revival mansion built around 1843. The offices of the Engelhardt Corporation are on the left. The stone block protruding from the grass to the left was once directly above the center of the tube. Continue across the lawn to Beach Road. At almost 5 miles into the hike you come to a large, rectangular stone building. It isn't known why this structure was erected here, but the tube is visible if you look through the gate on the river side.

Pass one of the Ossining fire stations to the right, and cross Snowdon Avenue to use the sidewalk. Walk up the four cement steps at the left of the sidewalk, and continue on grass to a wooden barricade. Cross two Ossining streets, Van Wyck and North Malcolm, through gaps in the protective wooden posts, and walk up the paved path with a children's playground on the left. Admire the gorgeous maple tree whose roots penetrate the tube 40 feet down, and walk down the shallow stone steps to the right of this venerable giant. Cross Ann Street to approach the Waste Weir, dated 1892. This weir was originally constructed to allow the flow of water through the tube to be controlled when inspection or maintenance was required lower down in the tube. The huge, solid cast-iron gate was dropped and the water diverted into the Sing Sing Kill. This Weir Chamber was one of a series that made it possible to drain the entire aqueduct line.

New Croton Reservoir Dam from the picnic area in Croton Gorge Park

The mechanism was also used to spill off, or "waste," water in times of flood. Old photographs indicate that when the aqueduct was in full operation in the early days, inspections were carried out inside the tube by engineers in boats—not an enviable occupation. Cross the bridge over the Sing Sing Kill, and turn left to reach your car.

Before leaving, make time to walk down to the viewing platform to see the double-arched bridge over the Sing Sing Kill. These bridges are one of the most prominent features of the Old Croton Aqueduct. The upper bridge, called the Aqueduct Bridge, was completed in 1839 and passes over the lower bridge, the Broadway Bridge. The lower bridge was originally made of wood and was rebuilt with stone in the 1860s. A visit to the museum here is recommended to complete your outing.

SJG

6

Blue Mountain Reservation

Total distance: 5 miles

Walking time: 3 hours

Vertical rise: 750 feet

Maps: USGS 7.5' Peekskill; Blue Mountain Reservation Mountain Bike Trail Map

Blue Mountain Reservation is open seven days a week from dawn to dusk with a $7 parking fee, reduced to $3.50 for those holding a Westchester County Park Pass. As the name of the recommended map suggests, mountain bikes are permitted in this reservation. The hiking, on approximately 15 miles of multiuse trails, is mostly on wide, gently undulating woods roads that pass by a delightful pond, and includes climbs to two high points with good views. The property was originally part of Van Cortlandt Manor purchased by Stephanus Van Cortlandt in 1677 from some Indians. At one time the Loundsbury family cut ice from the ponds, and when the need for ice diminished in the 1920s, they sold the land to Westchester County. During the summer of 1933, the Civilian Conservation Corps (CCC) built trails, fireplaces, and other structures. The park's present name was assigned by the park commission. Swimming, once permitted at Loundsbury Pond, has been discontinued, though the picnic area remains.

Exit from US 9 on Welcher Avenue at the south end of Peekskill, and drive east, continuing straight ahead through one crossroad to reach the tollbooth at the park entrance after 0.4 mile. Stop at the tollbooth to pick up a map, bear left for another 0.2 mile, and park in Lot #3. If maps are not available at the tollbooth, turn right and immediately right again onto a service road. Maps and other information are available from an office in a small brown building immediately on the left after crossing through

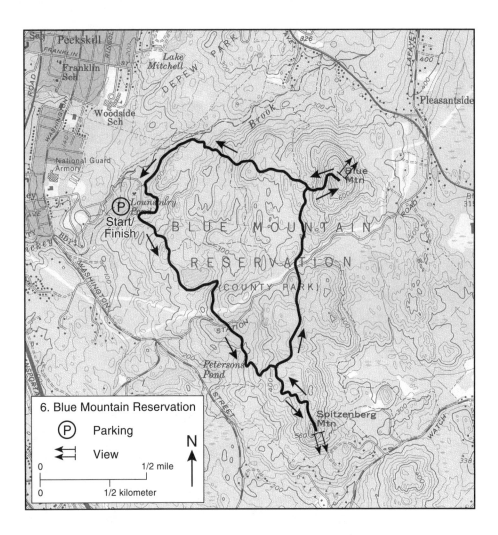

6. Blue Mountain Reservation

(P) Parking

⇄ View

N

0 — 1/2 mile
0 — 1/2 kilometer

a chain-link fence. A map may also be downloaded at www.wmba.org.

At one time many versions of park maps existed, often in conflict with one another. Blazes had faded, with the color often disagreeing with what was shown on the map. Improvements were made in the spring of 2001, and the blazes and the park map now agree. But one of the best guides to navigation are the wooden posts marked with white numbers seen along the route. Rely on these posts.

At the end of the parking lot #3, look for a wooden post at the front end, carrying green, orange, and yellow-gray blazes situated on the right-hand side of the wide, rocky road. (The gray paint blazes you may notice here and in other places in the reservation are old and blacked-out paint blazes.)

Our hike begins by climbing on the Orange-Green Trail. Ignore the yellow-marked trail that almost immediately enters from the left (post #1) because that is the trail on which you return. Continue straight

Horses on the road crossing the Blue Mountain Reservation

ahead on a rocky uphill gradient, and pass by the Orange Trail that leaves to the right (post #4). Just at the crest, turn right at the next junction (post #5) on orange blazes, leaving the Green Trail to its own devices on the left.

Ten minutes into the hike, the shore of the unnamed pond (some maps give this pond the name of New Pond) comes into view on the left. Here the big boulders make this place special and invite you to rest, even though the hike has only just begun.

Your route now skirts the side of the pond and crosses its outlet. Ignore any other posted numbers and the metal sign on a tree to the right of the trail with HORSE TRAIL in green lettering, until you reach post #12 at a junction. Do not bear left down the smooth red-marked path to the left, but turn right, climbing on a rocky and gullied trail. Faint purple blazes lead uphill, the trail first bending to the left, then to the right and passing through two boulders to cross a gas line (post #18). Look to the right for a limited view. Montrose Station Road can be glimpsed ahead, and firing from the range maintained by the park may now be audible. This noise is probably only heard on weekends, when the shooting range is available to the public.

Cross Montrose Station Road (post #19) after about an hour's walking from the start of your hike, and continue straight ahead to post #20, where arrows on a tree indicate that the Purple Trail travels in both directions. Turn left uphill on rocks, and within a few minutes at post #21 you may become aware that the purple blazes have ended, and the footway has merged into the Orange-Green Trail. Note this junction well because you need to turn here after you arrive back from the ascent of Mount Spitzenberg. In addition to post #21, a large tree grows in the middle of the junction and is a vehicle for many blazes.

Resume the ascent straight ahead. Post #22 indicates the last final push up rocks to the summit of Mount Spitzenberg, an excellent place to enjoy the panorama of the Hudson River, Hook Mountain, and High Tor. This point is close to 2 miles from your car. At an elevation of 540 feet the view is becoming limited through tree growth, and sounds of the firing range are somewhat obtrusive. The stone-cemented shelter at the summit is all that is left of a fire tower once used as a ranger station.

Retrace your footsteps to post #22, and bear left back to the junction at post #21. Turn right at the large tree previously mentioned, and walk downhill to Montrose Station Road (post #25), which you should reach after about 10 minutes. Cross the road toward post #26 immediately ahead. The trail recrosses the gas line and turns right along it for a short distance before leaving it to climb back into the woods on a wide rocky road at post #27. (Do not turn left to parallel the gas line because the Orange-Green Trail takes this route, and your route now switches to the Red Trail.)

In less than 5 minutes you bypass post #29. Follow the yellow arrow to the left, and after another 10 minutes look for post #30. Turn right onto a blue-blazed trail to the summit of Blue Mountain. The ascent of about 140 feet is well worth the effort, and the map indicates that mountain bikes are not permitted on this climb. Just before the summit a white trail on the right leads to the true summit. Here you'll find a derelict building. Woodland prevents any views, and although the trail continues beyond the destroyed building, do not go farther, but return to the main trail leading to the summit of Blue Mountain.

The view from the summit of Blue Mountain is one of the best—worthy of an extended break. This location, at 680 feet, is the high point of the hike. The vista from the summit boulders is located a few steps to the left of the trail and includes the Hudson River, Perkins Memorial Tower on Bear Mountain, Indian Point, and the fire-spoiled Dunderberg Mountain. There is now about another 1.5 miles of walking before you reach your car.

Return to the red-blazed trail at the base of the mountain, turn right, and when the trail splits only a few minutes after the descent, be sure to take the left-hand fork (post #31). In this stretch there are several numbered posts drawing attention to trails entering on the left (posts #33, #44, and #43), and within a few minutes you arrive at a junction (post #34) with a yellow-marked trail departing in both directions. Turn left to follow the yellow blazes that take you back to your car.

A few minutes down on the right you will see a bridge over Dicky Brook (post #38). Do not cross this bridge toward post #37, but bear left to parallel the stream for a while. As a paved road and the Blue Mountain Trail Lodge come into view, the trail bends left. The lodge provides dormitory accommodations and a kitchen and dining area for groups of up to 30 people. Reservations must be made in advance by calling 914-593-2634.

Any other signs you might see are for cross-country skiers, and a short walk now brings you to the trail junction (post #1) passed at the start of the trip. Turn right, and walk another few minutes back to your car.

SJG

7

Anthony's Nose and the Camp Smith Trail

Total distance: 4.2 miles

Walking time: 2.5 hours

Vertical rise: About 1,000 feet

Maps: USGS 7.5' Peekskill; NY–NJTC East Hudson Trails #1

The Camp Smith Trail summits the spectacular Anthony's Nose and traverses the side of Manitou Mountain in the northwest corner of Westchester County.

This beautiful trail was "a long time a-coming." Camp Smith, a unit of the New York National Guard, was acquired beginning in 1885 and extending into the mid-1920s. Public entry was prohibited, but hikers traditionally climbed to Anthony's Nose for its fabulous view of the Hudson. Routes from the nearby Appalachian Trail (AT) and an especially precipitous one from the east end of the Bear Mountain Bridge were commonly, if illegally, utilized.

Persistent efforts by officials of the New York–New Jersey Trail Conference (NY–NJTC) to gain limited public access finally paid off. In the early 1990s permission was obtained and a trail route planned. Construction by the Guard's ChalleNGe program for high-school dropouts and volunteers from the NY–NJTC was completed in 1995. The 3.7-mile route and the surrounding 100-foot wide corridor is managed by the Taconic Region of the New York State Office of Parks (845-889-4100).

This hike requires two or more cars. However, for hikes involving only one car or for a more strenuous outing, see the Options section at the end of this description.

Leave the end car at the old tollhouse on US 6, 2.6 miles east of the Bear Mountain Bridge (or 0.7 mile west of the Camp Smith entrance). Then return to the bridge (but don't cross it), and bear right onto NY 9D.

Park along a shoulder of NY 9D just north of the bridge.

NY 9D is narrow, and the shoulders provide limited parking. If a safe spot isn't available, consider an out-and-back hike from one of the two US 6 parking areas noted below. Alternatively, you could park at Bear Mountain (fee charged), and add the pleasant walk across the bridge to your day's outing.

The white-blazed Appalachian Trail leaves NY 9D a few yards into Putnam County (the Westchester-Putnam border is signed). Follow the AT as it climbs unrelentingly uphill close to the Camp Smith boundary. As you huff and puff, remember that AT backpackers using this route carry heavy packs weighing perhaps 30 to 60 pounds. Yours, hopefully, is much lighter.

After some 15 minutes, 500 feet of elevation gain, and just less than 0.5-mile distance, you reach a wide woods road. As the AT heads left along the road, turn right and head instead in the opposite direction, now following blue blazes.

The blue "viewpoint" trail continues along the rocky, wide woods road. It's still uphill, but much less steep—occasionally even flat for a short time. Another 15 minutes or so brings you up toward the summit and the famous view that opens up before you. Keep an eye open for the cairn (small rock pile) and three blue blazes that mark the official start of the Camp Smith Trail. This indistinct trailhead is just before you head out to the main rock-ledge view.

The view from Anthony's Nose is expansive and often attracts a crowd. North across the Hudson are the Crow's Nest on West Point property and Storm King Mountain, a state park. On your side are Canada and Sugarloaf Hills. To the south is the entire Bear Mountain Inn complex, including Hessian Lake, the ball field, an ice rink, and the new carousel building. Most

often there is boat traffic on the river (but, with any luck, not the loud whine of jet skis), and if you linger, trains are sure to pass by. Looking off to the southwest, Harriman's Bald and Dunderberg and Timp Mountains dominate. Bear Mountain's Perkins Memorial Tower is before you. You may catch the glint of cars on the highway to the top. The pink-rock top of Popolopen Torne and all of West Point rounds out the view.

So who was this Anthony with his magnificent nose? Although his identity is the subject of much folklore and speculation, the truth is no one really knows. Early maps called it Saint Anthony's Nose. Washington Irving spun his own humorous tale in the early 1800s. My favorite yarn was told to me by a hiker buddy who said, with a straight face, that as Henry Hudson sailed up the river later to be named for him, he had an Italian cook aboard named Anthony who, it was said, had previously lived with local Indians. When Henry spotted the cliffs he asked aloud, "What's that?!" One of his crew immediately responded, "Don't know sir, but you should ask Anthony. *Anthony knows*." One thing is sure: It was named long before the time of Revolutionary War General Mad Anthony Wayne.

Now return a few yards to the marked trail, and look for a cairn and three blazes marking the beginning of the official Camp Smith Trail. These blue paint blazes should be 2 x 4 inches rather than the 2 x 6-inch white ones followed so far. This trail starts with a small uphill scramble, and this knowledge should make it easier for you to find the beginning should the cairn be missing.

The short scramble brings you up to a rock outcropping and USGS benchmark, the true summit of the nose and another great view—one of about a half dozen more still to come.

The footway now becomes narrow and

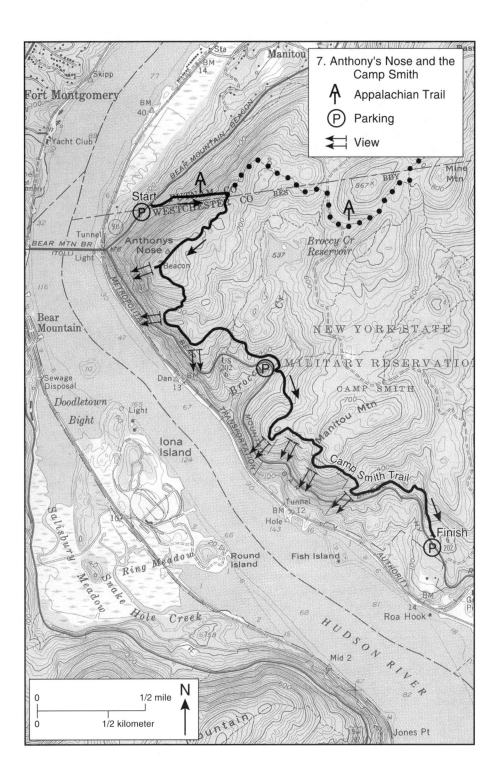

7. Anthony's Nose and the Camp Smith

🏹 Appalachian Trail

Ⓟ Parking

⇄ View

A view of the Hudson from the Camp Smith Trail

Stella Green

begins to descend, passing through a field of sweet ferns. Be sure to watch for the blue-painted blazes, and avoid unmarked deer paths. After a descent of just less than 300 feet, a rock outcropping provides yet another view of both the Bear Mountain Bridge and Bear Mountain Inn.

The trail alternatively swings inland away from the cliff edge and then returns. Occasionally you'll notice traffic noise on the nearby but unseen highway cut into the cliff below you. A small stream and gully are crossed, and then the trail joins a woods road.

After passing a register box, the first of many on the Camp Smith Trail, the trail continues to undulate and reaches the midpoint parking area at an hour plus into the hike and some 500 feet below the summit. Here there are spaces for a dozen cars.

The marked trail continues up as you begin the final 2 miles to the tollhouse.

You pass through a fire-scarred area as the trail again climbs. The effects of the 1993 fire are beginning to fade as the vegetation is making a hardy comeback: Sweet fern, blueberries, and even some small trees dot the surroundings.

More sweeping views down the Hudson are encountered as the trail levels off. The dominant building downriver is a waste recycling plant at Charles Point. On the other shore, farther downstream, the sharp outline of Hook Mountain (Hike 16) protrudes into the river.

As you climb up through a massive jumble of rocks, note the fine work of the trail crew. Each part of this difficult segment was carefully designed to minimize erosion and built to make the trail safe and enjoyable.

At just less than two hours of hiking, the "two pines" view is reached. You'll recognize it; it's one of many fine places for a stop. Rail lines on both sides of the Hudson, the wetlands of Iona Island (a noted bird habitat), and the domes of the Indian Point Nuclear Power facility are visible before you.

The next (and last) mile takes about 30 to 45 minutes. Parts of this section are through a burned area, so watch carefully for the blazes. Road noise may tease you into thinking you're at the end, but there are still some ups and downs and more views ahead.

After passing yet another register box, the tollhouse parking area is reached, after some 2.5 hours of walking.

Here bridge and road tolls were collected when the Bear Mountain Bridge and the spectacular approach road were first opened in 1925. Built and run as a private operation of the Harriman family, the tollhouse was abandoned when the state acquired the bridge in 1940.

The structure is now in ruins, but there is hope. In 1999 a $500,000 state grant was awarded to the town of Cortlandt to restore

the building as an information center—including a display on the history of the bridge and the impressive road (now US 6) leading to it. Additional parking is to be provided to encourage use of the new trail.

OPTIONS

For a shorter two-car hike, parking is also available at a U bend on US 6, 2.1 miles west of the Camp Smith entry or 1.1 miles east of the bridge.

For a more strenuous two-car hike, start at the tollhouse, and end on NY 9D. This backward hike adds at least 500 additional feet of elevation gain

Should you have only one car available, start from any one of the three parking areas noted above, and hike up and back to Anthony's Nose. From NY 9D it's a 2.2-mile round trip. From the tollhouse it's a 6.2-mile round trip, with additional elevation gain/loss and plenty of views. From the U bend its a 2.4-mile round trip, with a gain of 600 to 700 feet and many fine views.

HNZ

II. The East Hudson Highlands

Introduction to the East Hudson Area

State parks on this side of the Hudson Valley are managed by the Taconic Park Commission, a state agency with offices in Staatsburg. From the precipitous cliffs of Breakneck Ridge to the more gentle uplands of Fahnestock, the wide hiking choices available offer wonderful recreational opportunities.

FAHNESTOCK/HUBBARD-PERKINS

Astride the Taconic Parkway, this large area offers lovely lakes, swimming areas, and picnic and boating facilities. Many miles of trails can take you far from the crowds that regularly enjoy the more developed facilities.

The park has its roots in the 1929 gift of Dr. Ernest Fahnestock in memory of his brother, Clarence. Expansion in the 1960s and the more recent addition of the Hubbard-Perkins Conservation Area provide hikers with a park of impressive size: more than 11,000 acres.

The mines here once provided iron ore to the West Point Foundry at Cold Spring, where the ore was turned into Parrot artillery for the Union Army. The bed of the railroad built in 1862 to carry the ore from the mines now hosts a hiking trail.

Further back in its history, much of the land was purchased by Adolphe Philipse in 1691 and established as the Philipse Grant six years later by King William III. The vast and rugged wilderness surrounding the interior range of hills could not be farmed and never had many settlers. Only the 8-mile-long vein of iron ore that follows the ridgeline of the hills to the south managed to attract settlers—and then not until after 1800. Even the early miners regarded these dark woods with foreboding; because they have not been logged for many years, the woods probably look now very much as they did then.

The 4,400-acre Hubbard-Perkins Conservation Area was acquired in 1991 and 1995 by the Open Space Institute and is now administered by the Fahnestock park superintendent. In 1996 the New York–New Jersey Trail Conference opened a 22-mile network of trails, with two connecting into the adjacent Fahnestock State Park. Although not as mountainous as parkland closer to the Hudson, the varied terrain makes for peaceful excursions into woodlands and wetlands. Bow hunting is allowed in season, and some trails are open to mountain-bike and horse use.

The park is located off NY 301; the office phone is 845-225-7207.

HUDSON HIGHLANDS STATE PARK

"Eastward a high chain of mountains whose sides were covered with woods up to no more than half of their height. The summits, however, were quite barren; for I suppose nothing would grow there on account of the great degree of heat, dryness, and the violence of the wind to which that part was exposed." Thus, the Swedish botanist, Peter Kalm, observed the Hudson Highlands on the east side of the river in 1749. One highlight of his trip was his discovery and the first botanical description of the American mountain laurel, *Kalmia latifolia*, the shrub that grows on every slope from the Ramapos to the Shawangunks and whose blooms make walking here and everywhere in southern New York in late May and early June so special.

Hudson Highland State Park, also managed by the Fahnestock superintendent, consists of a series of units totaling almost 4,000 acres. Located generally along the Hudson in Putnam and southern Dutchess Counties, some portions surround the Appalachian Trail.

South of Garrison is the 1,000-acre Osborn Preserve. Here, old carriage trails provide for relaxed walking.

But by far the most impressive section of the park straddles the Putnam-Dutchess border north of NY 301 and protects a wonderful and rugged area. Mount Taurus, the aptly named Breakneck Ridge, and the impressive Sugarloaf Mountain (not to be confused with the nearby Sugarloaf Hill) rise steeply above the Hudson and provide numerous challenging climbs and spectacular views.

Behind these peaks, the 1,000-acre Fishkill Ridge Conservation Area was acquired by Scenic Hudson beginning in 1992. This preserve, also managed as part of Hudson Highlands State Park, connects with watershed lands owned by the city of Beacon. Standing as the northern gateway to the Highlands, the area's rocky outcrops offer panoramic views of the Hudson River and the Catskill Mountains. Bow hunting is allowed in season.

8

The Osborn Loop

Total distance: 5.5 miles

Walking time: 3.5 hours

Vertical rise: 1,000 feet

Maps: USGS 7.5' Peekskill; NY–NJTC East Hudson Trails #1

The Hudson Valley is rich in Revolutionary War history. The Beverly Robinson House, built by the Philipse family in 1758 on part of the Philipse Patent near Sugarloaf South, was confiscated and used as headquarters by Generals Israel Putnam and Samuel Holden Parsons in 1778 and 1779. In 1780 the house was used by General Benedict Arnold as his headquarters, and it was used as a military hospital during Arnold's command of West Point. Aboard the British ship *Vulture*, loyalist Beverly Robinson planned with Benedict Arnold and Major John Andre to deliver West Point to the British. When Arnold learned that Andre had been captured and that discovery of his treason was imminent, he fled from the house down a path to the river and then downriver to the *Vulture*; General Washington arrived only an hour or so later.

The Osborn Preserve, a separate 1,000-acre section of Hudson Highland State Park, came into being when William Henry Osborn II donated the land around Sugarloaf Hill in 1974. His grandfather, president of the Illinois Central Railroad, assembled the property for a summer home in the 1880s. The charming home, just north on Castle Rock, remains private. In the early 1980s the National Park Service purchased two additional tracts on the ridge to reroute the Appalachian Trail (AT) onto protected land. Many of the preserve's trails are easy-to-follow carriageways and old roads and are suitable for novice hikers.

This moderate hike, with one steep ascent at the start, is largely on old carriage

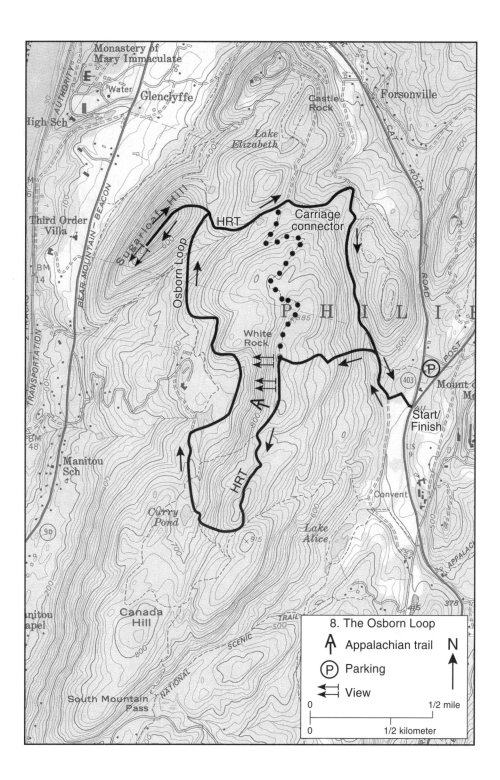

Monastery of
Mary Immaculate
Water
Glenclyffe
High Sch
Third Order
Villa
Castle
Rock
Forsonville
Lake
Elizabeth
Sugarloaf Hill
HRT
Osborn Loop
Carriage
connector
White
Rock
585
P H I L I
Start/
Finish
Mount
HRT
BEAR MOUNTAIN - BEACON
TRANSPORTATION
Manitou
Sch
9D
Curry
Pond
Convent
Lake
Alice
915
403
P
US
APPALAC
378
Canada
Hill
TRAIL
500
SCENIC
NATIONAL
nitou
apel
South Mountain
Pass

8. The Osborn Loop

Appalachian trail   N

P Parking

View

0   1/2 mile
0   1/2 kilometer

Along the Osborn Loop Connector Trail

roads, and occasionally equestrians are encountered. The highlight is an easy climb of Sugarloaf Hill—a name derived from the cone shape in which sugar was sold in colonial times.

The hike begins on the AT crossing of US 9 at its junction with NY 403 in Graymoor, Putnam County. This junction, easily located on a road map, is 3.8 miles north of the major junction of US 9, US 202,

and US 6 in Peekskill. Limited shoulder parking is available on the northbound side of NY 403 about 0.1 mile north of the trail crossing.

Begin the hike on the white-blazed AT that crosses at the junction of US 9 and NY 403. Head west through a field on some puncheons to a stone wall crossed by a stile. After some 10 minutes, the AT takes off sharp left from the woods road at a junction with the yellow-marked Carriage Connector Trail on which you return.

Continue until the AT tops out on the ridge at a junction with the blue-marked Osborn Loop trail. You have now hiked just less than a mile and have gained about 500 feet. Proceed on the AT, turning left on a wide trail. In a few more minutes, you'll pass a faintly blazed blue trail going right about 20 yards to the edge of the ridge.

This fine viewspot is known as White Rock. Across the river to the south is the Bear Mountain Bridge. Bear Mountain (Hike 26) looms above it, with the Perkins Memorial Tower peeking out on the top. To the north, again across the river, is Storm King (Hike 32), and directly across is the village of Highland Falls and Fort Montgomery.

Continue along on the AT for another 0.75 mile to a right-hand junction with the Curry Pond Trail, not yet on most trail maps. The junction is well marked, but you could pass it if you're not alert. Turn right onto this yellow-blazed trail as it heads generally downhill through mountain laurel stands, thick forests, and along some elegant rock outcroppings.

Twenty minutes from the junction, Curry Pond itself is reached. Your impression will depend on the recent weather; it can be just a big swamp during low water, but small wildlife abounds at this peaceful and seldom-visited spot.

Another 5 minutes brings you to the trail's end at a junction with the Osborn Loop. Turn right, now following blue blazes as the trail begins to climb, turns along a stone wall, and proceeds up to a cliff-top viewpoint. You are at 700 feet elevation and almost as high above the Hudson River.

The Osborn Loop now begins a switchback descent of 150 feet before resuming its northerly course. After a while you'll start to see the outline of Sugarloaf Hill, in front of you through the trees. Cross a small stream, and ascend the height-of-land to the intersection with the red-marked Sugarloaf Trail.

You'll return to this intersection, but for now turn left, following red markers for a short but steep side trip—a 220-foot climb to the summit of Sugarloaf Hill. Only a 15-minute trek, it's well worth the effort. The trail follows a narrow ridge over the top and then descends slightly to reach one of the best southerly views: Anthony's Nose, Bear Mountain, and Dunderberg Mountain frame the Bear Mountain Bridge. This is a good spot for a final snack. You may be able to spot the unusual patch of prickly pear cactus on the warmer south-facing slope.

From Sugarloaf, retrace your route to the intersection with the Osborn Loop. Continue with the blue-marked Osborn Loop trail up an old road. Soon you'll pass a large gazebo, rebuilt in the late 1990s by equestrian users of the area. Apparently someone is still caring for the flowers in the old planters nearby.

As the trail levels out less than 10 minutes from the gazebo, the Osborn Loop makes a sharp right turn. This point marks the junction with the yellow-marked Carriage Connector Trail, which begins ahead of you. Leave the Osborn Loop at this turn and hike downhill following yellow disks. The path soon turns sharp right and levels out, with the footway becoming gentle and sandy, making walking easy.

A hike of less than 30 minutes brings you back to the junction with the AT where your hike began. Continue ahead, now on the AT, back to US 9, about 0.5 mile away.

HNZ

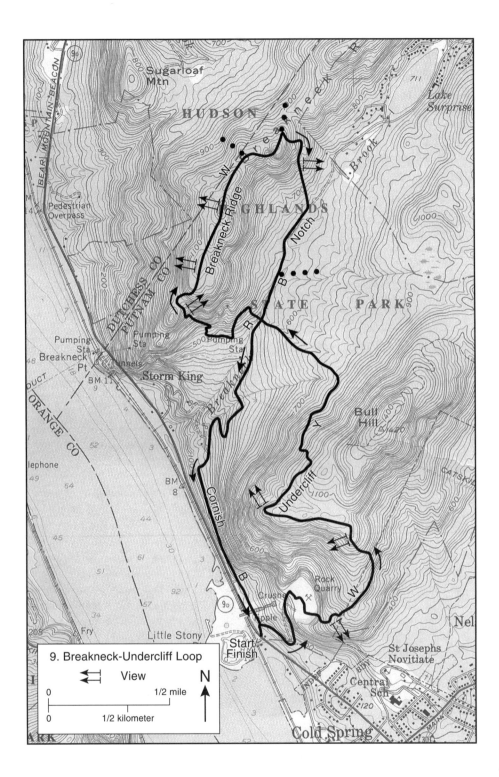

9. Breakneck-Undercliff Loop

View   N

0   1/2 mile

0   1/2 kilometer

9

Breakneck-Undercliff Loop

Total distance: 7.7 miles

Walking time: 5.5 hours

Vertical rise: 2,000 feet

Maps: USGS 7.5' West Point; NY–NJTC East Hudson Trails #2

The Hudson Highlands State Park had its inception in 1938, when 177 acres was donated as a gift to the state by the Hudson River Conservation Society. Land acquisition continued and resulted in the creation of one of the most spectacular hiking venues in the state, with acreage extending to approximately 3,800 acres. Here the Hudson River becomes narrow and winding as it curls between Breakneck Point and Storm King, with towering cliffs on both sides. Building NY 218 on the west and tunneling under the river to house the Catskill–New York Aqueduct were remarkable engineering feats. The handsome Bear Mountain Bridge was conceived in 1922 and opened in 1924, and in spite of its technological success, the suspension bridge, then privately owned, was a financial failure at first.

Climbing the Breakneck Ridge Trail is probably one of the most popular hiking adventures in the Hudson Highlands because of the strenuous effort and extreme exposure encountered while scrambling up the very steep face. However, the hike described does not use this trail, which is overused and can be dangerous in certain weather conditions. The route of this hike takes the walker on a new hiking trail constructed by volunteers from the New York–New Jersey Trail Conference in 1997, and has comparable views. The hike uses part of the Washburn, Undercliff, Breakneck Ridge, Notch, and Cornish Trails. The going is moderately strenuous with two sections of boulder scrambling on the Undercliff

Trail, so be sure to allow sufficient time to enjoy the outing.

Drive 0.6 mile north on NY 9D from its junction with NY 301 in the village of Cold Spring to a small parking lot on the east side of the road. Another small parking lot is available on the west side of NY 9D, where a bridge gives access over the railroad tracks onto Little Stony Point, where there are a few hiking trails. These trailheads can also be reached from the north by driving south on NY 9D approximately 2 miles from the Breakneck Ridge railroad tunnel.

For hikers without a car, the east side of the Hudson River can be reached using Metro-North's Hudson Line, which provides hourly trains daily into Cold Spring. The walk from the train station to the Washburn trailhead is 0.8 mile. Turn left at Fair Street across the street from the village hall, and turn left again when this street ends at NY 9D. This main road is busy, but the trailhead is just ahead on the east side of the road. For more information on train schedules call Metro-North at 212-532-5900 or outside New York City at 1-800-638-7646.

The Washburn Trail begins on the east side of NY 9D and is marked with three white blazes on a tree. Walk through the gate, and start uphill on a rough road that once was used for quarrying and is now marked with white disks. The quarry was opened in 1931 by the Hudson River Stone Corporation and closed in 1967. It is now growing in with grasses and small trees, though remnants of an old circular road on the quarry floor are still visible. Just before reaching the quarry, the white blazes lead sharply right and skirt the trail around the south end of the quarry rim. On the way you'll see old pieces of iron piping that remain as evidence of the quarrying operation.

The trail resumes its climb, leaving the eroded quarry road and going up over a hump on the ridge to the right, leading to a good viewpoint—the first of three. Proceeding uphill, for a total climb of 500 feet, the quarry becomes visible through the trees to the left, then swings away from it to the second viewpoint. The village of Cold Spring and Constitution Island to the south; West Point, Butter Hill, and Storm King across the river; and the slash where the highway cuts through make up the panorama. The Hudson River was chained from Constitution Island to West Point during the Revolutionary War to deter the British advance. The heavy iron chain laid in 1778 was never breached. At the time of this writing, all Storm King trails are temporarily closed because the fires caused by the drought during the summer of 1999 revealed some unexploded ordnance left from when the mountain was used as a practice range for West Point artillery until about 1930.

The trail continues to climb steeply to reach a cairn and three yellow blazes at the beginning of the Undercliff Trail. This trail junction is at the end of a steep section just before one of Bull Hill's false summits. Be alert at this junction as plans are afoot to extend the trail south to Nelsonville.

Turn left onto the Undercliff Trail at about 1,000 feet and 1.4 miles from the parking lot. The Undercliff Trail leaves the Washburn Trail slightly downhill but soon emerges on a rock slab overlooking the quarry on the left. At the right-hand end of this viewpoint, the trail meanders around a large glacial erratic, the first of several in the area. The first opportunity to see Breakneck Ridge comes after 45 minutes on the Undercliff Trail. The trail continues along the ridge to the right, passing several herd paths, and arrives at ledges that can be windy and chilly in cold weather but afford great views of Breakneck, NY 9D, and the railway tunnel. In clear weather the view includes the

A stone arch at the derelict Cornish Dairy Farm

Shawangunks, the Trapps, and the Catskills.

After the viewpoint the trail turns east, switchbacking down into a narrow valley on rocky terrain, the footway improved by man-made rock steps. Shortly, the trail crosses a creek on a small log bridge and swings to the left. Look to the left to see an incredibly large oak split at the base, perhaps by lightning, the two pieces falling in opposite directions.

Descend through open woods, paralleling a gully on the right that carries a tributary to Breakneck Brook, and emerge onto a woods road—the Brook Trail, marked in red. The hike uses the Brook Trail later. (Turn left and walk down to NY 9D if for any reason you wish to cut the hike short. When making this decision, be sure to take the blue-marked Cornish Trail rather than remain on the red-marked Brook Trail, which would lead you out on NY 9W north of your car.)

To continue on the hike, leave the woods road, cross Breakneck Brook on the bridge, and begin walking the most rugged and exciting part of the hike on the Undercliff Trail. Follow yellow blazes up a boulder field to the base of a cliff wall, and just as it looks as if the trail leads over the cliff edge in front, make a left turn downhill away from the cliff wall. Turn right to begin a switchbacked climb around and through large boulders, passing under cliffs on the way to the notch. Approximately 30 minutes walking from the bridge over the Breakneck Brook brings you to the end of the Undercliff Trail. Turn right on the white-blazed Breakneck Ridge Trail.

The walk along the ridge takes you up and down over several false summits. The Hudson River and the Beacon-Newburgh Bridge are visible over to the left when the leaves are off the trees, and on the way watch for an attractive but unexpected wetland filled with cattails on the right. Look down on Lake Surprise and Breakneck Pond

from the last rise to view some of our route back to the car. The camp on the shores of Lake Surprise is devoted to the arts.

The trail undulates along the ridge. Ignore the junction with the red-blazed Breakneck By-Pass Trail entering from the left at a large boulder. About 30 minutes from the junction with the Breakneck Ridge Trail, a quick ascent leads to a small rocky knob. The climbing for this hike is now completed.

After leaving this high point, watch carefully for the junction with the blue-blazed Notch Trail halfway down a steep rocky descent. From here the Notch and the Breakneck Ridge Trails commingle, and both blue and white markers are visible from the junction on trees straight ahead. Turn right. Be sure that you see only blue markers—although the first blaze to be seen is bleached from the sun and barely looks blue. The trail slabs downward along the side of the hill toward the right. Blazes are a little sparse, but Breakneck Pond may be visible through the trees to act as a guide. Turn right onto a woods road now used by the Notch Trail. Breakneck Pond is on the left.

Walking now on level ground, pass a man-made dam and several derelict buildings. These ruins are the remnants of a dairy farm once operated by the Cornish family as a gentleman's farm, and some feeding troughs can still be seen. The Notch Trail turns left past these ruins. Check for three red blazes on a tree to the right indicating the beginning of the Brook Trail, and continue straight ahead. At first Breakneck Brook is on the left, but eventually it flows under a sturdy, wide wooden bridge to parallel the trail on the right.

Watch on the right for the wooden bridge crossed earlier at the beginning of the Undercliff Trail, and continue to follow the red blazes of the Brook Trail. Breakneck Brook is on the right-hand side, and more remnants from the past—a small concrete building and a dam—line its course. Look up farther back to see the steep climb you made up to the notch earlier in the day on the Undercliff Trail.

At the upcoming fork in the trail, take the blue-blazed Cornish Trail to the left, and cross the Catskill–New York aqueduct. The road snakes down to NY 9D, swinging first left and then right, passing a cement water tank, an old greenhouse now almost covered with vines, and other derelict buildings. These extensive ruins are all that remain from the estate of Edward G. Cornish, chairman of the board of the National Lead Company, who lived here during the 1920s. The mansion was destroyed by fire in 1956.

The road swings again, this time closer to the river but still high above it. The road is now paved, and there is more evidence of the old estate in the stone wall and the high man-made wall to the left. Down to the right the railroad tracks and NY 9D can be seen. Turn sharply left just before the concrete pillars at NY 9D, and follow the Cornish Trail for another 5 minutes back to your car.

SJG

10

Fishkill Ridge Conservation Area

Total distance: 5 miles

Walking time: 3+ hours

Vertical rise: 1,700 feet

Maps: USGS 7.5' West Point; USGS 7.5' Wappingers Falls; NY–NJTC East Hudson Trails #2

The Fishkill Ridge Conservation Area was purchased in 1992 and 1993 by Scenic Hudson Land Trust with money from the Lila Acheson and DeWitt Wallace Fund, established by the founders of *Readers Digest*. The area is managed by the NY State Office of Parks and is open year-round, dawn to dusk. Supervision is provided by the staff at Fahnestock State Park, 845-225-7207.

Standing as the northern gateway to the famed Hudson Highlands, the area's rocky outcrops offer panoramic views of the Hudson River and the Catskill Mountains. Turkey vultures, eagles, hawks, and falcons soar high above the cliffs of this rugged 1,000-plus-acre site. This balloon hike includes a steep climb up (and back down, but the loop itself is quite moderate). Bow hunting is allowed in season (permit required), and the start of the hike is near a private shooting preserve. Therefore, this hike is not an appropriate outing during big-game hunting season (usually the Monday before Thanksgiving through mid-December).

To get to the trailhead in North Highland, proceed north on US 9 from its junction with NY 301 for 3.3 miles. Turn left onto Old Albany Post Road North, a loop formerly known as Uhl Road. If you reach the signed Putnam-Dutchess County border, you've gone past this turn. Go along Old Albany Post Road North, looking for shoulder parking. Some good spots are located near a bridge opposite a sign that traces the history of the road. The trail itself starts at a junction with Reservoir Lane (private, no

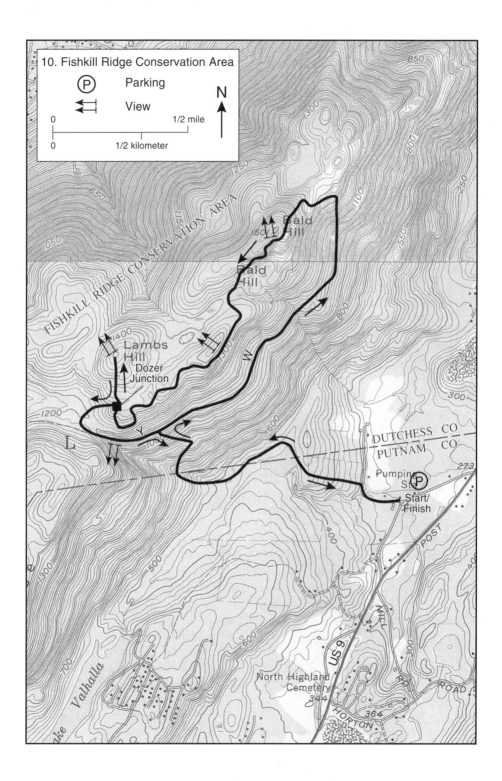

P   Parking

⇄   View

N

0   1/2 mile

0   1/2 kilometer

FISHKILL RIDGE CONSERVATION AREA

Bald Hill

Bald Hill

Lambs Hill

Dozer Junction

DUTCHESS CO

PUTNAM CO

Pumping St.

Start/ Finish

Lake Valhalla

North Highland Cemetery

US 9

POST ROAD

HORTON

parking). Additional parking opportunities are available along US 9.

Walk to the junction with Reservoir Lane where the yellow-blazed Wilkinson Memorial Trail begins, named after a fervent trail worker. Walk up the dirt road, passing a wooden gate. Soon after, the trail turns sharply left into the woods and begins a moderate climb.

In 10 minutes the climb eases off as the trail circles an unnamed pond that straddles the Putnam-Dutchess border. From here can be seen a good view up to Hell's Hollow, the rugged gap between the ridges.

Now the serious 600-foot climb begins. Some of the trail is on woods roads with switchbacks moderating the ascent, but other sections just go up—straight up.

As the Wilkinson Memorial Trail nears the ridgetop at almost 1,100 feet, it makes a sharp left onto a substantial woods road. This turn denotes a well-marked junction with the white-marked Fishkill Ridge Trail. Here begins the loop hike, which makes a counterclockwise circle and returns to this exact point for the hike back down. Leave the yellow trail, turning right, following the white markers in a mixture of formats: paint, plastic Scenic Hudson disks, and the smaller disks of the Taconic Park Commission.

The trail, on a woods road, loses a little elevation in the beginning and then starts to climb modestly. At about 1,200 feet the marked trail turns sharply left and climbs to the open summit of Bald Hill at 1,500 feet, about 45 minutes along the Fishkill Ridge Trail. The summit provides expansive views to the east, but as the trail begins to descend, there is an even better view from a rock outcropping just off the path. This overlook is *the* place for a break.

Far to the south, an unusual view of a bend in the Hudson looks more like a large lake. The grassy area on the mountaintop ahead is Glenwood Farm in Fahnestock State Park. The skyline of Manhattan as well as the tops of the George Washington Bridge towers can be seen on a clear day.

Fifteen more minutes along the trail is another fine view that includes a controversial quarry. The owners, Sour Mountain Realty, are trying to obtain a permit to mine some 50 million tons of rock over the next 140 years from the northeastern section of the ridge on which you are now standing (see www.fishkillridge.org). As you continue walking, more vistas ensue, including Lake Valhalla.

The trail then dips toward Hell's Hollow gap—you'll assume you're about to descend. However, steep dropoffs preclude a direct course. Instead, the trail bends right, climbs, and makes a short descent to a significant woods road.

Known by hikers as "Dozer Junction," this spot will probably be a marked trail junction by the time of your hike. A blue-blazed connecting trail is planned to begin here. As for the name Dozer Junction—to your left, down the road just a few yards, is the wreck of an old bulldozer thought to be at least 50 years old. Hop on up. The backdrop makes for fine photo, especially if the kids are along to climb into the driver's seat.

You'll shortly come back to this spot, but for now continue across the road on the yellow-marked trail for a 10-minute, 120-foot climb up to Lambs Hill (elevation 1,500 feet). The short climb is worth the effort, especially if you go a few yards beyond the summit where the views really open up.

You're at least 1,000 feet above the river. Below you the Hudson is stretched out in all its magnificence. To the north and west are I-84, the Mid-Hudson Bridge (Poughkeepsie), and the high peaks of the Catskills. North and South Beacon Mountains, with their

A trail sign in Fishkill Ridge

H. Neil Zimmerman

ubiquitous towers and a reservoir between them, are just to the south.

Look to the right of North Beacon Mountain and across the Hudson. On the far horizon, you should see a tower. That's New Jersey's High Point Tower, more than 40 miles away.

Retrace your steps to Dozer Junction and turn right, heading downhill on the woods road past the bulldozer. As noted before, the route you are about to travel will likely be marked as a blue trail, but if not, pay careful attention to these directions.

After 3 or 4 minutes of walking down the woods road from the old bulldozer, you'll pass some iron ruins. Just after this (but before big washout cuts across the woods road) turn left, following a clear trail downhill toward the gap between the two mountains.

After only a minute (at a low point), the trail reaches a T junction with another woods road. Turn left here, following the new woods road as it travels slightly uphill, and bear left at a fork. In less than a minute you'll see the yellow blazes of the Wilkinson Memorial Trail. Do not follow the blazes right (uphill), but instead follow them straight ahead.

Parts of this section of the Wilkinson Memorial Trail are on a woods road, parts on a narrow footway. One stretch even goes under a dramatic rock outcropping. After just 10 minutes or so you'll spot the three white markers of the Fishkill Ridge Trail where you began the loop earlier in the hike.

Stay with the yellow markers as you turn right and start steeply downhill retracing your earlier route to your car, some 45 minutes away.

HNZ

11

Hubbard-Perkins: Round Hill

Total distance: 7.5 miles

Walking time: 4 hours

Vertical rise: 1,100 feet

Maps: USGS 7.5' Oscawana Lake; NY–NJTC East Hudson Trails #3

This hike is on some little-used trails in the Hubbard-Perkins Conservation Area of Fahnestock State Park in Putnam County. The old rock walls seen on your hike are remnants from when the land was cleared for farming. The area was also once used for iron mining, and roads and railroads were constructed to transport the iron ore and farm produce to the Hudson River and elsewhere. The route of this hike is mostly through hardwoods with limited views, includes some moderate climbing, and ends with a pleasant walk by the side of an attractive stream. When you are in need of a low-key, quiet saunter, this circuit is the one to take.

Parking is available on the east side of US 9, just 0.1 mile north of the junction with NY 301. After parking, walk north on US 9 for 0.1 mile and turn right onto a paved road, where sometimes a sawhorse is placed as a barrier to vehicles. A little farther down pass a house on the left, and bear right onto a woods road to pass through a metal gate marked on its right-hand side with three Taconic Park Commission disks in white for School Mountain Road and three in blue for the Fahnestock Trail. This section of the trail is open to mountain bikers.

Follow both blue markers and white markers on School Mountain Road—a woods road that makes for easy walking in a tranquil setting and that, within 5 minutes, crosses Clove Creek on a steel-plate bridge. This crossing is shortly followed by two other similar steel-plate bridges. After

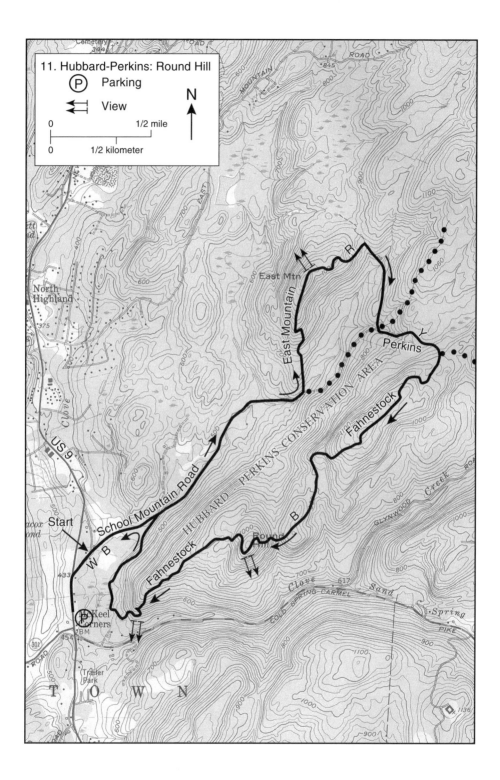

11. Hubbard-Perkins: Round Hill

Ⓟ Parking

◄ View

N

0   1/2 mile

0   1/2 kilometer

Cemetery
344

ROAD

ROAD

845

MOUNTAIN

600

800

1000

EAST

700

600

R

East Mtn

1060

North
Highland

375

East Mountain

Y

Perkins

Clove

600

HUBBARD - PERKINS CONSERVATION AREA

800

Fahnestock

1000

US 9

500

900

Creek

GLYNWOOD

1000

Start

School Mountain Road

B

W B

Fahnestock

Round
Hill

700

617

800

ROAD

Clove

COLD SPRING CARMEL

Sand

Spring

acox
ond

433

McKeel
Corners

454
BM

301

ROAD

500

600

Trailer
Park

700

600

PIKE

900

700

1100

800

1000

1000

T   O   W   N

900

1000

900

1136

A cedar tree on Round Hill

walking for about 15 minutes, watch for a brown plastic post on the left and two stone pillars flanking a woods road leading to the site of the old Hubbard mansion. The pillars are just before the third bridge, and immediately on the other side of the bridge, the Fahnestock Trail, marked with blue disks, enters from the right. At the end of the hike you return to this junction before retracing your steps on School Mountain Road.

Continue ahead on the white-marked School Mountain Road, crossing two more steel-plate bridges and beginning a steady ascent between old rock walls. After crossing a deteriorating wooden bridge, bear left on the red-marked East Mountain Loop, leaving School Mountain Road to continue to the right. The East Mountain Loop rejoins School Mountain Road farther north. Just after traversing a stream on wide logs, look for the three red markers indicating the beginning of the East Mountain Loop. There is also a brown plastic post here indicating that mountain bikes are no longer permitted. Follow red markers as the trail bears left to hug an old rock wall on your right. The footway passes through another wall, then snakes upward to the summit of East Mountain with a view of the Fishkill Ridge—a good place to rest a while. The footway is a little obscure at times, but the route is well marked.

The East Mountain Trail now drops, sometimes routed on top of rock slabs, until it crosses a seasonal watercourse and turns immediately right to continue its downward trend on a woods road. Walk for approximately 10 minutes on this woods road to reach the end of the East Mountain Loop, confirmed by three markers on a tree to the right. Traversing this loop will probably take the best part of an hour before you rejoin School Mountain Road. (If you wish to end the hike here, follow the white blazes back to your car.)

Otherwise turn right onto School Mountain Road, and almost immediately cross over a dilapidated wooden bridge. Look for the three yellow disks of the Perkins Trail in the woods to your left, and turn promptly toward them. The trail climbs, sometimes on rocks, by the side of a cascading stream, until after about 15 minutes it arrives at the junction of the blue-marked Fahnestock Trail. Here you are probably a little more than 2 hours into the hike.

Blue markers can be seen in both directions at this junction. Be sure to turn right. If you still see yellow markers as well as blue ones, turn around and follow only blue markers because you are walking the wrong way.

The Fahnestock Trail proceeds to climb, then descends into a low-lying area before undulating along the ridge, and beginning the ascent of Round Hill. The first vista to the southwest on a clear day offers a view of the Bear Mountain Bridge; the second, a view to the west. The area is dotted with many beautifully shaped red cedars. All the climbing is now finished, so tarry awhile before starting downhill. The trail jogs along on the ridge before recommencing its descent. Very soon now you begin to hear traffic on US 9, and in fact you'll get a view of the junction with NY 301.

The trail flattens and reaches a distinct woods road. Turn right, and walk for about 10 minutes by the side of a stream containing many moss-covered rocks until School Mountain Road and the junction noted earlier are reached. Turn left and walk the 0.5 mile back to your car.

SJG

12

Hubbard-Perkins: Jordan Pond

Total distance: 6.6 miles

Walking time: 3 hours

Vertical rise: 300 feet

Maps: USGS 7.5' West Point; USGS 7.5' Oscawana Lake; NY–NJTC East Hudson Trails #3

The hike described opens up in one place that may remind you of walking in southern England. The portion in the vicinity of Clove Creek is particularly beautiful, and visiting this area in June when the laurel blooms is especially rewarding. Most of the trails are rocky and interrupted by small streams, usually dry in summer. It uses the Charcoal Burners Trail, parts of the Fahnestock and Perkins Trails, and the Cabot Trail. Mountain bikes and horses are not allowed on these trails.

The park can't be reached by public transportation, and for this hike a shoulder of NY 301 is used for parking. Drive east from the junction of US 9 and NY 301 for 3.45 miles. Watch carefully on the north side of NY 301 for a white cross painted on a rock and a brown plastic post indicating that hiking is the only permitted recreation. From the NY 301 junction with the Taconic State Parkway, the distance to parking at the white cross is 2.9 miles. Pull off to the side of the road to park.

Climb the berm, ignore the herd path straight ahead, and turn right onto the Charcoal Burners Trail into the woods, almost immediately crossing a small stream. Within a couple of minutes the yellow-marked Perkins Trail (named for the former owners) leaves from the left. Stay with the red blazes. The walking is flat and easy through a forest of hardwood trees and laurel. Fifteen minutes in, turn left at a cairn and three white blazes onto the Cabot Trail.

Ignore the herd path straight ahead when the Cabot Trail makes a 90-degree turn to the left. In about 10 minutes from the junction, Jordan Pond becomes visi-

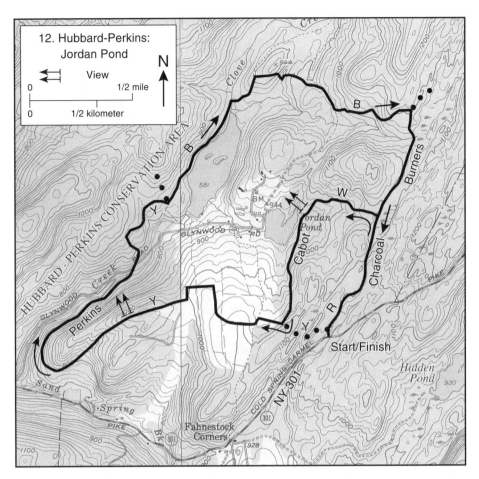

ble. Within another 5 minutes a herd path down to the shore invites the walker to rest at the bench placed conveniently on a rock slab overlooking Jordan Pond–a wonderful spot.

Continue on the white-blazed Cabot Trail to emerge into a clearing with lovely fir trees on the right, a woodpile, and an old gate. The Perkins Trail comes in from the left slightly farther down, marked by yellow blazes on a tree. (Walking back to your parked car from here along the Perkins Trail makes a good 1-hour trip for children.)

The route becomes more open and the footway wide and grassy. Markers direct you toward the right through the fir trees

and a gate carrying a sign requesting that hikers stay on the trail. Walk ahead to the private gravel road, turn left, and almost immediately go right through a metal gate and out on a grassy field. This part of the hike is on private land, so please close all the gates used, and keep your presence as low-key as possible.

Continuous views abound over farm fields that attract many butterflies, insects, and birds. A stone wall and a fence mark the perimeter between two such fields, with intermittent yellow markers on fence posts on the right-hand side. Go through the gate at the end of this first field leading through the old stone wall to proceed through a thicket of undergrowth. Turn right into another field, noting that the trail markers are on the fence posts. The trail continues at the edge of a farmer's field, and it is interesting to glance over to the field on the right to wonder at the large number of boulders lying there. Did these rocks all come from the cultivated fields?

Ignore the cart track that continues ahead, and follow the one bending to the left that soon passes through another old stone wall and veers left. Here the fields are on the right and the undergrowth and hardwood on the left.

At about an hour into the hike, the cart track bends right around the edge of another field, then forks. Ignore the left fork, bear right into another open space, and walk to the right around the edge of the field (farmers prefer that walkers do not go straight across). The path, now slightly uphill, enters woods back onto state land—an orange stake is visible to the right just before the land drops away.

The trail now climbs to a slab with an outlook toward the northwest, with a view of Wicoppee Pass to the right and Round Hill (Hike 11) to the left. The trail then descends an old woods road through a mixed forest with some tall evergreens and laurel and in 20 minutes makes a 90-degree bend to the north. Shortly a woods road joins from the left. Glynwood Road can be seen over to the left through the trees, and the gurgling of Clove Creek can be heard. The trail now follows Clove Creek in a splendid stretch through a plantation of young trees. The trail at first climbs above Clove Creek, then drops down to the level of Glynwood Road and the water, which is crossed on a wide-plank bridge.

After crossing the bridge and Glynwood Road, climb for 5 minutes, and turn right on a dirt road. Walk downhill for about 6 min-

utes, then turn left onto a woods road, ignoring the one on the right. Just a few steps down, the yellow-marked Perkins Trail and the blue-marked Fahnestock Trail commingle, until the Fahnestock Trail leaves to the left. Turn right and follow the blue markers (you are going in the wrong direction if you continue to see yellow markers), and head northeast, passing to the left of a lake locally referred to as "Large Lake." A better view of the lake may be obtained by following a herd path to the right in about 0.5 mile. Walk over the inlet to the lake on two man-made bridges about 2 hours into the hike.

Watch carefully at the crest of the hill, and turn right when two markers indicate a change of direction. Here the woods road continues ahead, and the turn is by a large downed tree that probably will be there for quite a while. Begin descending on switchbacks traversing a steep drop on the left-hand side until the trail climbs again on boulders, giving a different experience from that already encountered on this hike. Be alert here, and stay with the blue-blazed Fahnestock Trail, ignoring any cairns and unmarked woods roads entering from either side. At one point the trail makes a definite 90-degree turn before continuing to a T junction, where a right turn is made onto the Charcoal Burners Trail. Note that the Charcoal Burners and the Fahnestock Trails commingle now for a short spell. The time taken to this point is probably about 2.5 hours.

Beaver Pond soon comes into view. The trail does not go across the dam but turns right on a cement bridge over the outlet just before the man-made structure. Within 10 minutes a brown-plastic sign indicates that the Fahnestock Trail leaves the Charcoal Burners Trail to the left. The white-marked Cabot Trail taken earlier enters on the right, and you are now retracing your earlier route back to your car.

SJG

13

Hidden Lake Loop

Total distance: 6.5 miles (3.3-mile alternate)

Walking time: 2.5 to 3 hours (1.5-hour alternate)

Vertical rise: 500 feet

Maps: USGS 7.5' Oscawana Lake; NY–NJTC East Hudson Trails #3

This pleasant woods walk, which could also be done on cross-country skis, passes peaceful lakes, lush swamps, and even uses a Civil War–era railroad bed. As the park's terrain is generally higher than surrounding areas, snow accumulates faster, is often deeper, and stays longer than city-folk might suppose. As you walk along, picture the rural communities that once dominated this region. Old stone walls, foundations, historic mine pits, and woods roads are all that remain of the active history of this now quiet area.

To reach the parking area on NY 301, take the Taconic State Parkway to the well-signed exit for NY 301 east (Cold Spring). Proceed east for 1.3 miles to a modest-sized parking area on the north side of the road, between two sections of Canopus Lake. If full, a second parking area is located a short distance farther east, at the Appalachian Trail (AT) crossing.

Walk over to the other side of NY 301, and head a very short distance west (back the way you came) along the shoulder. Hop the road barrier, and scramble down to Three-Lakes trailhead, indicated by the blue-plastic markers of the Taconic Park Commission. Trails in Fahnestock are primarily marked with these disks supplemented with paint blazes.

The Three-Lakes Trail begins on a wide trailway. Rock cuts and piles of stone (called talus) are dramatic evidence of the mining activity from the late 1700s through the late 1800s. The blue markers are somewhat sparse, but the wide trail is easy to follow.

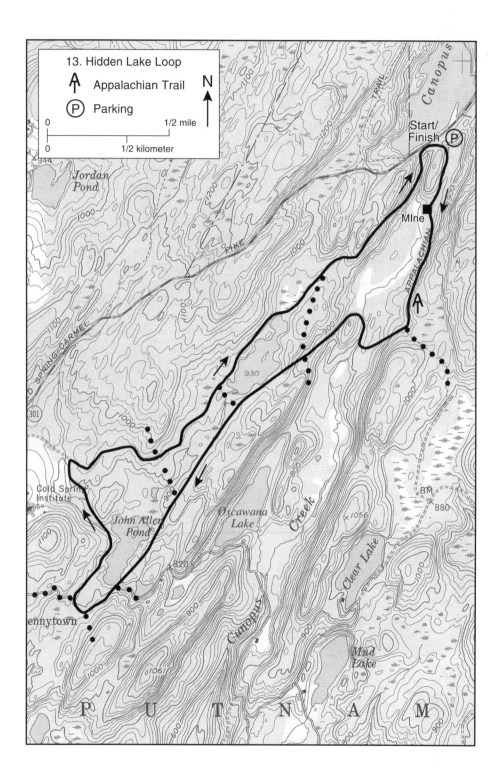

Appalachian Trail

N

P Parking

0   1/2 mile

0   1/2 kilometer

Jordan
Pond

Canopus

Start/
Finish

P

Mine

APPALACHIAN

TRAIL

PIKE

COLD SPRING CARMEL

301

Cold Spring
Institute

John Allen
Pond

Oscawana
Lake

Canopus

Creek

930

820

900

Clear Lake

BM
880

1056

ennytown

1061

Mud
Lake

Canopus

P   U   T   N   A   M

The first mine you pass, identifiable only by its tailing pit, belonged to Richard Hopper, who opened it in 1820. The mine remained a small operation until the Civil War, when Philipse heirs sold the mineral rights to Paul S. Forbes, the builder of the railway. The mining survived until the panic of 1873, and the surrounding land was obtained by Dr. Clarence Fahnestock in 1915 after a series of intervening land sales.

Less than 15 minutes along, the route passes a lovely marsh with an extensive stand of cattails that rustle in the wind. There are many birds here, heard but often unseen. Soon the woods open up, and old stone walls offer evidence of long-gone settlements.

Remember, you are following the blue blazes, not just the obvious footway. There are several points on this hike when the marked trail abruptly leaves a woods road and turns onto a narrower footpath.

One such point comes just 0.5 mile into the hike as the blue trail turns right, leaving the woods road. If you notice green markers you've passed the turn and are heading toward the Clear Lake Boy Scout Reservation.

The Three-Lakes Trail turns right past fields of hay-scented fern and down to a charming little brook. A small picturesque gorge just upstream is worth the short detour for a peek.

The trail crosses the brook on large rock slabs placed there by the volunteers of the East Hudson trail crew and then arcs back north along the stream almost to a meadow. Zigzagging to the left the route now takes you up to a ridge in the impressive forest, certainly one of the more handsome second-growth forests in southern New York.

It should have taken no more than 35 minutes to walk the mile-plus distance to the intersection with the white-marked AT. Cross the intersection, and continue on the blue-marked Three-Lakes Trail, watching for Hidden Lake on your right.

As Hidden Lake comes into view, you'll travel through a canyon of mountain laurel and approach the shore of this graceful pond. At a T-junction with a woods road, turn right, off the marked trail, and head to a dam for a fine view of the lake.

For those wanting a shorter hike (so far you've walked 1.8 miles), the dam can be crossed (except at times of high-water flow), and on the far side you'll spot the Old Mine Railroad Trail. Turn right onto this yellow-blazed trail for about 0.75 mile to its end at a junction with the AT. Continue ahead, now on the AT, for less than a mile back to NY 301. Walk right along the road to your car, a short distance away.

For those walking the full loop, return to and continue on the Three-Lakes Trail, which shortly leaves the woods road. About 0.5 mile from the lake, you'll pass the southern terminus of the Charcoal Burners Trail (red), easily missed in the midst of a laurel grove. Another 0.5 mile (and just more than an hour into the hike) brings you to the vicinity of John Allen Pond, a genuinely charming spot. The island with its fine stand of evergreen trees is especially memorable.

Someday when I'm here in winter and the lake absolutely frozen solid, I intend to walk over to the island to see for myself if it is truly as special as it looks from this spot.

The footpath wanders along the shore of the pond and then crosses a cement section of the spillway/dam. Continue ahead as the trail leads away from the water.

Time has altered the features of the mines and ponds, but a 19th-century observer once wrote about a spot not far from here that was the destination of an 1887 picnic. The trip to Pine Swamp was described by E. M. Hopkins, one of the picnickers who spent a summer afternoon

Hidden Lake Loop

Hidden Lake from the dam

exploring the Sunk Mine, an enormous cleft "gently filled with green slimy looking water." All the accessible ore had been removed, and "one end of the cleft terminates at the surface of the sloap; for the other a lateral drift, whose mouth is partly concealed by water extends into the mountains. . . . None now living can remember when it was in operation." Two picnickers entered the mine, guided by dry birch-bark torches. Inside they discovered the canoe of one Levi Marshall, deceased, who had claimed once to have found a silver mine. Thinking they had discovered Marshall's lost silver mine, they walked deeper and deeper into the mine until they found a pile of silver objects: teapots, plates, and other items. Leading up from the cache was a ladder that led the picnickers into Marshall's cabin. The residents at the time were charged with burglary, putting an end to the rumors that silver could be mined with the iron in these hills.

Turn right when the Three-Lakes Trail comes to follow Skunk Mine Road (sand and gravel). After a 4- or 5-minute walk on the road, watch for the blue-marked route to leave the road to the left. Careful–here is where you leave the Three-Lakes Trail.

Continue instead on the road for a minute or two to a bend. On your right, you'll see the start of the 2.2-mile yellow-marked Old Mine Railroad Trail. Turn onto this trail as you now begin to head back north. The hiking is easy. The trail is wide, at first flat and then descending toward John Allen Pond. Markings are few, but the route is easy to follow.

After 10 minutes the trail crosses a small stream on rocks. I hope you, too, will see the lush underwater plants that were so obvious on our visit. Note also how well the trail is constructed and elevated. No, volunteers did not build this. They just used the features that gave the trail its name–literally an old mine-railroad bed.

During the Civil War a narrow-gauge railroad was built to service the iron mines in the area. More track was laid in the mid-1870s, but the better economies of open pit mines in the Midwest brought these operations to an early end. Starting a new life, much of the railbed was opened as a hiking trail in 1994.

A few more minutes along, the marked trail makes a sharp right. Follow the blazed route, avoiding the woods road that branches left and leads to private land.

Some 2 hours into the hike, an easy-to-miss junction with the red-blazed Charcoal Burners Trail is passed. Just beyond, look for a large glacial erratic. Doesn't it appear that two trees are supporting the rock?

In another 10 minutes you again approach Hidden Lake dam, this time, of course, on the other side. Continue ahead, following yellow. The path is now narrower and raised above the surrounding land. Occasionally there is open water on both sides of the footway.

A half-mile or so beyond the dam, the Old Mine Railroad Trail ends at a junction with the AT. Turn left, now following white blazes, again along an old railbed. Here, the elevated rock roadway is sometimes 15 feet above the surrounding land. The path continues through a rock cut and skirts high on a ridge overlooking the marsh passed near the start of the hike.

Soon you'll begin to hear the traffic sounds of NY 301 and pass an AT sign-in register box. Follow the AT up to the highway, and turn right back to your car—or turn right onto a distinct woods road paralleling the highway that takes you back to the hike's starting point.

HNZ/BMcM

14

Pawling Nature Reserve

Total distance: 7.2 miles

Walking time: 4 hours

Vertical rise: 700 feet

Maps: USGS 7.5' Pawling, NY-CT; USGS 7.5' Dover Plains, NY-CT

The Appalachian Trail (AT) traverses Hammersly Ridge from southwest to northeast through the 1,000-acre Pawling Nature Reserve. Combining parts of the trail with a walk on Quaker Lake Road and some of the reserve's other trails makes not only for a fair hike but also gives a delightful chance to observe a variety of flora, from a deep hemlock gorge to wet meadows to swamps. You may see wild turkey, deer, and an occasional beaver, coyote, or bobcat; but remember to take precautions against the bites of deer ticks when you are walking here.

Three trailheads for the reserve are on Quaker Lake Road, but only one, the main entrance, has good parking. To reach the trailheads, turn east off NY 22 north of Pawling at Hurd Corners, and continue on County Route 68 (CR 68) for 1.5 miles to Baker Corner, where you turn left onto Quaker Lake Road. A figure-eight walk can be started at the main entrance, 1.3 miles north on Quaker Lake Road, just beyond the private lands of Quaker Lake. Three small patches of the reserve line the road, but all the rest of the roadside is posted.

There is no parking at the southern red-marked trailhead near the height-of-land south of Quaker Lake; this spot is 0.4 mile from CR 68. There is room for only one or two cars at the northern parking area for the yellow-marked trail at 2.7 miles. But Quaker Lake Road is a quiet, mostly dirt road, so with a 2.3-mile walk along it, you can make a figure-eight loop over the top of Hammersly Ridge. Alternatively, you can walk several shorter loops through the reserve.

The East Hudson Highlands

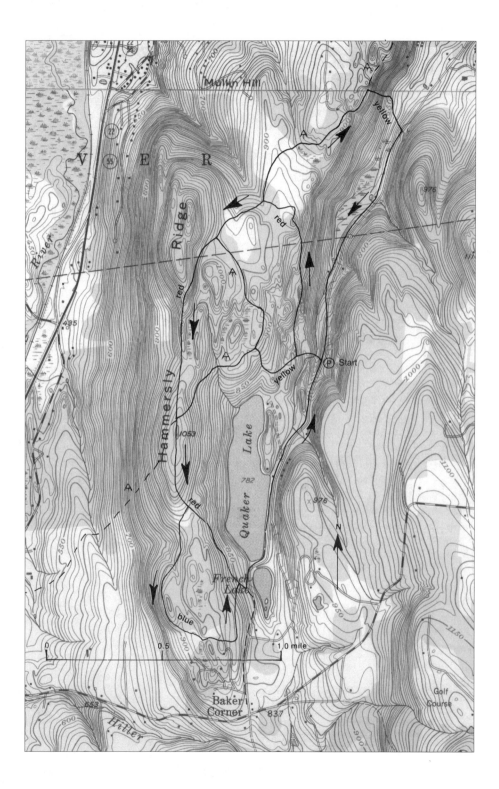

A yellow-marked trail from the main entrance immediately enters the gorge with its charming waterfall and lush ferns. The trail continues briefly beside the stream and crosses it before mounting the rocky slopes of the ridge. In 5 minutes you reach the red-marked trail, which forks right. Stay on the yellow-marked route, and after 0.5 mile, the trail swings along the ridge, then intersects the white-marked AT at an acute angle. Your continuing walk north has both yellow and white markers. Wildflowers such as pinksters, many ferns, and marsh plants fill the wet areas along the ridge, areas that were cleared and farmed sometime before the Revolutionary War. In another 0.3 mile the red-marked trail forks right, and you could follow it back to the start for a shorter loop. If you choose to continue on the AT, the next 20 minutes, about 0.9 mile, is a walk along the ridgeline.

When the AT goes straight ahead, take the yellow trail 0.3 mile down the eastern slope of the ridge. The trail crosses the outlet stream on a shaky bridge, then turns right to emerge at the northern parking area. New flagging, mixed with the yellow blazes, makes it possible to follow the route through the brush to the small parking lot. Walk south for 1.3 miles along Quaker Lake Road, past lovely stands of hemlock that line the valley beside the Quaker Lake outlet. The ridge is quite close to the road, and when the leaves are off, the steep slopes are clearly visible.

From the main entrance, begin the second half of the figure-eight walk as you started, but this time turn right on the red-marked trail and follow it north to the AT, then turn south on the AT briefly, walking this 0.3-mile segment in the opposite direction from your earlier walk. Near the top of the ridge, watch closely, for the AT makes a sharp turn left. Go right onto the red-marked trail, and enjoy the lovely walk south along the ridgeline. The AT crosses this red-marked trail just below the crest of the ridge. (An alternative entrance to the reserve is along the AT from the large parking area on NY 22, 0.25 mile north of CR 68.)

Stay on the red-marked trail; it will lead you past small wet places and beside truly wonderful stands of hemlocks as it descends to Quaker Lake Road. Another variation is inviting: A blue-marked trail makes a loop to the reserve's southern boundary, returning to the red-marked trail within 100 yards of Quaker Lake Road. This loop circles more marshes, and its northern leg takes you through a large area of blowdowns. A short walk north beside Quaker Lake, about 1 mile and no more than 20 minutes, takes you back to the main entrance.

BMcM

15

Dutchess County Backpack

Total distance: 14.6 miles

Walking time: 2 to 3 days

Vertical rise: 2,300 feet

Maps: USGS 7.5' Poughquag; 7.5' Pawling; NY–NJTC/ATC Appalachian Trail Map #1 (1998).

First proposed in 1921, the Appalachian Trail (known by hikers as the AT) extends from Maine to Georgia, some 2,150 miles across 14 states and is the result of the tireless efforts of many thousands of volunteers and eight decades of advocacy and work.

The first section was built by the New York–New Jersey Trail Conference (NY–NJTC) on Bear Mountain in 1923, but there was not much additional progress for several years. Serious efforts resumed in 1925 with formation of the Appalachian Trail Conference (ATC) to coordinate efforts. The Civilian Conservation Corps completed the last section on a ridge in Maine in 1937.

The route did not last. After World War II, highways, housing, and other developments encroached on the trail, forcing many sections onto highways. As the situation became more serious, the hiking community turned to Congress and President Lyndon Johnson for assistance. The result was a system of National Scenic Trails, with the AT and Pacific Crest Trail being the first designees. Slow progress led President Jimmy Carter to sign the Appalachian Trail Bill in 1978, and true protection efforts finally began. Some $90 million dollars was appropriated to acquire a corridor for the trail where it was not already in a public park or forest. Today only a few miles remain unprotected.

Under a unique agreement, the ATC has been entrusted by the National Park Service with the primary responsibility for maintaining the footpath and associated facilities (mostly shelters). The 88.5 miles that lie in

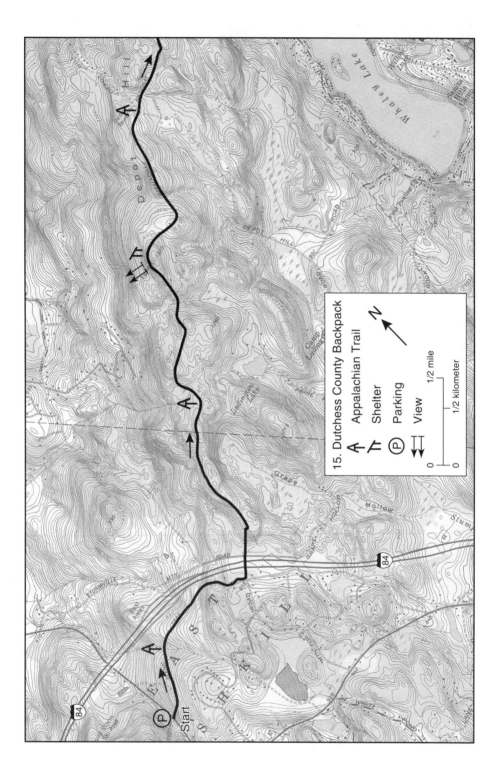

15. Dutchess County Backpack

Appalachian Trail

Ⓟ Shelter

Ⓟ Parking

View

0   1/2 mile

0   1/2 kilometer

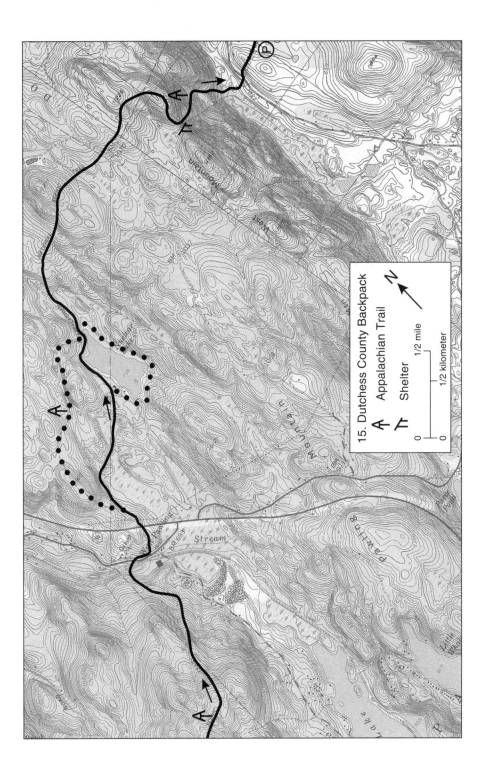

15. Dutchess County Backpack

Appalachian Trail

Shelter

0   1/2 mile

0   1/2 kilometer

New York State are maintained by volunteers of the NY–NJTC and some of their member clubs. At some 4,000 acres, the AT corridor constitutes Dutchess County's largest park.

This two-night "family" backpack consists of a short 4-mile hike to the first lean-to, a moderate 7.6-mile day to the next lean-to, and a short 3 miles out on the final day. It can be started on Friday afternoon and end early on Sunday. The full distance can also be done as a vigorous day hike. For a longer backpack, see Options at the end of this hike.

Backpacking requires preparation. If you are not experienced, get advice from a backpacking basics book or a good specialized outdoor store. In addition to normal day-hike equipment, you'll need at least a good sleeping bag and pad, food, a cooking pot or two, dishes, utensils, backpacking stove, matches or lighter, flashlight, and a tent (in case the lean-to is full). The more you take, the heavier your pack. Take what you need and only what you need (easier said than done). Many outdoor-equipment stores offer backpack equipment checklists, and these are also available on the Internet. AT guidelines require overnight groups to be no more than 10 people. Be aware of seasonal conditions. For example, if you're going during an unusually dry period, check with the NY–NJTC to see if the water supply is sufficient—and they may need a few days notice to get this information for you.

The end point on NY 22, 2.4 miles north of the center of the village of Pawling and 1.8 miles from the Trinity–Pawling School footbridge. The parking area is located on the northbound side of NY 22 just west of the trail crossing. NY 22, a major thoroughfare, is accessible from I-84 exit 20 and I-684 exit 10. If you have two cars available, spot one at the end, and then drive to the start. Otherwise, you'll have to arrange with a friend for a pickup or drop-off.

It's worth noting that there is a special weekend/holiday Metro-North rail station here, which could provide your transportation home. This site is also less than 2.5 miles from the full-time Pawling rail station. For information call 212-532-4900 or 800-METROINFO.

To get from NY 22 parking to the hike's start on NY 52 (see below), take NY 22 south about 3 miles to NY 55, then turn right onto NY 55 for 7 miles to its junction with NY 216 in Poughquag. Turn left onto NY 216 for another 7 miles to NY 52. Turn left again onto NY 52 for about 2 miles (going under I-84) to the parking area (left side) near the crest of the hill. If you come to Leetown Road, you've gone 0.4 mile too far.

If you don't need to shuttle a car, you can get directly to the beginning of the hike on NY 52, using I-84 exit 16. Proceed north on the Taconic Parkway for less than 1.5 miles to NY 52. Turn right (east) onto NY 52 for just less than 4 miles. Pass under I-84, and head up a hill to a small AT parking area off the left side of the highway.

Day One
Distance: 4 miles
Walking time: 1.5 hours
Vertical rise: 800 feet

From the parking area off NY 52 (800 feet elevation), proceed through the boulders on a blue-blazed connector trail intersecting the AT within one minute. Do not turn right, but continue straight ahead on the AT, blazed with a white rectangle. Continue up-hill to one of many information signboards you'll pass. They're placed on both sides of almost all the road crossings. About 10 minutes in you'll cross an old stone wall (again, one of many in this area) and a seasonal stream. The trail undulates and skirts a grassy field with young saplings. Portions of this field are cleared as part of an open-areas management plan to increase natural diversity. The views to the north and north-west are of the Catskills and Shawangunks. As you leave the field area, note the huge tree next to the trail. This magnificent white oak has been measured at more than 20 feet in circumference!

Soon the roar of traffic on I-84 fills the air as the trail ascends a small hill and bears left down to the paved Stormville Mountain Road. Turn right a short distance to Mountain Top Road, where a left turn takes you over I-84 to Grape Hollow Road (very limited parking). You've come about a mile and a half in 30 minutes.

The trail immediately reenters the woods down an embankment on some stone steps and begins a moderate ascent of ridges leading to Mount Egbert (1,329 feet). Soon you'll pass a small pond (a swamp in dry seasons) and some nice rock outcroppings. At just more than an hour into the hike, you'll pass a yellow-blazed access trail on the left that leads from a cul-de-sac in the town of Beekman. The trail passes over the crests of small hills, crosses seasonal streams, meanders through patches of mountain laurel, and comes to an attractive rock cut before ascending the first ledges of Mount Egbert with its fine views. In another 0.25 mile, after cresting the summit, the shelter is reached (75 feet to the right of the trail).

The Morgan Stewart Memorial Shelter, named for a deceased trail worker, was built in 1984 by local volunteers with $2,500 in funds donated by IBM. This raised floor three-sided lean-to accommodates six (first come, first served), so you should bring a small tent (especially on weekends or in summer) in case it's occupied. There's a fireplace, a privy 200 feet to the side, and a water pump downhill about 400 feet. The round concrete ruin near the shelter is the remains of a cistern that served a farmhouse that once stood nearby.

All backcountry water should be boiled, chemically treated, or filtered before use. We find using a good backpacking filter is the best and easiest method. The filtered water has no unpleasant taste and is still cool and refreshing.

Bears have been seen here. You're unlikely to encounter any bears, but smaller animals are common. Bring a rope to hang your food high from a tree branch.

Day Two

Distance: 7.6 miles
Walking time: 5 hours
Vertical rise: 1,000 feet

Leaving the shelter, the AT undulates through the woods. There are no views except near the start, and the terrain is generally gently down. You cross the gravel Depot Hill Road in about 20 minutes. Depot Hill is a state reforestation area. The area is naturally regenerated from farmland abandoned in the early 1900s. In 1971 thinning by the state eliminated diseased and poor-quality trees. Selected timber harvests are done periodically and a small sign is posted explaining this in detail.

About an hour from the start, you'll pass a large balancing boulder. Immediately after is a viewpoint east down to Whaley Lake. Now begins a 15-minute, 700-foot descent ending with a crossing of a railroad track (the yellow paint markers are the boundary of the railroad right-of-way). Note the stand of Japanese knotweed (looks just like bamboo) on the far side of the track. Continuing down an embankment, the trail crosses an outlet stream of Whaley Lake on a bridge and continues up to cross Old NY 55. Bear right across the road and through some boulders, and reenter the woods. The route now parallels and then ascends through a large rock outcropping. Heavy pack? Short legs? This scramble can be bypassed by bushwhacking around to the right, and relocating the main trail to this easier alternative is being considered.

Soon the trail crosses NY 55 (parking is available just north of the crossing) and enters the Nuclear Lake section. This property, which was acquired by the National Park Service in 1979, derives its name from the previous owner, United Nuclear Corporation, which conducted nuclear fuel reprocessing research there until the early 1970s. The buildings were removed, the area cleaned, and the lake declared safe for unrestricted use.

After passing a signboard and a blue-blazed trail to a parking area, another blue-blazed trail is reached. This alternate route, still maintained, was used before the 1998 opening of Nuclear Lake for public use. Stay on the AT, which skirts along the side of a hill through mixed hardwoods and hemlocks, continuing for more than a mile before crossing the Nuclear Lake outlet stream three times. After paralleling the stream for a short distance, the trail passes through a rock crevice, an area heavy with mountain laurel, and continues to the lake.

Completely surrounded by public land, Nuclear Lake (yes, it needs renaming) is most often a peaceful area—a great place to stop and explore. The lake is large. At-your-own-risk swimming is OK . . . and it's only 3 miles more to the shelter. Construction of a yellow-blazed, around-the-lake loop trail was begun in the summer of 2000 and will likely be completed by the time you take your hike.

The walk along the lake takes 10 to 15 minutes, and it's just less than 0.5 mile to the junction with the blue bypass. The route, which has been undulating, now begins a steady ascent to a stone wall, then levels off on a 1,200-foot-high ridgetop and begins a descent, crossing a swamp area on puncheons. An old dirt road (Penny Road) is reached. You have now hiked just less than 7 miles from the Morgan Stewart shelter.

For the next 0.5 mile the trail passes a swamp and then ascends to the summit of West Mountain. Here there are fine views to the north. The green pastoral countryside is so peaceful. One is hard-pressed to admit just how close this spot is to our nation's largest city. It's now just 0.3 mile to the Telephone Pioneers Shelter and night two.

This small shelter, a short way off on a side trail, accommodates six. There's a privy with water usually available from a stream at the trail junction. Built in 1988, the shelter was funded by the White Plains Chapter of the Telephone Pioneers of America, whose members also helped build it.

Day Three
Distance: 3.1 miles
Walking time: Less than 2 hours
Vertical gain: 500 feet
The hike out is fairly short and mostly downhill. It begins by paralleling the stream, with the descent sometimes steep. After about 0.5 mile, the AT descends over some rock outcroppings (slippery when wet, but they can be bushwhacked around) with some lovely cedars. Stay on the trail whenever possible because there's considerable poison ivy around. The trail passes through some fields (follow posts) before crossing West Dover Road (County Road 20—parking available).

Cross the road, passing a huge white oak to the left of the trail, and proceed into a very wet area of fields. Trail builders have placed many stringers in this area, but they can be slippery—take your time.

About an hour from the lean-to, the trail

Take the time to hug a tree.

reenters the woods and soon begins to descend Corbin Hill. This area had a major encroachment in 1997 when a contractor, through a series of misunderstandings, built logging roads and began cutting timber on this federally protected land. The activity was spotted and reported by a NY–NJTC volunteer. Although it was soon stopped, the area nevertheless sustained serious damage.

The trail continues its descent and passes through several stone walls before crossing the Swamp River on a wooden bridge. Crossing a major marsh on puncheons, the trail then follows a short dirt road, passes around a gate, and crosses the Metro-North railroad tracks at their Appalachian Trail station. NY 22 is just beyond, with the parking lot on the far side of the road about 0.1 mile north (left).

OPTIONS

Day one can be lengthened by about 5 miles by beginning near the AT crossing of the Taconic State Parkway near Miller Hill Road. No parking is available on the Taconic, but limited parking is available along Rock Ledge Road (50 feet east of the parkway) or Hortontown Road (0.3 west of Parkway). Miller Hill Road crosses the Taconic about 1 mile north of the Dutchess-Putnam County line and about 2 miles south of the its intersection with I-84 (exit 16). The trail in this area traverses a side of Housner Mountain and crosses the multiple summits of Stormville Mountain. It adds about 1,100 feet of elevation gain. There are numerous fine views.

There are several other options to shorten the route. Midhike parking areas are mentioned in the text.

HNZ

III. Rockland County and Harriman Park

Introduction to the Ramapos: Harriman–Bear Mountain State Parks and Rockland County

The Ramapo Mountains run from northern New Jersey into Rockland and Orange Counties. Their eroded slopes have risen above nearby seas for nearly 600 million years, making them among the oldest land masses on the continent. These mountains are part of the Reading Prong, which extends from Reading, Pennsylvania, to the Hudson Highlands and north to the Green Mountains of Vermont. This Precambrian formation is the result of periods of intense folding and metamorphism of sediments deposited more than a billion years ago and of intrusions of magma that occurred several times in the Precambrian era. Although these forces leave a complicated picture for the geologist, later events, the Ice Ages, are much clearer. The striations and polished rocks and the ubiquitous glacial erratics are obvious to the hiker on any walk through the Ramapos.

Whether the name *Ramapo* derives from a Native American name for the potholes that mark the Ramapo River or whether it comes from a Leni-Lenape word that means "place of slanting rock" is not known. The latter is certainly more descriptive, for the views of uplifted faces of various metamorphosed layers are also a part of each hike.

HARRIMAN AND BEAR MOUNTAIN STATE PARKS

Bear Mountain and Harriman State Parks span most of the Ramapos in New York State. Their origins are unusual. In 1908 the state proposed building a prison at Bear Mountain. Among the many who protested this desecration of beautiful and historic lands was Mary Harriman, widow of the railroad tycoon, who offered to give the Palisades Interstate Park Commission (PIPC) 10,000 acres, the nucleus of the modern parks. In return it was agreed that the commission's jurisdiction would be extended north along the Hudson, and plans for the prison would be dropped. Subsequent gifts and purchases have expanded the park to its present 54,000 acres and allowed for scenic parkways and the building of dams to create or enlarge the numerous bodies of water that dot the park.

PIPC (pronounced *pip see*), under the leadership of its president, George W. Perkins, and chief engineer, Major William A. Welch, fostered much development. Lakes were formed, roads and children's camps were built. During 1910 and 1911 a dock for steamboat excursions and a railway station were built, and the park officially opened for public use in the summer of 1913. By 1914 it was estimated that more than 1 million people a year visited the park.

The Bear Mountain Inn, completed in 1915, still offers hospitality to visitors. It was constructed with huge boulders and chestnut logs and at that time guests paid $4.50 for a room and three meals. Upstairs the magnificent fireplace was constructed with stones from old walls.

Establishment of facilities for winter sports followed, a Trailside Museum was established, trail shelters were constructed, and at the time of this writing a new building is under construction to house a large carousel.

Although officially separate, the two contiguous parks are jointly administered and offer today's hikers several hundred of miles of marked trails. The present foot-trail system within the parks was the vision of early "trampers" belonging to infant walking clubs in New York City. During the summer of 1920, Major Welch, working with others, formed a permanent federation of hiking clubs known as the Palisades Interstate Park Trail Conference—the roots of the present New York–New Jersey Trail Conference (NY–NJTC). Their first venture, the building of the Tuxedo–Jones Point Trail (later to be called the Ramapo-Dunderberg Trail) enabled trampers to catch the ferry to New Jersey and the railway to Tuxedo on a Saturday afternoon, spend one night in the woods, and emerge in time to catch a train back to the city on Sunday evening. The first section of the Appalachian Trail was created at Bear Mountain in 1923 and now extends more than 2,000 miles from Georgia to Maine.

By 1930 new trail building had come to an end, but quite soon trail wars broke out between competing outdoor clubs. Hiking groups accused one another of establishing their own trails and, worse, of painting out blazes put on trees by rivals. In addition, individuals began to paint routes for their own use. Kerson Nurian was one of these culprits (Hike 20). It was at this time that trail maintenance standards were established under the guidance of the NY–NJTC. No new trail cutting was permitted without reference to the group, and the willy-nilly proliferation of new trails ceased.

Today the HBM (as hikers call it) is the most popular hiking destination for city residents because several bus routes and a rail line connect with numerous trailheads. These parks often attract throngs of people who enjoy the skating, waterfronts, and picnicking in the more developed areas. However, escaping the big crowds is not hard if you are prepared to walk.

Hikes in Harriman and Bear Mountain State Parks provide great loops that include segments of many different trails. Many trails here involve frequent small undulations that may not be specifically detailed in hike narratives or on the maps. Those seeking real solitude should walk during the off-season or during the week. Sites of old mines, cemeteries, and other signs of human habitation can easily be found, and maps and guidebooks educate the walker. Much detailed history, specifically keyed to the trail system, can be found in *Harriman Trails: A Guide and History*, by William J. Myles. Many of the trails are suitable for family outings.

Parking is permitted but only in designated areas; you may not build fires or disturb flora and fauna. Equestrians (permit required) and mountain bikers are permitted on multiuse trails designated for those activities. Overnight backcountry camping is permitted only at designated shelters.

OTHER STATE PARKS

From the New York–New Jersey border north to Haverstraw, a string of smaller parks is administered by PIPC and provide a local route for the Long Path. Tallman Mountain, Clausland (a county park), Blauvelt, Hook Mountain (Hike 16), the highly developed Rockland Lake, and High Tor (Hike 17) provide for a variety of walking and hiking as well as more developed recreation, including swimming and golf. Descriptions of each are provided in the New York Walk Book.

16

Hook Mountain

Total distance: 11 miles

Walking time: 6 hours

Vertical rise: 1,200 feet

Maps: USGS 7.5' Haverstraw; USGS 7.5' Nyack; NY–NJTC Hudson Palisades map #4B

The towering cliffs of the Hook have awed travelers to southern New York State for centuries. Henry Hudson and the sailors who followed made note of this impressive headland as they made their way up the Hudson River. The constructed cliffs of abandoned quarries further etch the skyline into sheer red-brown walls that appear to continue the Palisades. Whether walking to the high point in spring or fall to watch the hawk migration or bicycling along the paths that hug the shores, you'll find much to enjoy in the parklands run by the Palisades Interstate Park Commission that stretch from Nyack to Haverstraw on the Hudson's western shore.

A portion of the Long Path takes the high route from Nyack across the Hook and the hills called the Seven Sisters. You can make a circuit walk along the hills and back on the bike path along the shore, enjoying the best views of woods and water. If you have two cars, you can just hike over the hills, avoiding the bike path return walk. Driving directions for the "half hike" are at the end of this narrative.

The hike begins at Nyack State Park at the end of Broadway in Nyack, where a seasonal parking fee may be charged. Walk back to the tollbooth, and on a utility pole you'll see the three blazes denoting the start of a white-blazed connector trail. The trail travels along the road and turns right onto Larchdale Road to its end. Note the cliffs on your right—that's the top of the Hook, where you're headed. At the end of Larchdale, the trail turns left and after 50 yards turns right,

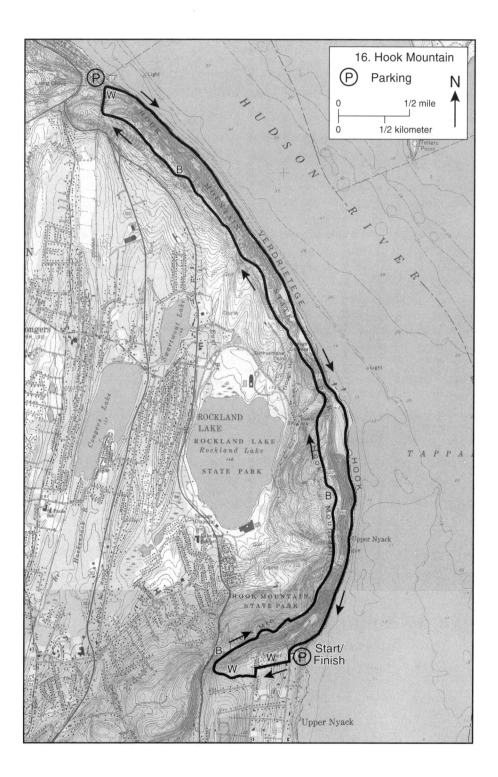

P Parking

N

0   1/2 mile

0   1/2 kilometer

HUDSON RIVER

Long Clove

W

B

HOOK

MOUNTAIN

VERDRIETEGE PATH

Golf Course

Trough Hollow

ROCKLAND
LAKE

ROCKLAND LAKE
Rockland Lake

STATE PARK

Congers Lake

Swartwout Lake

Hackensack R.

Bethsemane Cem.

Kom Sch

Hook Mountain

HOOK

B

Upper Nyack

TAPPA

HOOK MOUNTAIN
STATE PARK

B

W   W   P   Start/
Finish

Upper Nyack

this time into the woods. After a 10-minute, sometimes wet, walk, the connector trail ends at a junction with the turquoise-blazed Long Path, about 0.75 mile from your car. Turn right, and begin following the Long Path.

Much of the trail here follows the (thankfully) never-completed Tweed Boulevard, part of a 1870s scheme by cohorts of the infamous Boss Tweed to build a road from Nyack across Hook Mountain to Rockland Lake—complete with a hotel on the summit.

A 20-minute walk brings you to the top of the Hook with views toward New York City and north to the quarry behind Rockland Lake. Beyond the quarry lies the massif of Dunderberg that ends in the Timp. Farther north and on the other side of the river lies the ragged contour of Breakneck Ridge leading up toward South Beacon. The Hudson River, wide here at Tappan Bay, is pinched to the north by Croton Point. Farther north it opens out into its widest segment at Haverstraw Bay before becoming choked into the narrows of the Hudson Highlands.

You are standing on the 736-foot peak of the Verdrietege, or tedious headland, so-called by early Dutch sailors who struggled to sail upwind around it. But the landscape at your feet is not what the Dutch sailors saw, and the history of that landscape accounts for a good portion of the preservation movement that resulted in the parks now lining the Hudson's shores.

The Palisades' traprock diabase, which is volcanic in origin, surfaces here through the base of Triassic sandstone and shale. Quarries along the river to the south were active in the 1820s, and the columnar cliffs of the Hook were quarried extensively in the 1870s and 1880s with the introduction of dynamite and heavy earth-moving equipment. The basalt columns were crushed for traprock for macadam roads and, later in the 1890s, for concrete for Manhattan buildings. Angered at first only by the ear-shattering explosions heard up and down both sides of the river, residents of both New York and New Jersey began to speak out against the quarries. It was not until 1894 that a well-organized group opposed the visual desecration of the cliffs caused by the quarrying.

Finally in 1900, after several years of legislative debate fueled by the argument that "preservation would largely benefit those who enjoyed the view from the New York side of the Hudson," a study commission report was accepted. It called for a permanent interstate park commission and the acquisition of land along the Palisades for recreational purposes. With both private and public funds, the acquisition program progressed from acquiring lands from the top of the cliff face to the river to adding cliff-top lands north to Nyack. The Hook was still threatened until the Palisades Interstate Park was extended northward in 1906. By 1915 all of the Hook was acquired by the Palisades Interstate Park Commission.

The cliff-top trail continues north through Hook Mountain State Park by first heading down the incredibly narrow and sinuous ridge. Trees block the views here, but you'll climb a handful of open summits before the day is over. One opening discloses Rockland Lake and the landing from which the lake's ice was shipped to New York City. A 40-minute walk brings you into a valley, and shortly beyond is the second hill with several view spots on its summit.

The descent from this hilltop is marked by a left fork that takes you across an old roadway that once led toward Rockland Landing. Beyond the low point, another roadway comes in from the left. As you start to climb, you'll be amazed at the amount of rock work that was used to construct these

Croton Point

Stella Green

old roadways, making an especially lovely base for the trail to follow. Gentle ups and downs ensue. The curved stone wall and old foundation beside the trail are sure to intrigue you.

As you begin to climb again, about 2 hours into the trip, watch for a path that leads up to the right to a promontory overlooking Croton Point, unquestionably one of the best views of the day.

This is a good place to observe the clues to the second major industry of the region's past, clues that are much less obvious than those of the quarries. At the shore below are the remains of old docks, the successors to Slaughter's Landing, a settlement begun in 1711 by John Slaughter from Rockland Lake. An ice business was started at Rockland Lake in 1831 when Moses G. Leonard impressed New York City hoteliers with the cleanliness and purity of the lake's ice. In 1855 the business became the Knickerbocker Ice Company, the largest in New York, employing as many as 1,000 men. Ice was cut from the lake and stored for shipment south to New York City. It was moved from the lake via an endless conveyor cable to the landings, where three pairs of tracks led across the docks whose ruins are guarded by an old lighthouse. Four-hundred-ton loads were carried south on barges.

Return to the trail, and within a few feet you meet what appears to be a trail intersection. The way right is steep and unmarked. Turn left for an almost equally steep descent behind a row of houses and old foundations; follow it to a road that could provide an alternate trailhead for a portion of this walk. This point also can be reached by car from Rockland Lake State Park, which is to your left (west). Rockland Landing is on the waterfront to your right. The 3.8-mile walk to this point along the summits should take around 2.5 hours.

Immediately north of the stanchions that bar vehicular traffic into the park, the turquoise-marked Long Path continues, first passing an early 19th-century cemetery. The first hilltop with a view is scarcely 5 minutes from the road, a perch atop the first in a string of smaller quarries north of the landing. Just beyond, you'll be amazed to see Dutchman's-breeches blooming in spring only a short distance from the prickly pear cactus that seems to enjoy this dry location. The trail continues on the west side of the ridge, emerging to a series of more or less obscure views, depending on the season. At one spot you look down on red-brown cliffs and pine seedlings that are filling in a second quarry.

The trail descends, turns left past a filtration plant, and heads up the next ridge bordered by vine-covered stone walls. For a short time the trail follows the park boundary. Just beyond, a side trail (right) leads to a lookout with spectacular views atop a third quarry. A series of gentle ups and downs ends in a sharp, short drop into a hemlock-filled valley. Immediately you emerge with views to the north and northwest. The next downhill leads off the ridge.

The way out of the small valley is viewless, its taller trees making the segment feel like a remote woodland trail where the roller-coaster effect of the ridge continues for a delightful 45-minute walk. One summit yields views of narrow DeForest Lake. As the trail turns sharply east and heads steeply down toward the river, almost above the railroad tunnel, you feel suspended above the water. The hemlock-covered bank parallels the shore 400 feet above it. As the trail descends along the ridge, keep an eye open for a white-blazed trail (if you reach a major power line, you've gone too far). This fairly recent trail provides a connector to the bike path, avoiding a walk into Haverstraw. This point is 3 miles from Rockland Landing Road. Your trek from the Hook across the hills of the Seven Sisters—and surely twice that number of small knobs and crests—has taken about 4.5 hours.

Now follow the white trail as it switchbacks down the steep hillside toward the river. In about 10 minutes it brings you to the shore bike path. The three-sided old stone structure was probably used to store explosives when the quarrying was active. The newer ruin was an administrative structure for Haverstraw beach, where swimming was allowed. Unless you've spotted a return car (see Options, below), turn right and follow the wide path south.

Bicyclists, joggers, and strollers will join you for the return, but the lack of privacy does not detract from the pleasant route. The mostly level 4.8 miles back to Nyack State Park are easily walked in 2 hours, unless you stop to examine the quarries en route.

OPTION

You can shorten the hike to just more than 6 miles by spotting a return car at the northern end of the bike path. From the junction of US 9W and NY 304, drive north on US 9W for about 1 mile. Turn right onto Short Clove Road, crossing the railroad tracks and continuing down a short distance to Riverside Avenue. Turn very sharply right onto Riverside, and continue about 1 mile to its end at the bike path parking. Leave one car here. Return to US 9W, and drive south 6 miles, then turn left onto Christian Herald Road. In 0.3 mile turn sharply left onto Midland Avenue to its end, then right onto Larchdale Street to its end at North Broadway. Turn left into Nyack Beach State Park.

BMcM/HNZ

17

The Tors, High and Low

Total distance: 4.5 miles

Walking time: 3 hours

Vertical rise: 850 feet

Maps: USGS 7.5' Haverstraw, NY–NJTC Hudson Palisades map #4B

High Tor is one of Rockland County's most conspicuous landmarks. Rising 800 feet above the Hudson River and with its broad view of the surrounding area, the peak of High Tor has served as both signal and sentinel. During the Revolutionary War, beacons were placed on the mountain to alert of possible British attack. In Celtic lore, "high tor" is a place in which to commune with the gods, "tor" being a gateway.

The Maxwell Anderson play *High Tor* (1937) signaled the beginning of a campaign to protect the mountain from quarrying. The end result was purchase and transfer to the Palisades Interstate Park Commission (PIPC) of 564 acres in 1943. In 1995 Scenic Hudson purchased a 54-acre former vineyard on the south face of the mountain. It will be managed as part of the park and be linked by foot trail to the Long Path, the trail used on this hike. Because some short rock scrambles are involved, this hike is not appropriate in wet or icy weather.

From Palisades Interstate Parkway exit 11, go east on County Road 80 (CR 80, New Hempstead Road) 1.4 miles to a T junction with Main Street in New City. Turn right, and then turn quickly left at the light, continuing east on CR 80 to a junction with NY 304. Turn left (north) onto NY 304, and continue for about 3 miles to its end at an intersection with US 9W. Turn left onto 9W, and after 1 mile turn sharply left onto South Mountain Road (a.k.a. Old Route 304 and CR 90, poorly signed). Good shoulder parking is available on the right, just beyond

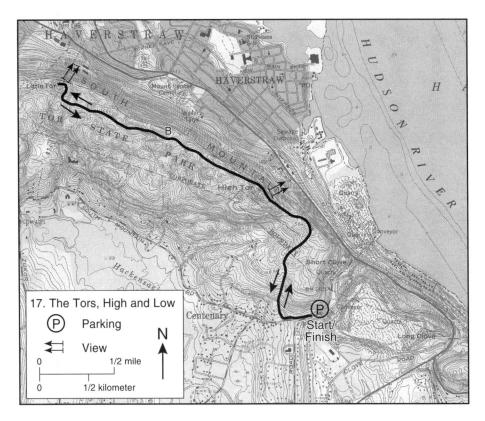

17. The Tors, High and Low

(P) Parking

⇇ View

N

0   1/2 mile

0   1/2 kilometer

a junction with Scratchup Road. If you reach the junction with CR 23, Ridge Road, you've gone about 20 yards too far.

Hike west along the road (the direction you were driving) for a short distance, passing four utility poles on your side of the road. The route is marked with the turquoise rectangles of the Long Path, which turns into the woods opposite house number 330, just after passing the fourth pole.

The footway is now a narrow hiking trail, flat only for a short stretch and then it starts up–sometimes steeply up. A few sections are quite rocky, evidence of quarrying that still continues nearby. The land in this section is owned by the Tilcon Company and used with their permission. The route was moved in the mid-1990s after some of the quarrying operations came too close to the

old route, which is still shown on most hiking maps.

After 20 minutes of uphill hiking, the trail crests the ridge and makes a sharp left turn. Now begins the ascent to High Tor itself. The first climb is quite steep, up 150 feet including an exciting rock scramble. Here the first view opens up, and it's a great one. To the south the skyline of New York is on the horizon with the Hudson River below you. The curved shape of Hook Mountain spreads out along its shores. Press on; three more short climbs brings you up to the summit and an even better view.

Although only 832 feet high, the 360-degree view is truly superb. DeForest Lake (a reservoir), the skyline of New York City, and even part of Newark are visible to the south. The two round domes to the north are reac-

The Manhattan skyline visible in the distance from High Tor

H. Neil Zimmerman

tors for the Indian Point nuclear power plant. To the northwest are the rolling summits of Harriman State Park. Forested areas of Rockland County and northern New Jersey spread out to the west. Below you is Haverstraw, with its active waterfront. The long curved mountain along the Hudson Shore is Hook Mountain, another PIPC-protected park (see Hike 16). The old footing at your feet is the remains of an airplane signal beacon.

Linger if you wish, but the hike is not over. Carry on to Little Tor (a.k.a. Low Tor) by continuing on the Long Path as it heads downhill away from the river. The short descent is steep and very rocky. The marked route now follows a fire road as it parallels the ridge just below the crest. There are numerous opportunities to take a short bushwhack up to the crest for a fine view. You're guaranteed to find a spot you can call your own.

After about 30 minutes a gravel road bisects the trail. To the right, faded arrows on a large boulder direct you to take a right turn for the short hike up to Little Tor with a fine view. Haverstraw is some 700 feet below. You're more likely to have company here because it's just a short 1-mile walk to Central Highway, which crosses the ridge to the west.

Hike back the way you came. We find it rewarding to allow time for another break on High Tor. Be extra careful going down the rock scramble because descending can often be harder than climbing up.

HNZ

18

Southern Ledges of Harriman

Total distance: 8 miles

Walking time: 6 to 7 hours

Vertical rise: 1,000 feet

Maps: USGS 7.5' Sloatsburg; NY–NJTC Harriman Trails #3; PIPC Harriman Park map

A walk along these ledges of Harriman State Park can take you away from the crowds. The southern area of the park often gives one a feeling of remoteness. The many ups and downs will ensure a rewarding workout and plenty of fine views. If possible, start this hike early because the parking areas are often full by 10 AM on weekends.

Take the New York Thruway (I-87) exit 15A, and proceed north on NY 17 through and past the village of Sloatsburg to a traffic light. Turn right onto Seven Lakes Drive, and proceed for 2 miles into the park. This loop hike starts at the parking area adjacent to the Reeves Meadow Visitor Center (open seasonally). Overflow parking is available across the road.

Walk east on a roadway through the field behind the center for less than 100 yards to a right fork blazed with three white squares, indicating the beginning of the Reeves Brook Trail, which heads uphill and to the south, following a small tributary of Stony Brook.

The Reeves Brook Trail winds a tortuous course over almost every convolution of the terrain. It passes beautiful rock ledges and crosses a small stream. In 15 minutes the road the trail has been following forks right. Follow the white-blazed trail left, climbing some more to pass a small cascade. You pass a huge glacial erratic on a knoll to the right and then a wet swale to the left. Zigzag south and then east, across a small valley and then up. As you ascend, watch carefully for the trail markers along this serpentine

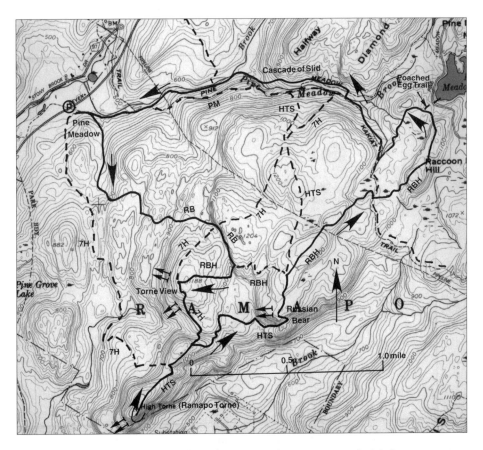

stretch of trail! The trail threads through a very handsome hemlock grove and continues to climb. Still climbing, you become aware of the bare rock escarpment ahead, to the east.

After 45 minutes you reach a four-way intersection where the Seven Hills Trail crosses, marked white with blue squares. The left branch of this trail heads steeply up slope; its right branch is slightly less obvious. Stay on the white-blazed trail for another 10 minutes as it continues paralleling the cleft beneath the cliffs to the east. Soon the trail ends at a T junction with the Raccoon Brook Hills Trail, blazed with black dots, squares, or Rs on a white background. Turn right on this trail, heading up slope for

10 minutes to a wonderful view west.

Follow the trail downhill for another 75 feet. You reach a second T intersection, this one with the blue-blazed Seven Hills Trail, which would have been a slightly shorter and slightly less interesting route.

Turn left onto the Seven Hills Trail, and enjoy more views, some of them across to Ramapo Torne, your next destination. Head very steeply at first down to a deep draw, then up a rubble-filled hillside at a scramble that ends at the intersection with the Hillburn-Torne-Sebago Trail, recently reblazed with orange blazes. This last section is about 0.5 mile, but with the rough walking it may take you more than 20 minutes. Just off the trail on the ledge above you is an overlook with views south to New York City.

At this intersection, you could detour south along the joint Hillburn-Torne-Sebago Trail and Seven Hills Trail, staying left on the Hillburn-Torne-Sebago Trail when the trails split. This trail climbs to the rock knob of Ramapo Torne, which has more southerly views. Return north on the trail to the intersection, and fork right.

Continuing the loop from this intersection, follow orange markers east on the trail. You descend and then climb a small ridge around boulders to a bare, fire-scarred expanse, beyond which you can see the deep gorge that lies between you and the Russian Bear, which is the southern tip of the sharp escarpment to the east. You descend from this broad ridge, steeply at first, then cross the head of a draw with its small stream. As you get closer to the jagged cliffs, look up to discover a cave. As the trail turns to climb the promontory, you see a free-standing rock slab that has fallen from the cliffs of Russian Bear. At this point you also have views back to the knob of Ramapo Torne.

The trail swings back left on top of the cliff to a vantage to the southwest and a pretty view back to the ridge you were on about a half hour earlier. The orange markings lead you across the broad hilltop through tall oaks on high ground, for a 15-minute walk to an intersection with the Raccoon Brook Hills Trail. Turn right onto this white-with-black-blazes trail, which leads you northeast on high ground, across bare rock through another fire-scarred area. This trail is a route of fire and ice: strange yet beautiful compositions of fire-ravaged trees and stumps in a landscape punctuated by huge erratics and boulders dropped by the glacier.

Ten minutes from the intersection, as you begin to descend, you can glimpse the cliffs of the Raccoon Hills through the trees. The trail crosses the slash of a gas pipeline, then makes a rubble-strewn, sharp descent to intersect with the white-blazed Kakiat Trail. This last segment on the Raccoon Brook Hills Trail takes almost 30 minutes. If you're tiring, turn left onto the Kakiat to shorten the loop by more than 1 mile.

To continue on the main loop, turn right through a lovely laurel glade to follow the combined Kakiat and Raccoon Brook Hills Trails. (Kakiat is the contraction of a Native American name for the patent granted by the governor of the province of New York in 1696. The patent encompassed much of northern New Jersey and southern New York.)

Stay on this part of the Kakiat Trail for only 100 feet, and turn left onto the continuing Raccoon Brook Hills Trail, which heads downhill to a rubble-strewn draw beneath the cliffs, then across open rock and up behind the cliffs. Winding along the hilltop, the trail offers several views across the deep valley to the east. Pine and hemlock shelter knolls where you walk on bare rock. Twenty-five minutes from the cliff top, you begin to descend and overlook Pine Meadow Lake with Pine Meadow Mountain in the background. A short, steep descent brings you to an intersection with the "Poached Egg" Trail. A detour of 200 yards on this yellow-on-white-blazed trail leads you to the lake. Caves to the right of the trail have yielded Native American artifacts. Marvelous cliffs line a promontory to the north across the lake.

Returning to and continuing on the Raccoon Brook Hills Trail, you cross another knob, and descend southwest into a draw and across a deep, rubble-filled valley. A steep descent follows the next height-of-land, and then the trail leads up to a marvelous circle of erratics, a veritable

A stream in South Harriman State Park

Stonehenge built by the glacier. You meet a small stream coming in from the left—you'll follow it as it grows and joins with others, all the way to your car.

Across the stream the Raccoon Brook Hills Trail climbs 30 feet to end at its second intersection with the Kakiat Trail, after making a 1.4-mile loop. Turn right—downhill on the easier footing of the Kakiat—high above the amazing mass of boulders below. This trail gradually swings northwest, descending constantly to the deep, cool valley of Pine Meadow Brook. After less than 10 minutes on the Kakiat, you reach a major intersection with both a red- and a blue-blazed trail. Turn right to follow the union of all three trails across the bridge over Pine Meadow Brook. At this point you are less than an hour from your car, and you have several choices for the return, including the red-blazed Pine Meadow Trail, which stays on the south side of the brook by clinging above it on the steep hillside.

For the most spectacular return, turn left onto the white-blazed trail, the continuing Kakiat, on the north side of the bridge, and stay on it after the intersection 100 yards downstream where the Seven Hills Trail forks right and uphill. The Kakiat here is close enough to the brook that you can enjoy its quiet pools and rock cliffs. In 10 minutes the valley of the brook begins to fall away quickly. Your white-blazed trail crosses the orange-blazed Hillburn-Torne-Sebago Trail, just north of a bridge that carries that trail across the brook.

Stay along the brook as it enters a deep gorge and plunges through the Cascade of Slid for the best part of the walk. Hemlocks shroud the cliffs and shelter small waterfalls, making them too dark to photograph except in late afternoons near the summer solstice. In less than 15 minutes, the cascades end at a bridge that crosses the brook, just upstream from its confluence with Stony Brook. Looking downstream from the bridge, you can see a second bridge that crosses Stony Brook. Cross to the south side, pass the bridge that carries the Kakiat north, and continue on the old roadway.

Stony Brook descends fairly steeply. The roadway crosses the gas line, then picks up the red-blazed Pine Meadow Trail, which joins at an acute angle. Two huge erratics frame a small waterfall on the brook and mark the place where the brook becomes quiet. From the boulders it is but 10 minutes along the roadway back to the beginning of the hike. The ease of this stretch should take the kinks out of your legs—kinks that are inevitable when you consider the tortuous route this loop makes through the southern border of the park.

BMcM/HNZ

19

Ladentown Ramble (or Breakneck Mountain Loop)

Total distance: 6.75 miles

Walking time: 3.75 hours

Vertical rise: 900 feet

Maps: USGS 7.5' Thiells; NY–NJTC Southern Harriman Bear Mountain Trails, #3

This hike uses parts of the Tuxedo–Mount Ivy, Breakneck Mountain, Suffern–Bear Mountain, and Red Arrow Trails to make a "balloon" hike (out and back on the same trail with a loop in the middle). The terrain is almost entirely through deep woods with occasional stands of laurel and a few open slabs. Except at the start, the climbing is gentle and steady, and the route makes for a leisurely saunter in a peaceful atmosphere embellished by birdsong. Rocky footing at the beginning and the end may pose a slight challenge to the inexperienced hiker.

Take Exit 13 from the Palisades Interstate Parkway (signed for US 202/Suffern/Haverstraw), and drive west for approximately 1.75 miles to a junction with Old Route 306. Turn right, then right again at the stop sign only a few yards ahead. Turn left after 0.2 mile onto a dead-end road signed for a summer camp—RAMAQUOIS—bear left, and turn left again within another 0.2 mile onto Diltz Road, a private road. Continue along Diltz Road for 0.2 mile, and just before the overhead power lines cross the paved road, turn right into an occasionally muddy lot where the sign indicates HIKERS PARK HERE.

Park and walk toward the wire gate at the back of the circular track, and pass through the gate. The Tuxedo–Mount Ivy Trail is blazed with a horizontal red dash on a white background. Look for the three red blazes on the right indicating the beginning of this trail and follow single, similar blazes uphill on a wide service road. Bear right as

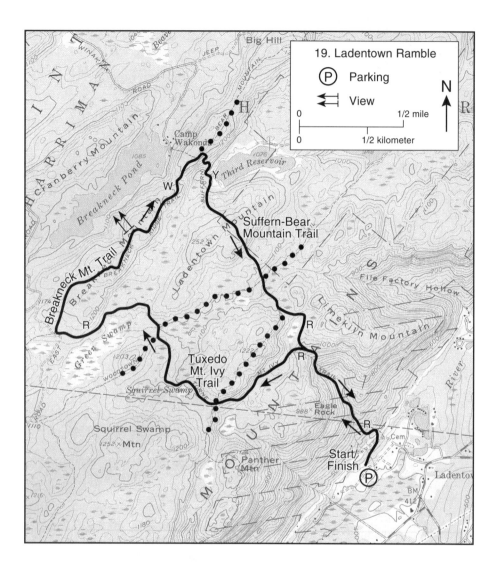

you approach the power line. Follow this rocky road, possibly crossing a couple of wet patches. Pass one pylon, bear left under the power line to a Y junction, and take the left fork uphill. Confirming red blazes are on the rock underfoot. Almost immediately the Tuxedo–Mount Ivy Trail leaves the service road and the route of the pylons and makes a right turn into the woods.

Continuing ahead, the Tuxedo–Mount Ivy Trail ascends gradually on rocks. Cross a stream on stepping-stones, ignore a woods road coming in on the right, and follow the red-paint blazes. After about 15 minutes of climbing from where it entered the woods, the trail makes a sharp left turn. This section of the Tuxedo–Mount Ivy Trail is used for the return trip, so look around at this point to ensure that you recognize this turn when you come back to it at the end of the hike.

At the time of this writing there is a log across the incorrect route.

Within 2 minutes the Red Arrow Trail enters from the right. Three blazes with a red arrow on a white background are painted on a rock to the right. Two cairns and RA painted in red on a rock in the middle of the trail alert you to this junction. The Red Arrow Trail is used as part of this hike, and you return to this junction later on.

The footing is still rocky but becomes narrower until the Tuxedo–Mount Ivy Trail crosses the Suffern–Bear Mountain Trail in about 15 minutes. There is a pleasant batch of rocks to the right of the trail if you wish to take a break. The Suffern–Bear Mountain Trail, as its name implies, runs for just more than 23 miles from Suffern to Bear Mountain. Proposed in 1924 by Major William A. Welch, then general manager of the Palisades Interstate Park Commission, the Suffern–Bear Mountain Trail is the longest trail in the park.

The Tuxedo–Mount Ivy Trail now enters a laurel thicket and, after an hour's walking from where the trail entered the woods, emerges onto Woodtown Road, a legally designated horse trail, which the foot trail uses for a very short distance. Turn right onto Woodtown Road, cross a wet patch with a wooden bridge on the left, and immediately leave this major woods road and turn sharply left into the woods, continuing to follow the paint blazes.

After a stream crossing, Green Swamp is visible as an open area to the left of the trail. Watch carefully now as the Tuxedo–Mount Ivy Trail turns right–the blaze at present is on a log to the left of the trail. If you miss this turn and emerge onto a major woods road, the Pine Meadow Road East, backtrack to find the missed turn.

Within 5 minutes make a right turn onto the Breakneck Mountain Trail, indicated by

three end markers in white. The Tuxedo–Mount Ivy Trail continues ahead, and, again, if you miss this turn and reach another part of the Pine Meadow Road East, turn back to find the correct route of the hike.

Breakneck Mountain was once known locally as Knapp Mountain from the name of the original owner. This trail, too, was blazed at the suggestion of Major Welch in 1927. The trail gives the impression of being on high ground and from time to time emerges onto open rock slabs. Follow the white blazes, watching for an unexpected turn downhill on the right. One particularly beautiful section traverses an open slab with large boulders left by the glacier that was once here. Notice the large cracks in the rock underfoot caused by winter's freeze-and-thaw cycles.

Another 10 minutes on the Breakneck Mountain Trail, and Breakneck Pond can be glimpsed through the trees to the left, followed within a few minutes by a clearer view of the lake. Along the trail, two balsam firs make an unusual sight by the side of the footway. Voices from Camp Lanowa on the shores of Breakneck Mountain can often be heard in summer, but please ignore the unmarked paths down to the camp.

Very soon the end of the Breakneck Mountain Trail is indicated by three white blazes, and the Suffern–Bear Mountain Trail is met. Do not turn left up the rocks, but follow the yellow blazes downhill to the right toward the waters of the Third Reservoir glimpsed ahead through the trees. The Suffern–Bear Mountain Trail passes the western end of the reservoir and is an appealing spot to rest. The water is tranquil and inviting, but swimming is forbidden. The Third Reservoir, built in 1951, is the most recently built water cache to serve Letchworth Village and the now closed Letchworth Village State Developmental

Glacial erractics along the Breakneck Ridge Trail

Center. Even with three reservoirs, Letchworth Village still runs out of water in dry years, and when this happens a pipe is laid over Breakneck Mountain and water is pumped out of Breakneck Pond.

The Suffern–Bear Mountain Trail climbs away from the Third Reservoir over Ladentown Mountain and within 10 minutes emerges onto Woodtown Road. In this section the trail is sometimes marked with yellow metal markers rather than paint blazes. Go straight over the road, and continue on the Suffern–Bear Mountain Trail, crossing two watercourses before reaching the junction with the Red Arrow Trail, which is easy to spot. Turn left onto the Red Arrow Trail, abandoning the Suffern–Bear Mountain Trail, which leaves to the right. The Red Arrow Trail now skirts the edge of an unnamed swamp, with Limekiln Mountain in the background, and descends, passing remnants of old rock walls.

Ten minutes more, and the end of the Red Arrow Trail is indicated by the markers passed earlier at the junction with the Tuxedo–Mount Ivy Trail. Turn left and retrace your earlier route. Remember to make the sharp right turn noted earlier, and then turn left at the pylons to reach your car.

SJG

20

Kerson Nurian Revisited

Total distance: 8.25 miles

Walking time: 4.5 hours

Vertical rise: 1,000 feet

Maps: 7.5' Sloatsburg Monroe; NY–NJTC Northern Harriman Bear Mountain Trails #4

The route taken on this "balloon" hike (out and back on the same trail with a loop in the middle) is all on marked trails using the Nurian, Dunning, White Bar, and Ramapo-Dunderberg Trails. Highlights are the clamber through the massive rocks called the Valley of Boulders, walking by Green Pond (one of the most beautiful spots in the park), and the exhilarating traverse of the open slabs of Black Rock. Traffic noise is detrimental at the beginning of the hike but soon abates after the initial climb.

Kerson Nurian, born in Bulgaria and employed as an electrical engineer at the Brooklyn Navy Yard, was one of the first enthusiastic trail builders. In the 1920s Nurian often found himself in conflict with other active cutters of hiking trails in the park. In these early days most hiking devotees would travel from Manhattan to the woods by train, and a real camaraderie grew between these lovers of the outdoors.

Begin your hike at the Red Apple Rest (cafeteria). Easy to find on NY 17, the Red Apple Rest was a major stop in the 1940s and 1950s for travelers to the great resorts of the Catskills. Coming from the south (through Sloatsburg and Tuxedo) on NY 17, Red Apple Rest is on the east side of NY 17, 3.5 miles north of Tuxedo Railroad Station and a little less than 1 mile from the junction with NY 17A. Approaching from the north, the Red Apple Rest is approximately 6 miles south of exit 16 from the New York State Thruway (I-87). The Red Apple Rest is on the left, 0.2 mile south of Orange Turnpike, where it joins NY 17. Park at the extreme northeast corner, close to the cell telephone tower.

Walk down to the railroad tracks from the northeast corner of the parking lot, and turn north (left) along the tracks. Remember that this is an active rail line, and there are no blazes to follow until the trail officially begins when it leaves the railroad tracks. To find the beginning of the marked trail, count thirteen poles, including the utility pole immediately in front as you leave the parking lot, before looking right to a larger high-tension pole numbered #162 behind the smaller utility poles. The walk along the railroad tracks takes about 7 or 8 minutes.

Immediately opposite the beginning of the Nurian Trail is a private home on the west side of the tracks. Look for the three white blazes indicating the start of the Nurian Trail, and walk right into the woods. Continue south on the west bank of the Ramapo River, and cross a substantial bridge. Nurian built his trail in about 1929. Several of the bridges he originally used to cross the Ramapo were washed out before the present steel bridge was constructed by the park in 1950.

Continue toward the New York State Thruway, and cross on the overpass commonly called the Nurian Bridge but officially named the Southfield Pedestrian Bridge. The western end of the Nurian Trail was closed during the thruway construction in 1953, pending the building of this bridge. The trail was threatened again when the thruway was resurfaced and refurbished in the early 1990s. This "improvement" caused the existing bridge to be too low to accommodate tractor trailers, and it was only through the efforts of the New York–New Jersey Trail Conference that it was raised and rebuilt for hikers to use.

After crossing the bridge, turn left, and walk along the Old Arden Road—a wide grassy woods road paralleling the northbound New York State Thruway. The trail turns right from this road into the woods as you reach the first stand of conifers and just before a watercourse in a gully. The climb of approximately 350 vertical feet to the top of Green Pond Mountain takes about 10 minutes, in two pitches, before beginning to descend. On the way down, look to the right. The rectangular cement tank on the rise above the trail once served the latrine for a camp operated by Grace Church of New York City.

The trail continues downhill, crosses a woods road, emerges onto a paved road now falling into disrepair, and continues on a bridge over the outlet to Lake Stahahe. The dam—the most recent of several built here—can be seen to the right as the bridge is crossed. Hikers should stay away from the camp buildings, particularly during the summer season when children are in residence.

Step over any chain gating the road, and turn left, still on the gravel road. The road forks almost immediately, and the trail continues along the upper right-hand road, thus avoiding the concrete septic tank below. The trail now requires some rock hopping as it ascends, following pretty Island Pond Brook on your left. The ravine you are now walking through is called the Valley of Boulders, and soon the trail continues upward through some impressively huge rocks after about an hour into the hike.

Emerging from among these massive boulders, the trail descends slightly and then curls right, around the end of a long sloping rock in a hemlock grove. About 15 minutes from those large boulders you reach the beginning of the Dunning Trail, indicated by three yellow markers on a tree at its junction with the Nurian Trail. Note this junction because the hike will return you to this spot later.

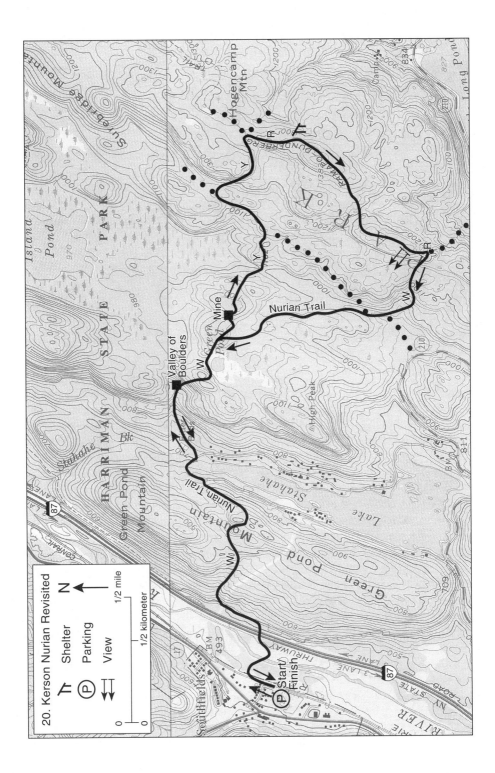

20. Kerson Nurian Revisited

N

⊤ Shelter

Ⓟ Parking

View

0 — 1/2 kilometer
0 — 1/2 mile

HARRIMAN STATE PARK

Surebridge Mountain

Island Pond

Hogencamp Mtn

Nurian Trail

Green Mine

Valley of Boulders

Green Pond Mountain

High Peak

Stahahe

Lake Stahahe

Green Pond

Nurian Trail

Mountain Trail

Southfields

Ⓟ Start/ Finish

RAMAPO-DUNDERBERG TRAIL

Long Pond

Camp

RAMAPO RIVER

NY STATE THRUWAY

87

87

Along the Ramapo-Dunderberg Trail

Switch to the Dunning Trail, which leads straight up a rocky pitch and over toward Green Pond. Pick your way down through rocks and blowdowns in a fire-damaged area, taking your eyes from your feet long enough to appreciate the beauty of Green Pond. The Dunning Trail circles the north side of Green Pond almost to lake level, and the Nurian Trail follows a similar route only a short distance away. Green Pond is atrophying. Enjoy it now because growth is slowly taking over. Eventually, in an undetermined number of years, Green Pond will be Green Swamp. However, until that happens, the surrounding rocks make an appropriate place to rest and admire the scenery.

Do not cross the inlet of Green Pond, but turn to your left, leaving the stream on your right. The Nurian Trail joins the Dunning Trail from the left for a very short stretch but leaves to the right within 75 feet. Stay with the yellow blazes. Turn left when the Dunning trail reaches a cairn-marked junction with Island Pond Road (a woods road), and walk a few hundred yards. Watch carefully for the turn to the right that takes you to Boston Mine. This mine has been inactive since 1880 and is now flooded. Ore from the mine was sent to the Clove (anthracite) Furnace at Arden, and many tailings remain in the area.

Turn right at the mine, and continue uphill. The trail undulates through hemlock and laurel, passing underneath a large rock outcrop, and begins to climb more seriously again at about 1 hour 35 minutes from the car. Turn left within 10 minutes when the White Bar and the Dunning Trails commingle, and follow both yellow and white markers for approximately 0.25 mile. After a few minutes along these combined trails, look right to see the dramatic effect of fire on the landscape. Cross a seasonal stream on slabs that are sometimes slippery, and after walking through a low-lying area, turn right uphill on the yellow-marked Dunning Trail, ignoring the White Bar Trail that continues straight ahead.

After a climb of approximately 60 feet, the trail continues through a more open area protected on the left by a rocky escarpment. Ten minutes from where the White Bar Trail separated from the Dunning Trail, you arrive at the T junction with the Ramapo-Dunderberg Trail. The intersection is marked with a cairn. Leave the Dunning Trail that continues straight ahead, and turn right to follow the Ramapo-Dunderberg Trail, which is marked with a red dot on a white background. Look right to find this blaze on a tree, and climb for about another 80 feet onto open slabs in a fire-damaged area. The Bald Rocks shelter is visible ahead and to the left.

The Ramapo-Dunderberg Trail was the first trail to be built by the New York hiking clubs in Harriman State Park. First blazed in 1920, its route was suggested by Major William A. Welch, the general manager of the park at the time.

Now begins an invigorating walk across the Black Rock ridge on open fire-scarred slabs that always remind us of a Salvador Dalí painting. The first summit reached is dotted with large rocks and affords almost a 360-degree view. Blazes are sparse, and you may need to hunt and peck a little before finding the correct route, which bears to the right halfway across the ridge. The trail continues in this wonderfully open area for almost 0.5 mile, reaching another high point before dropping down a couple of pitches between slabs of rock to a junction at the terminus of the Nurian Trail. This junction is marked with a cairn and three white blazes. Follow the Nurian Trail to the right, disregarding the Ramapo-Dunderberg Trail, which turns to the left steeply downhill.

The Nurian Trail here also drops steeply down to the level of a small, possibly seasonal stream. Cross the water on stepping-stones, and walk uphill to a T junction with the White Bar Trail. Turn right. These two trails use the same woods road for about 0.1 mile, and 5 minutes' walking brings you to a fork. Do not take the White Bar Trail to the right, but turn left, still on the Nurian Trail. The trail passes first through a lovely stand of hemlocks, followed by an equally beautiful laurel grove, and traverses a "damp in season" patch before bearing left onto higher ground. Emerge onto Island Pond Road, and turn right. Sharp eyes might spot a yellow blaze of the Dunning Trail some distance ahead, and you should then recognize the turn made earlier in the hike. Follow the white blazes of the Nurian Trail, perhaps noticing where the Dunning Trail intermingles for a very brief time. Do not miss the right turn marker that leads you uphill and onward to the junction with the Dunning Trail. Green Pond will be partly visible to the left as you walk this section, and by this time you have walked almost 3.5 hours.

When you arrive at the three markers of the Dunning Trail, retrace your footsteps on the Nurian Trail for about an hour to get back to your car.

SJG

21

Rockhouse Loop

Total distance: 7.3 miles (or 5.8 miles)

Walking time: 3.5 to 4 hours (or 3 hours)

Vertical rise: 1,000 feet (or 800 feet)

Maps: USGS 7.5' Thiells; USGS 7.5' Peekskill; NY–NJTC Harriman-Bear Mountain Trails #4; PIPC Harriman Park map

This relatively easy balloon hike travels through central Harriman State Park, an area once rich with farms and mines going back to colonial times. Circling but not climbing Rockhouse Mountain, the walking is easy, with just a few short climbs. However, at more than 7 miles, it can be a bit long for young children or beginning hikers. There are several interesting historic places to explore, so choose a nice day and start early. The hike is all on marked trails except for a short section toward the end on an easy-to-follow woods road.

The road to the parking area is closed to vehicles in winter (December 1st through April 1st). However, an alternative year-round access, which also shortens the hike by 1.5 miles, is available as an option (see note at end).

Leave the Palisades Interstate Parkway at exit 16 (Lake Welch). Proceed for 0.5 mile to where the road splits. Bear right onto Tiorati Brook Road, and continue for 1.1 miles to a large parking area, just after a bridge, in a field on the right. Or you can travel to the parking area from Tiorati Circle (see note at end for directions to the circle). The parking area is 2.4 miles south on Tiorati Brook Road on your left.

From your car, cross to the other side of Tiorati Brook Road, and begin hiking by following the dark-blue markers of the Beech Trail as the trail heads southwest. This is one of the newer trails in the park, blazed in 1972 (most trails go back to the 1920s and 1930s). There are lots of beech trees along the route, but it was named after Art Beach,

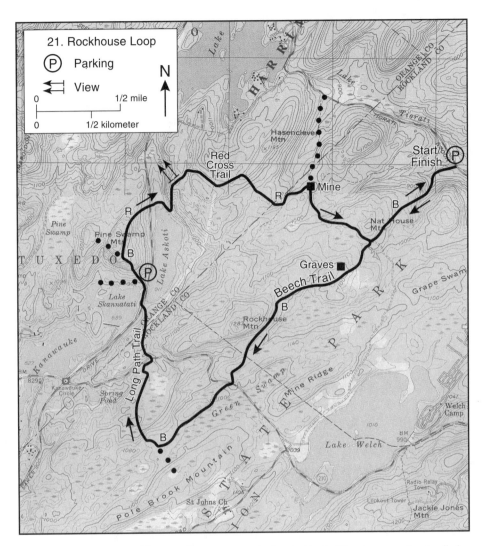

21. Rockhouse Loop

P Parking

⇄ View

N

0 — 1/2 mile
0 — 1/2 kilometer

a tireless trail worker. The spelling was changed to circumvent a park policy against naming trails for living persons.

The trail follows a woods road, which shortly forks. Bear right, and follow the markers as the path runs alongside a gully. Soon you'll enter an area filled with blueberry bushes and mountain laurel; observe how the old road was built up from the surrounding ground. Be careful crossing a small stream on some slippery wooden planks. As the trail begins a moderate climb, you may note a fine cascade just 0.3 mile from the start. Trail builders named it Arthur's Falls to honor a crew member.

After climbing just more than 200 feet, the trail reaches an intersection with Hasenclever Road, still occasionally used by park vehicles. Note this location because you will need to recall this junction when you return here near the end of the hike.

The Beech Trail jogs right along the road

for only 5 yards and then reenters the woods. Cross another small stream, and continue for another 10 minutes or so. You'll begin to notice a change in vegetation. You are nearing a old farmstead that we've spent hours exploring.

To be sure you're in the right area, it's best to stay on the trail until it passes an old cemetery on your right. Cleaned and restored as an Eagle Scout project in 1990, the graves are from the Babcock, Youman, and Jones families. Most of the readable inscriptions are from the mid- to late 1800s.

If you have the time and desire to explore the farm area, go back along the trail, and look for a route through the thornbushes toward a massive Norway spruce, now sadly dying. Some routes are better (hurt less) than others. In this area you can find the remains of stone foundations and even an old root cellar.

When you're ready to start hiking again, continue ahead on the blue trail. It begins to level off and passes a large glacial erratic to the left.

A little more than an hour into the hike, the trail crosses County Road (CR) 106. Just before reaching this crossing, be alert for the marked route to bear left, off the woods road and onto a narrower footway. As you continue along, observe the attractive jumble of rocks to the right of the trail and the wonderful stand of laurel, which in June will be ablaze with large white and pink blossoms.

Some 15 minutes after crossing CR 106, the Beech Trail ends at the junction with the turquoise-blazed Long Path. Turn right.

The Long Path, a major trunk trail, currently extends more than 300 miles from the George Washington Bridge north to John Boyd Thatcher State Park just south of Albany. Plans are under way to extend the trail into the Adirondacks, perhaps even to the Canadian border. You, however, are not going that far—at least not today.

The Long Path traverses a lush wet area and emerges in a pine plantation, probably planted by the Civilian Conservation Corps (CCC) in the 1930s. Once again you reach CR 106, about an hour and a half into the hike. The trail crosses the road and goes right along the pavement for about 30 yards before reentering woods, just as the highway begins to bend.

The blazing may be poor for a short distance, but the trail quickly joins a woods road, and the blazes again become easy to follow. This 0.5-mile section quickly leads you down to Seven Lakes Drive, which you'll cross. It goes under a phone line, where you'll see an abundance of sweet fern. Pull off a leaf and crush it in your fingers for a pleasant smell. The leaves, I'm told, make a refreshing tea and have also been used to treat poison ivy rash.

As Seven Lakes Drive and Lake Askoti (Native American for "this side") come into view, the trail heads down to the highway. Cross the highway bridge and continue down on the far side of the road to a major parking area at Lake Skannatati (Native American for "the other side"). This parking area is an alternative place to start the hike, especially when Tiorati Brook road is closed for the winter (see end of hike description).

Cross the parking lot to the far end near the lakeshore. The Long Path enters the woods close to the shore, but instead you need to switch to the Arden-Surebridge Trail, known by hikers as the ASB. This trail, which starts just a few feet farther away from the lakeshore, is marked with red triangles (often just blotches) on a white background.

The ASB trail heads up Pine Swamp Mountain, a very short but 200-foot ascent. Cresting after going through some rock out-

Ducks at Lake Askoti

croppings, the footway levels off and comes to the clearly marked beginning of Red Cross Trail (red cross on white background). You'll need to turn right onto the Red Cross Trail, but about 20 yards ahead on the ASB there is a fine viewpoint down to Lake Skannatati that's worth the short detour.

Now on the Red Cross Trail, climb moderately another 80 feet through open woods, and then head down to recross Seven Lakes Drive. A large rock slab jutting into Lake Askoti appears soon after. This lovely spot is marred only by the road noise and occasionally some irritating litter.

More than 2 hours of walking have now brought you to the homeward leg. Another short, steep climb brings you to another viewpoint, strangely not indicated on the New York–New Jersey Trail Conference's map. At 1,100 feet above sea level, you can look back across the road toward Pine Swamp and Surebridge Mountains.

After crossing under a phone line and over some wet areas, the path bears left, joins a woods road, and continues on it for 0.25 mile to a major junction. You are now at the center of the Hasenclever Mine complex, where the hike leaves the marked trail.

In 1765 Peter Hasenclever, while traveling through, discovered a large deposit of iron ore. He immediately bought 1,000 acres, including most of Cedar Ponds, now Lake Tiorati. His intention was to construct a furnace, but he was recalled to England before it could be built. However, mine operations under a succession of owners continued on and off for almost a hundred years. In the mid-1850s one owner planned a railroad from the mine to the Hudson at Stony Point. Never completed, the trench in which it was to run can still be seen—as can stone foundations and other remnants of the human activity. At its peak, some 20 to 30 men worked this area. The NY–NJTC's

Iron Mine Trails, by Edward J. Lenek (1996), provides an extensive history and guide for exploring this area in depth.

Abandon the marked trail, which follows a significant woods road left. Instead, turn right onto an unmarked section of the same significant road. This location is immediately before the marked trail reaches the main mine pit. (While this turn is easy to find, an alternate route—especially if you're worried about darkness or weather—is to stay on the marked Red Cross Trail, which reaches the paved Tiorati Brook Road in little more than a half mile. Turn, right and walk along the road for the mile back to your car).

The complete hike continues on an unmarked woods road that crosses a small bridge with concrete abutments and begins to travel upward. In a few minutes the surface footing gets smoother, and the grade moderates. Some 10 to 15 minutes from the mine keep a sharp eye out for a junction with the blue-paint blazes of the Beech Trail. This is at the location you noted near the beginning of the hike. Blazes are visible on both sides of the road.

Turn left onto the Beech Trail, and head back to the parking area, about 20 minutes away.

OPTIONS

During the winter months when Tiorati Brook Road is closed—or for those wanting a shorter hike (5.8 miles), park at the Lake Skannatati access just off Seven Lakes Drive. To reach this area, take the Palisades Interstate Parkway to exit 18 and the Long Mountain Circle. Go around the circle to Seven Lakes Drive (not Route 6), and continue past Tiorati Circle (at 3.8 miles) for another 2.6 miles to a right turn down to the Lake Skannatati parking area. Begin the loop hike on the Arden-Surebridge Trail as noted in the text above.

HNZ

22

Iron Mine Walk

Total distance: 8 miles

Walking time: 5 hours

Vertical rise: 1,050 feet

*Maps: USGS 7.5' Monroe; USGS 7.5'
Popolopen Lake; USGS 7.5' Thiells;
USGS 7.5' Sloatsburg; NY-NJTC
Harriman-Bear Mountain #4*

Harriman State Park is full of historical walks, and the one that touches on a few of the region's 19th-centiry iron mines blends good hiking with the annals of that time. Iron mining in the Ramapos actually dates back to 1742, although the colonies had been an exporter of iron ore since 1817; and at the onset of the Revolutionary War they were producing 14 percent of the world's iron. The iron ore of the Ramapo Hills, the nearby watercourses to power the bellows for the furnaces, the heavily wooded slopes whose timber yielded the necessary charcoal–all attracted entrepreneurs. The furnaces at Sterling near Monroe, at Greenwood near the Ramapo, at the Queensboro Furnace, and at the Forest of Dean Furnace all produced iron for guns for the American Revolution and the Civil War. Mines were scattered throughout the Ramapo Hills, furnaces were built, and settlements grew up around the furnaces.

The mines varied in depth from 10 to 6,000 feet, the deepest being the Forest of Dean Mine on U.S. Military Reservation property. That mine's entrance has been sealed. Many of the mines are water filled and dangerous. This walk takes you past a few of the mines that can be inspected safely from the trail.

The mines you'll walk past are in the Greenwood group, suppliers of the Greenwood Furnace at Arden. This and other furnaces are described in *Vanishing Ironworks of the Ramapos* by James M. Ransom, a book to read if you wish to delve deeply into the history of the area. The Greenwood

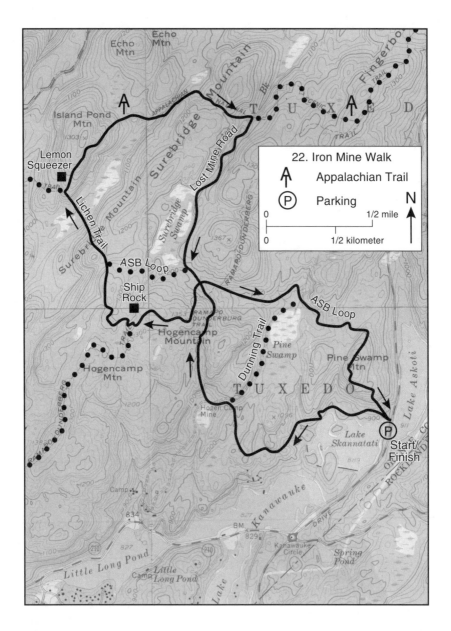

Furnace was established about 1810 and supplied cannonballs to the American forces during the War of 1812. Robert Parrot acquired an interest in the furnace and surrounding lands in 1837, and he and his brother Peter managed the ironworks and became sole owners of it. With coal transported by the newly built railroad through the Ramapo Valley, the furnace's output increased until yearly production reached 5,000 tons of pig iron, destined for fine hardware and stoves. During the Civil

War the iron was used for the famous Parrot gun, the most effective artillery weapon of the Union army. This gun was made at the West Point foundry at Cold Spring under the direction of Robert Parrot. The ore supplied by the Greenwood, Surebridge, Pine Swamp, O'Neil, and Clove Mines was hauled to a kiln about a half mile above the Greenwood Furnace, where the ore was roasted to drive off sulfur, stamped to reduce it to the size of a "pigeon's egg," and then smelted in the furnace, which was built in the charming glen beside the outlet of Echo Lake.

The mine walk starts at the Lake Skannatati parking area off Seven Lakes Drive. Take the Palisades Interstate Parkway to exit 18 and the Long Mountain Circle. Go around the circle to Seven Lakes Drive westbound (not US 6). Continue driving past Tiorati Circle (3.8 miles) for another 2.6 miles to a signed right-hand turn down to the Lake Skannatati parking area. Two trails begin in the northwest corner of this lot, one marked with three red dots on a white blaze and the other with the turquoise-blue rectangle of the Long Path. Take the latter, which begins along the lakeshore, leaving it near a northwest bay, to make a hop-a-rock crossing of an intermittent stream about 20 minutes from the trailhead.

A gentle uphill climb takes you to a gorgeous rock on your left; the route runs through an open parklike area of tremendous oaks with laurel and blueberries beneath. Over a second ridge, 30 minutes from the start, you reach an abandoned roadway. Turn left onto a road marked with the yellow of the Dunning Trail as well as the blue of the Long Path. Within 100 yards turn right, away from the road, following the Long Path as it angles along the rocky hillside. The next half an hour takes you over hills, across ridges, and beside a lovely hemlock-forested gorge with balancing rocks along the trail to a second intersection. Turn left to join the Arden-Surebridge Trail (known as the ASB). Your route is marked with the red of the ASB as well as the blue of the Long Path.

In 200 yards you reach the large erratic of Times Square. Six roads or trails intersect in the vicinity of Times Square. The continuing blue-marked Long Path and the red-marked ASB fork left from the intersection, following an old road. A second red-marked trail, the Ramapo-Dunderberg, also crosses the intersection. For this loop you want the red-marked Ramapo-Dunderberg Trail, which is a left fork just south of the erratic.

The Ramapo-Dunderberg Trail heads southwest, up steeply through a hemlock draw. In 10 minutes you reach bare rock and an area that was ravaged by fire in 1988. You pass wonderful rock clefts, climb again over bare rocks with glacial striations, and enjoy views, mostly south over lovely rolling terrain falling away from Hogencamp Mountain at 1,353 feet. Many additional markings guide you through the burn area.

From the broad summit the trail zigzags down across a ridge with signs of glaciers and fire everywhere. In 10 minutes you reach Ship Rock, which looks like a bottom-up prow of a boat. Just beyond it the trail makes a sharp right turn.

Watch for a second right turn, this one marked with a blue L on a white blaze, which indicates the Lichen Trail. This 0.5-mile connector will take you to the combined red-marked ASB and the blue-marked Long Path. The picturesque Lichen Trail features tall laurel, ledges, and hemlock, with occasional openings with views. The trail drops sharply through an evergreen-covered hillside to intersect with the ASB. Turn left beside a swamp, and head down a very pretty hemlock-covered hillside

The view south near the end of the mine walk

with a stream. As the trail levels out at the bottom of the hill, it makes a sharp right turn to pass a wet area and reach another intersection, where the Long Path forks right (northeast) and a white-marked trail forks southwest. Stay straight on the red-marked ASB, the middle route, which crosses a little stream, follows it briefly, then begins to climb beside cliffs with handsome rock formations. The tiny stream contrasts with the violent forces of water and ice that over the years have created this scene with its impressive overhangs. Such a variety of impressions in only two hours of walking! The hill to your right now adds to the drama as it is beginning to recover from the devastation of the fires.

Five minutes from the intersection, your route intersects the white-marked Appalachian Trail (AT). Turn right (north) onto the AT. This route quickly splits. The right fork leads you on a scramble through the aptly named Lemon Squeezer. After you squeeze between sheer rock walls and pull yourself over ledges through this miniature chasm, you find that the two routes rejoin. The left fork is the easier way. Continue following the blazes to the peak of Island Pond Mountain. In winter there are views south of Island Pond and east to the valley between you and Surebridge Mountain.

Stay straight on the white-marked AT as it descends into a valley beside a dry streambed and then north for a 5-minute walk to a right turn up through a draw. Near the top of the draw, a hemlock perches on a rock like a brontosaurus on a giant egg.

Beyond the tree the trail may be hard to follow as you continue climbing through the rocky draw. Just about three hours into the hike, you cross a hill beyond the draw, through a broad open forest. A short descent through a small bridge brings you to an abandoned roadway below ledges that define the eastern side of this small valley. From this intersection with the Surebridge Mine Road, you can see the tailing pit of the Greenwood Mine. Walk left (north) for a short distance along the road to examine its pit, which between 1838 and 1880 produced ore from three veins. Turn south along the road for one of the more charming parts of the walk. The roadway passes a handsome swamp, where signs of mining abound; tailing piles are everywhere, and a few pits of the Surebridge Mine lie to the east of the road. As the road bends right, it follows a causeway built up of tailings and heads south across Surebridge Swamp. An arch of rhododendron shades the causeway, from which there are glimpses of the twisted stumps and wildflowers in the sphagnum bog.

A small rise leads to an intersection just short of Times Square. Return to the erratic of Times Square by turning left on the red-marked ASB, which follows another old mining road past charcoal pits and more mine areas.

Stay on the red-marked ASB for one more mountaintop view. The ASB continues along a roadway, passing another mine hole near the intersection with the yellow-marked trail. A quarter mile beyond that intersection, the red-marked ASB leaves the roadway to follow a narrower path that winds up and over Pine Swamp Mountain. This 20-minute climb offers a superb overlook across the lakes where the walk began, and a steep 15-minute descent brings you to the trailhead.

BMcM/HNZ

23

Black Mountain

Total distance: 4.75 miles

Walking time: 2.5 hours

Vertical rise: About 900 feet

*Maps: USGS 7.5' Popolopen Lake;
NY–NJTC Harriman-Bear Mountain Trails
#4*

As part of the celebration of its diamond anniversary, volunteers of the New York–New Jersey Trail Conference cleared and marked the Menomine Trail on Labor Day 1994 as a convenient connection between the Appaachian Trail (AT) and the Long Path. More importantly, it was the first marked trail to utilize the large Silvermine parking area that, unlike many others, is maintained (plowed) in winter.

This hike includes the 1,200-foot summit of Black Mountain, one of our favorites. The route up the mountain, on a well-constructed trail, includes some lovely views, and the peak has an extensive view of the Hudson Valley down as far as the Manhattan skyline. Although the last part of the hike is not on a marked trail, the route is pleasant, easy to follow, and includes less than 10 minutes of walking along an active auto road.

To reach the Silvermine parking area, leave the Palisades Interstate Parkway at exit 18. Proceed around the traffic circle to Seven Lakes Drive (westbound). The parking area is on your left 1.4 miles along the road. A fee is usually charged from Memorial Day to Labor Day.

Begin the hike on the yellow-blazed Memomine Trail by crossing the wide bridge at the bottom of the parking area and bearing left across the field toward two small wooden outbuildings. From here the trail parallels the lakeshore.

After about 20 minutes of walking, the trail heads away from Silvermine Lake and begins a modest 100-foot ascent on a

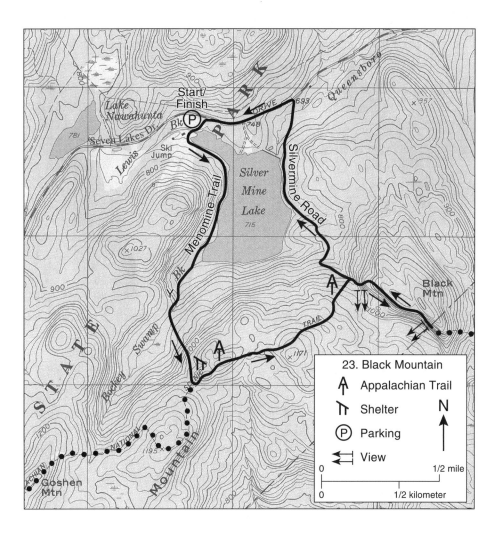

23. Black Mountain

Ӿ	Appalachian Trail
⍑	Shelter
Ⓟ	Parking
⇇	View

N

0 — 1/2 mile

0 — 1/2 kilometer

woods road to a crest, where it makes a sharp left and continues climbing another few hundred feet to its end at the William Brien Shelter, 1.35 miles from the hike's start. The junction with the co-blazed AT (white rectangle) and Ramapo-Dunderberg Trail (red dot on a white background) is at this shelter.

The William Brien Memorial Shelter, built in 1933, was later named for the first president of the New York Ramblers, a still-active local hiking club. A short blue-gray trail from

the shelter leads to an old well (all backcountry water must be treated before drinking). This area is popular with backpackers and long-distance AT hikers as it is one of only a dozen or so legal places to camp within the park.

From here, the hike proceeds east (north) on the AT/Ramapo-Dunderberg co-blazed trail. From the shelter look ahead about 40 yards to the boulder-covered hill. The trail blazes will be clearly visible. Make a left onto the trail and up the hill.

Owl Swamp and the breached dam from the Owl Lake Swamp Road

Alternatively, a clear but unmarked trail at the side of the shelter also ascends on an easier route to the blazed trail.

The co-blazed trail meanders along the top of a ridge through open hardwoods and in about 30 minutes descends to a substantial gravel road before crossing and beginning the climb up Black Mountain. Now known as the Silvermine Ski Road, it was built in 1934 as a fire-control road and will be the route you later use to complete this circuit hike.

For now, continue ahead on the AT/ Ramapo-Dunderberg Trail as it climbs steeply up the side of Black Mountain on a fine footway. The full climb up takes only 20 minutes, but there's a viewpoint after 5 minutes. A rock outcropping provides a fine view back toward the area just traversed and to Silvermine Lake, where the hike started.

The Silvermine Lake area has an interesting history. In the early 1900s the area was called Bockey Swamp, "bockey" being a local term for the woven baskets used by charcoal burners. During the 1920s, beavers–which had just been reintroduced– built a dam, killing many trees. The park cleared the dead trees and planted rice, which they hoped would attract birds to the area. Instead, deer ate the rice (sound familiar?). In 1934 the CCC built a 600-foot dam, and the new lake was named Menomine (wild rice) by Major William A. Welch, the first general manager of the park.

In 1936 a ski slope and rope tow were added, and the area was named Silvermine after a legendary (only legendary) Spanish silver mine on Black Mountain. In 1942 a second ski slope was added, and in 1951 the lake was renamed Silvermine. The parking lot was enlarged in 1968, but the ski area has been closed since 1986–snowfall was just too undependable. The name Menomine was brought back to the area only when the trail was dedicated in 1994.

Rockland County and Harriman Park

Continue climbing more gently on the AT/Ramapo-Dunderberg Trail to the broad 1,200-foot summit of Black Mountain to enjoy the spectacular views of the Hudson and surrounding area. The small lake ahead of you is Owl Swamp. Farther afield, on the west bank of the river, are the dramatic shapes of the Tors (Hike 17) and Hook Mountain (Hike 16). On a clear day the skyline of Manhattan breaks the horizon.

You'll want to linger—this spot is one of our favorites in the park. When ready, retrace your steps down the mountain back to the gravel Silvermine Ski Road. Turn right, downhill, toward the lake. The road is unmarked but very easy to follow. In 15 minutes you'll pass by the dam (crossing is prohibited and unsafe) and 5 minutes later cross a stream on a substantial bridge. Almost immediately after the bridge, two green-and-black painted-metal posts flank the road. Here, turn left and bushwhack up about 40 yards to Seven Lakes Drive (passing cars will be apparent). Turn left again, and walk the shoulder of the road back to your car, less than 10 minutes away.

HNZ

24

Anthony Wayne Loop

Total Distance: 4.8 miles

Walking time: 4 hours

Vertical rise: 1,000 feet

Maps: 7.5' Popolopen Lake; NY–NJTC Northern Harriman Bear Mountain Trails #4

This hike is one of our favorites. It uses portions of several trails in Harriman State Park and includes part of one of the longest trails: the Suffern–Bear Mountain Trail, a mellow walk through trees and a wonderful ridge walk with extensive views both to the east and to the west.

Parking for the hike is at the Anthony Wayne Recreation area, in the first of two large lots once used by visitors to the now disused swimming pool, which had its heyday in the years after it opened in 1955. Leave the Palisades Interstate Parkway at exit 17, and drive past the tollbooth to park in the first lot on the right-hand side. Parking is normally free, except sometimes during the summer. For information call the Palisades Interstate Park Commission at 845-786-2701.

Walk back toward the tollbooth and through two cement-block gateposts with signs on the barrier indicating that hiking trails begin here on the right-hand side of the paved auto road. Our hike begins on the white-blazed Anthony Wayne Trail. Here the trail is used as part of a bike trail, and you may notice the blue-on-white markers. The title for the trail was taken from the name of the recreation area called after the famous general "Mad Anthony" Wayne, who was believed to have marched with his men through the area in 1779 during the American Revolution. The road at first is paved and climbs gently to cross another gravel road before the paving deteriorates and reaches a T junction, where the Anthony Wayne Trail turns left. Look immediately to

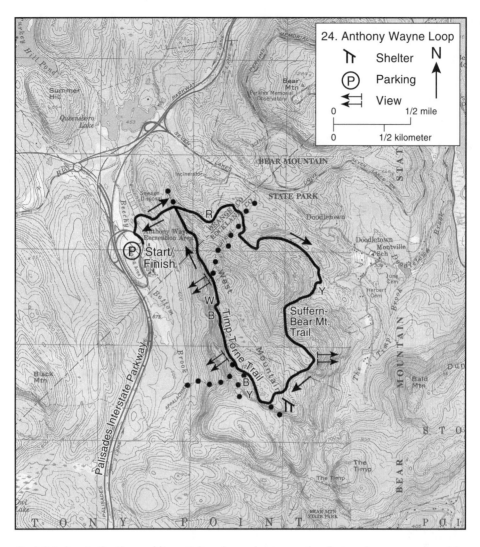

24. Anthony Wayne Loop

the left to locate the three white metal markers, each with a red *F* indicating the beginning of the Fawn Trail. In accordance with usage, it is deemed to be a red trail. The beginning of the Fawn Trail has recently been relocated and now is only correctly shown on the 2001 (eighth) edition of the New York–New Jersey Trail Conference map. The trail climbs, and when the metal markers change to paint blazes, you know that you're walking on the old route. The Fawn Trail was

shown on the first park map produced in 1920 but was badly damaged by bulldozers making a fire lane during the fire of 1988.

After climbing more ruggedly on rocks, the Fawn Trail meets the blue-marked Timp-Torne Trail. Take note here because the hike will bring you back to this junction later on. Ahead is a good view of Bear Mountain and the Perkins Memorial Tower (Hike 26). The Fawn Trail bears left at this junction, going gently downhill at first, bending left again

Along the Suffern–Bear Mountain Trail

after a while, and undulating along through a peaceful hardwood forest to its end at a junction with the Appalachian Trail (AT) after about 45 minutes into the hike.

Turn right uphill on the white-blazed AT (which uses a wide woods road here), ignore the woods road entering from the right in a couple of minutes, and continue to follow the white AT blazes to the left for only a very short distance. When the AT leaves to the right, your route continues on the wide woods road that has been cleared for use as a ski trail. You may occasionally see ski markers, but this road is not marked as a hiking trail. The sturdily constructed road you are following is part of the Doodletown road system. The hamlet called Doodletown was first inhabited by the Junes (or Jouvins), descendants of the French Huguenots, probably from 1762 until 1965. Although records show that it had already been named "Doodletown" by the time of the

British arrival, there are other suggestions for the derivation of the name. One of the most interesting is that the British derided the settlers by playing the tune "Yankee Doodle" as they marched through town. It is believed that 300 people may once have lived in Doodletown, and for many years after the hamlet's abandonment, the school, the church and other buildings remained standing. Today only foundations of the buildings can be discovered, mostly covered by the nonnative barberry.

The yellow-blazed Suffern–Bear Mountain Trail joins the ski trail from the left and leaves after about 0.75 mile past the junction of the Fawn Trail and the AT. Turn right now, and follow yellow blazes uphill on a rocky and gullied trail. The Suffern–Bear Mountain Trail crosses the Doodlekill and climbs seriously to reach a short rocky climb over talus, followed by a more gentle section. The Suffern–Bear Mountain Trail then passes through a small rocky outcrop. Do not linger here, but continue ahead to a viewpoint just off the trail to the right—a good place for an extended break, as you are now about midway through the hike. From this overlook there is a good view of the Timp and the Hudson River.

Within 20 minutes of starting off again after your break, the blue-marked Timp-Torne Trail joins the Suffern–Bear Mountain Trail from the left. The Timp-Torne Trail takes its name from two of Harriman–Bear Mountain State Parks's prominent summits—the Timp, which you have already seen from the recent overlook, and Popolopen Torne. For 0.3 mile the Timp-Torne Trail and the Suffern–Bear Mountain Trail are joined, so follow blue and yellow blazes until the Suffern–Bear Mountain Trail (yellow) goes off to the left, leaving only blue blazes to guide you. Fire once consumed part of this trail, but now birch, cedar, and pines are thankfully making a comeback, and your route on the ridge is open to the sky.

The AT joins the Timp-Torne Trail after another 0.1 mile. This junction is clearly marked with a wooden signboard. Take a few minutes to enjoy the extensive panorama before turning right to follow the white blazes of the AT and the continuing blue blazes of the Timp-Torne Trail. Your hike for the next 0.65 mile is along the spectacular west ridge of West Mountain, offering many fine outlooks both to the west and to the east as the trails jog from one side of the ridge to the other, tempting you to linger.

The dual blazes lead over several open flat rocks and up over some short rock ascents before beginning a descent to where the AT leaves the Timp-Torne Trail to the right, thus leaving you to follow blue blazes only for the next 1.1 miles. The Timp-Torne Trail wanders through a cleft in a rock and continues downhill, mostly over rock slabs, to the junction with the Fawn Trail, where you were previously. There is a downhill jumble of rocks leading down to this junction that may alert you to watch carefully to make a left turn onto the Fawn Trail. Retrace your earlier footsteps back to your car.

SJG

25

Dunderberg and the Timp

Total distance: 7 miles

Walking time: 5 to 6 hours

Vertical rise: 1,200 feet

Maps: USGS 7.5' Popolopen Lake; USGS 7.5' Peekskill; NY–NJTC Harriman-Bear Mountain Trails #4

The eastern end of the Dunderberg massif pinches the Hudson River to create the entrance to the narrows at the southern end of the Hudson Highlands. Its western end is sharply defined by the cliff-faced Timp. The mountain stretches 3 miles in an almost east-west direction to form the northern border of Haverstraw Bay. This ponderous hulk inspired Washington Irving in *The Storm Ship* to tell of the Dutch goblin who "keeps the Donderberg [sic]" with speaking trumpet. Sailors reported hearing him in "stormy weather . . . giving orders in Low Dutch, for the piping up of a fresh gust of wind or the rattling off of another thunder-clap." Hikers will find that the loop walk along Dunderberg's summit ridge to the Timp and back is one of the favorites in Bear Mountain State Park, especially if their trips are planned to avoid the goblin's storms and give clear weather for the spectacular views.

The parking area is on the west (inland) side of US 9W, 4.25 miles south of the Bear Mountain Traffic Circle and opposite Old Ayres Road to Jones Point. If traveling from the south, this spot is 0.25 mile north of the Anchor Monument.

Walk south of the parking area for 100 yards to the co-marked beginning of the blue-blazed Timp-Torne and red-on-white blazed Ramapo-Dunderberg Trails. The Ramapo-Dunderberg Trail was relocated after major fires destabilized the route still shown on most maps. This new route allows for a circular hike without the necessity of walking along busy US 9W.

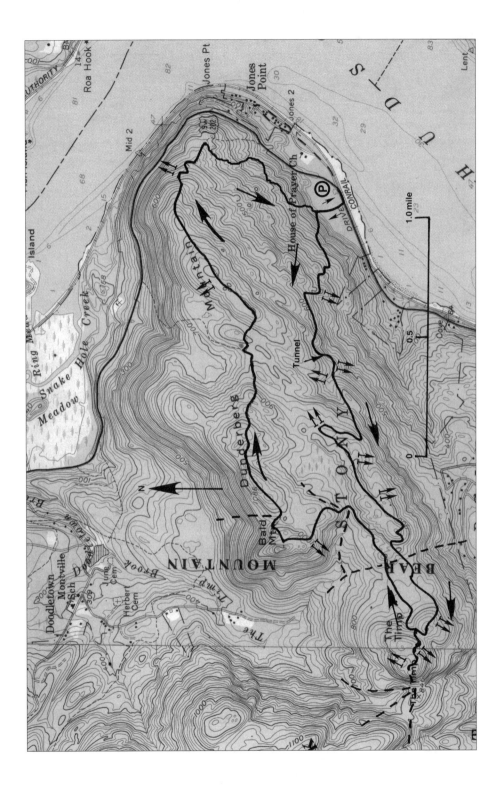

Follow the trail along the level, then steep, incline, as it begins to climb the flanks of Dunderberg. Within 10 minutes you zigzag up the beautiful cut-stone tunnel of the failed Dunderberg Railroad. Your walk today will take you across many sections of that incline railway, 13 miles of which were completed in the early 1890s before the failure of the project to construct the line to a hotel and restaurant that were to be built on the top of the mountain.

When after only 0.2 mile the two trails split, take the blue-blazed left fork. You continue zigzagging in tight S-curves up the steep flanks; then make a long traverse south below the crest. Already through-the-trees views reveal Haverstraw Bay, High Tor, the Hook, and Verplank Point, although the Indian Point Nuclear Plant and other power and resource-recovery plants intrude on this wonderful vista.

Turning to climb again, within 30 minutes you cross another section of the incline railway, and make a hairpin turn at the head of a deep hemlock draw. Rock work and the parallel tracks of the railway are visible. At about 1 mile you're following a track along an almost-level stretch when double trail markers point you uphill to the higher level of track at a point where the railway was supposed to emerge from a tunnel cut into the hillside. Stop to explore this partially cut tunnel. The trail then returns to the lower level, where it is built up into a sharp curve from which there are excellent views. The curve ends in a cut. Then the trail crosses a stream and a roadway and heads steeply uphill into the woods.

This trail was constructed to take advantage of the views and points of interest along the railway, and the route at times seems illogical. Stay with it because it sometimes follows roadway, sometimes narrow footpaths that are impossible to find without the markers. Be careful not to stray from the trail in these sections.

From a distance Dunderberg appears as a smooth hillside, but it's covered with rock outcrops, cliff-faced knobs, and various geological warts. You do a lot more climbing up and down than the 1,200-foot vertical rise indicates, so just enjoy the way the trail seems to wind over so many bumps. The New York–New Jersey Trail Conference map shows many of the intersecting roads and trails, but even its 20-foot contours give few clues to this contorted terrain.

The climb through the woods takes you steeply up to a viewpoint on top of the ridge. From here you look back northeast. You are about an hour into the walk, and at this point you start zigzagging steeply again, passing a balancing rock, then heading north on the almost-level trail. In another quarter hour you reach a lookout that's the sum of all those preceding it. At this point, just short of a deep draw separating your ridge from a northern part of the mountain, you make a hairpin turn to head southwest, zigzagging again, and in 10 minutes you reach an opening beside a balancing rock, where you have a breathtaking view down the Hudson, past Croton Point and the Tappan Zee Bridge.

After descending from this knob, you climb along a narrow path to a high point, marked with a cairn and winter views to the north. A series of rugged ups and downs follows. In one cut between little cliffs you can see Bear Mountain. The tortuous route reaches a vehicle track. Downhill from the track and about two hours into the hike, the blue-blazed trail crosses the 1777 Trail. The trail's name commemorates the roadway used by the British on their march to capture Fort Montgomery.

More jagged ups and downs follow, then a minor lookout and a descent to a valley with an intersection with the Ramapo-Dunderberg Trail, blazed with a red dot inside a white square. Turn left, following the red-with-white and the blue markers for a 10-minute climb to the Timp, that wonderful overlook that encompasses the Bear Mountain Bridge, Bear Mountain itself, several small lakes with islands, and the Manhattan skyline.

From the Timp, 2.5 miles from the trailhead, retrace your steps to the intersection, but this time turn left along the Ramapo-Dunderberg Trail. Head steeply down, through stands of laurel, and 25 minutes from the Timp you cross the 1777 Trail again.

Your route now heads over a knob, then winds through tall laurel around the head of a draw, where 30 minutes from the Timp it crosses a small stream and joins a roadway. Shortly the roadway turns right, and the trail continues straight ahead and up the side of Bald Mountain. There are several overlooks along this stretch—the northernmost looks straight down at the graceful Bear Mountain Bridge. Bald Mountain's slopes at this western end of Dunderberg are precipitous.

Bald's summit is 1.3 miles from the Timp. To the north of it is a rubble-and-tailing pile that marks the Cornell Mine. The trail east hugs the very steep northern slopes of Dunderberg, quickly intersecting the blue-blazed Cornell Trail that forks left and heads sharply downhill. Within 10 minutes you reach another summit in the chain, this one with views to the northwest as well as north up the Hudson. The trail winds over a wooded summit, descends to a marsh in a swale, and reaches a second draw, this one with a roadway. Forty minutes from Bald's summit, the trail crosses a portion of the incline railway, climbs, descends to a deep draw with a tiny, dark pond, then climbs to a knoll with a lovely view to the north, with glimpses of Taurus, Beacon, and Storm King.

The trail then briefly joins a roadway to climb another knob. This point, an hour from Bald, marks the end of climbing along the ridge. The trail follows a narrow course through the woods, traversing across the head of a steep ravine and up a short grade with a view northeast across Iona Island with its bird sanctuary. The island was once known as Weyant's Island after its first owner. Dr. C. W. Grant inherited it from his father-in-law in the 1850s. He farmed choice fruits there, maintained a vineyard, and gave it its curious name when he claimed, "I-own-an-island."

Below the knob the trail begins its steep plunge off the mountain. Some sections of the route are rubble-strewn and dangerous. A short white-blazed spur trail leads to a knoll with a superb lookout north and east.

With just about 0.75 mile to go, the marked trail now travels its new route using sections of the incline railway. Views west and south include the Indian Point Nuclear Plant and the town of Haverstraw.

A large stone wall marks the place where the footpath turns sharply east and descends steeply down the cable incline of the old railroad. The last 0.2 mile of the hike is along the same co-marked Ramapo-Dunderberg/Timp-Torne Trails on which you started the hike, and you'll soon be back to your car.

The distance between Bald Mountain's summit and US 9W is 2.5 miles, and the 3.8-mile return from the Timp along the Ramapo-Dunderberg Trail takes upward of 3 hours.

BMcM/HNZ

26

Bear Mountain

Total distance: 3.75 miles

Walking time: 2.5 hours

Vertical rise: 1,127 feet

Maps: USGS 7.5' Peekskill; USGS 7.5' Popolopen Lake; NY–NJTC Northern Harriman Bear Mountain Trails #4; park map

This loop hike, although short, is taxing because it uses the Major Welch Trail to the summit of Bear Mountain, perhaps the steepest climb in the park. The Appalachian Trail (AT), used for the descent, while not quite as steep as the Major Welch Trail, is popular and becoming badly eroded. It is sometimes difficult to see the correct trail route, but it is important to stay on the marked route and avoid the many developing herd paths. The views from the summit are exceptional, and you should allow enough time to climb Perkins Memorial Tower. At each window at the top of the tower, photographs are provided that enable the visitor to pick out the geographical points of interest which, on a clear day, include four states and Manhattan. If you find you have spare time at the end of the hike, a visit to the carousel, the Bear Mountain Zoo, and the Trailside Museum would add interest to your trip.

To access the hike, drive south for 0.4 mile on NY 9W from the Bear Mountain traffic circle at the northern end of the Palisades Interstate Parkway, just west of the Bear Mountain Bridge. Turn right at the light, then right again to park at the Bear Mountain Inn for a $5 charge at the weekend (less on weekdays).

From the parking lot, take the paved paths (or walk across the playing field) to the back of the inn, and turn right along the west side of Hessian Lake. Follow the blazes with a red dot on a white rectangle, which indicate the Major Welch Trail. This trail continues to the summit of Bear

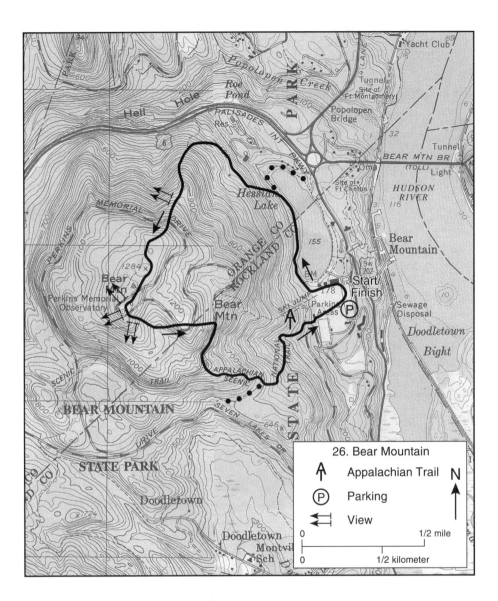

Mountain and beyond. (The blazes should not be regarded as graffiti depicting the Japanese flag–there have been some comments on the resemblance.)

At the base of the mountain facing you is the abandoned ski jump and the blazes of the Appalachian and Suffern–Bear Mountain Trails that commingle here. Your official route

back uses these trails, but a shortcut is recommended at the end of this hike description.

Walk along a paved path on the west bank of Hessian Lake, following the red-dot-on-white blaze. This lake has had several name changes. The small pond that existed here in the 1740s was called Lake Sinnipink and was later enlarged by the construction of three

---

small dams. Ice was cut here and shipped to New York City in prerefrigerator days.

Watch for a turn sign on the Major Welch Trail after about 11 minutes from your car, and turn left steeply uphill into the woods. Twenty minutes into the hike, Overlook Lodge, a Bear Mountain Inn facility, can be seen downhill from the trail. Soon afterward, a large tank, part of the Bear Mountain water system, can be seen uphill to the left of the trail. From here water is pumped from the reservoir to Perkins Memorial Tower and other Bear Mountain facilities.

After crossing the stream (ignore the woods road leading to the right down to Overlook Lodge), the trail turns right onto the woods road for about 20 yards before leaving it on the left. The climbing has been tough, but now the trail flattens out, following the 400-foot contour around the mountain. When there are no leaves on the trees, the Palisades Interstate Parkway can be seen below.

Following this short respite, the trail resumes its punishing upward climb. Small boulders underfoot become larger as the trail ascends, until the blazes eventually lead the hiker across large slabs. Rest awhile at the viewpoint reached about 50 minutes into the hike, and enjoy the view of the Hudson River and the graceful Bear Mountain Bridge. This bridge was opened in 1924, and at that time it was the longest span in the world.

The Major Welch Trail soon crosses Perkins Memorial Drive, bearing slightly to the left. A few minutes later, look for a significant stone monument about 5 feet tall to the left of the trail. West Point was one of the original owners of land on Bear Mountain, and this edifice is one of the old boundary markers.

Most of the climbing is now over as the trail flattens out about 5 minutes from the road crossing. The footway is now less rocky and passes through dense laurel. Just ahead, after the trail crosses a gravel road, is the true summit of Bear Mountain at 1,305 feet (Perkins Memorial Tower is at 1,280 feet and up to this point has been hidden from view). Evidence of the old fire tower, moved to Diamond Mountain, remains on top of the massive gray-and-beige-shaded rock. The trail does not go over the true summit but skirts the base of the summit rock toward the left, uses a gravel road that almost immediately becomes paved, crosses Perkins Memorial Drive again, and leads up to Perkins Memorial Tower. The bathrooms on the left-hand side are open only during the warmer months.

Perkins Memorial Tower is a landmark and can be seen from many locations in the park. Once used as a weather station for the U.S. Government, then as a fire tower, it was dedicated in 1934 in memory of George Walbridge Perkins, who served as one of the commissioners to the Palisades Interstate Park Commission. Vehicles may be driven to the summit of Bear Mountain via the Perkins Memorial Drive. Both the road and the tower were dedicated in 1934, although the road's original route was subsequently changed.

The several levels and staircases of the tower are decorated with tiles detailing historical events, including interesting snippets of information such as: "In 1920 a good meal could be purchased at Bear Mountain Inn for as little as $0.50." Look up to see the compass painted on the ceiling. Perkins Memorial Tower can be climbed seven days a week, except for the winter season, without charge.

After walking up and down the 57 steps of the tower, look for the white rectangles of the AT, and walk toward the view of the Hudson. On the way you pass a rock-

Ascending the Major Welch Trail

mounted plaque dedicated to Joseph Bartha, Trails Committee Chairman of the New York–New Jersey Trail Conference from 1940 to 1955. Near are two separate AT blazes, one marked with N for North and the other S for South. Be sure to travel north.

Five minutes down, the trail uses stringers over a wet patch and a little later makes two crossings of Perkins Memorial Drive. As you approach the third crossing, be careful to stay on the marked trail, even though it may be difficult because many alternative routes offer themselves. The AT on Bear Mountain has been relocated many times because of erosion.

Turn right at the third crossing of Perkins Memorial Drive and walk the paved road (finding blazes on boulders lining the road on the left-hand side) for almost 0.3 mile until a loop in the paved road is reached. Road walking can be tedious, but this short section is memorable for the views to the left. The trail blazes switch to the right at the loop. Leave the auto road between two boulders onto a badly eroded paved road, and almost immediately turn left downhill into the woods. The trail now descends through laurel and pines until the Suffern–Bear Mountain Trail (yellow blazes) joins from the right, about 45 minutes from the tower.

Turn left, and follow the joint blazes to a cement-slab stream crossing. Turn right downhill on a woods road, ignoring the gravel road entering from the left. Almost immediately the blazed trail turns left and leads you back to the rear of the inn. However, we suggest taking a shortcut by continuing straight ahead down the steep road, toward the ice-skating rink. Skirt the skating rink on its right-hand side, and cross the playing field to your car.

SJG

Bear Mountain

IV. The West Hudson Hills

Introduction to the West Hudson Area

New York's Orange County, known by hikers as the West Hudson area, has four distinct hiking areas: privately owned Black Rock Forest and Schunemunk Mountain, the new Sterling Forest State Park, and historic Storm King Mountain.

BLACK ROCK FOREST

Black Rock Forest is a 3,785-acre preserve dedicated to scientific research, education, and conservation of the natural ecosystem that once covered this entire region. Only 50 miles north of New York City, the area is home to numerous ponds, wetlands, and great biological diversity.

The land remains relatively pristine thanks to the foresight of Dr. Ernest Stillman, who in 1949 established and endowed it as a Harvard University research forest. In 1989, after Harvard decided the tract was no longer needed for its programs, the land was acquired by philanthropist William Golden, who established the not-for-profit Black Rock Forest Preserve.

Today, the forest is used as a field station by the Black Rock Forest Consortium, comprising of 22 private and public educational and research institutions, including the New York–New Jersey Trail Conference (NY–NJTC). The consortium provides a center for research and teaching at all levels and serves as an information network linking students, researchers, teachers, administrators, and institutions.

Public access continues. A feature of any walk in the forest is the sight of distinctive plots of native trees, each with differing timber-management techniques. All but one of the half-dozen ponds are parts of water systems for nearby towns, so laws prohibit use of them in any way. Dirt roads connect the different plots and are used by the forest's managers, but public vehicular traffic is not permitted. The Black Rock Fish & Game Club has sole permission to hunt the numerous deer that populate the forest. The property is closed to the public during deer season and may also be closed during times of high fire danger and for occasional special events. Call 845-534-4517 for information. Organized groups such as hiking clubs must call to preregister.

SCHUNEMUNK MOUNTAIN

Schunemunk sits in solitary splendor, its long, gently rounded form isolated from the Hudson Highlands and the Shawangunks as completely as its rocks are separated by the ages from their surroundings. Light grayish and pinkish sandstones, shales, and conglomerates crown its summit ridge. Hikers marvel at the unique conglomerate bedrock, commonly called puddingstone, so apparent when walking along either of the two distinct ridges. In many places the bedrock has been ground down to a smooth surface by the movement of glaciers. The purplish hue of the main rock houses different sizes of pink- and lavender-colored rocks as well as attractive white quartz pebbles.

The name Schunemunk is believed to mean excellent fireplace and was given to the Leni-Lenape Native American village once located on the northern part of the mountain that is such a familiar sight to travelers on the thruway.

The northern half of the ridge was saved from development by Star Expansion Industries, the Ogden Family Foundation, and the Storm King Art Center, who, under the leadership of H. Peter Stern, formed the Mountainville Conservancy. In 1996, using a grant from the Lila Acheson and DeWitt Wallace Foundation, the Open Space Institute acquired 2,100 acres that will eventually become the core of a new state park. The Nature Conservancy owns an additional 163 acres, but the rest of the ridge remains in private hands.

The foot-only trails are open from dawn to dusk. Hunting is not permitted, but violations are not uncommon. Most hikers avoid the mountain during deer season.

STORM KING STATE PARK

To the east of Black Rock Forest stands mighty Storm King Mountain. In 1922 Dr. Ernest Stillman donated 800 acres to the Palisades Interstate Park Commission to ensure its preservation. Little did he know of the controversy that would surround the mountain just four decades later when Consolidated Edison announced plans for a pumped storage power project that would have forever altered the area.

Some prominent local citizens, the NY–NJTC, and the Nature Conservancy joined forces to fight the project. Along with others, they founded Scenic Hudson Inc., the organization that today is still working to preserve the Hudson Valley's natural heritage. The landmark legal battle that ensued, not finally settled until 1980, now forms the basis of the environmental law movement championed by organizations such as the Natural Resources Defense Council.

In the summer of 1999 the Storm King

area was ravaged by a forest fire. It had been exceptionally dry, and the fire's heat went deep into the topsoil. To everyone's surprise, explosions followed. Long-forgotten unexploded shells, mostly from World War I, detonated under the intense heat. Fortunately, no one was hurt. The park was closed and a U.S. Army Corps of Engineers cleanup began in 2000. It is expected that at least the northern section of the park, including Storm King Mountain, will be opened for public use by 2003. However, before hiking, you are strongly advised to contact the Palisades Interstate Park Commission or the NY–NJTC for the latest information.

Except for hiking trails, the park is undeveloped and managed from Bear Mountain. Seasonal deer hunting is permitted.

STERLING FOREST STATE PARK

Sterling Forest is known for its role in the early mining and smelting industry. Old (and not so old) woods roads crisscross the area. A score of historic mines and the remains of two 19th-century furnaces are found on the property, one visited on Hike 29. Although many of the mines have been filled in and closed, the park still shows signs of this activity as well as more recent prepark logging operations. Most of the logging was responsibly done, and Mother Nature has restored most of the woodlands.

In late 2000 a 15-year effort by environmental groups and government agencies to create Sterling Forest State Park was all but completed with the acquisition of one of the last parcels of private land. The Trust for Public Land and the Open Space Institute raised almost $8 million for this final 1,065-acre purchase. A corridor of federal land surrounding the Appalachian Trail bisects the park at its northern end. Passaic County, New Jersey, owns a 2,000-acre tract in the south, acquired by eminent domain. All told, the protected open space is now close to 20,000 acres.

All during the 1990s the campaign to Save Sterling Forest dragged on and on. Ever so slowly, the pieces began to fall into place. The original $55 million acquisition included money from an intricate variety of sources. The federal government, the states of New York and New Jersey, and numerous private sources combined to purchase the original 14,500 acres.

Once owned by the Harriman family, the land was offered to the state as parkland in the 1940s, but the offer was declined and the property sold to private interests. In the late 1980s the corporate owners proposed a massive development: homes for 35,000 people, along with abundant office and commercial space. From the beginning, hikers had a strong interest in preserving this rugged forest. Spearheaded by NY–NJTC Executive Director JoAnn Dolan and her husband, Paul, a public-private coalition was formed that, over time, developed into a formidable force. The result, after many tortuous ups and downs, was our newest state park.

Contiguous with Harriman Park, the park is separately administered and currently in the midst of a master planning process. Hiking is allowed but, so far, only a limited foot-trail system is available. The park permits seasonal turkey and deer hunting (permit required), and to accommodate these users, many of the old logging roads are paint-blazed to facilitate navigation.

A generous donation of $1.75 million from the family of retired U.S. Senator Frank Lautenberg (D-NJ) has endowed a visitors center near Sterling Lake. Construction began in 2002. A temporary office is located nearby (845-351-5907).

27

Sterling Ridge to the Fire Tower

Total distance: 6.6 miles (8.6 miles for end-to-end hike with car shuttle)

Walking time: 3 hours (4–4.5 hours for end-to-end hike)

Vertical rise: 500 feet (800 feet for end-to-end hike)

Maps: USGS 7.5' Greenwood Lake; NY-NJTC Map #100, Sterling Forest State Park; park map

New York's newest state park provides a vital link in the Highlands greenway connecting Pennsylvania with Connecticut. This hike travels along one of the main ridges, with some moderate ups and downs, to an active fire tower with stunning views.

The Sterling Ridge Trail parking area is located on the south side of NY 17A, 5.4 miles west of its junction with NY 17 (junction is 6 miles north of Tuxedo, New York) or 1.8 miles east of the NY 17/210 intersection in Greenwood Lake village. The Allis Trail starts across the road. The trailhead turnoff is well marked with brown signs on NY 17A. The parking area has a chemical toilet.

This hike is out and back. However, you can do the entire 8.6-mile trail with a shuttle by placing a car at the south end in Hewitt, New Jersey. This interstate walk is highly recommended. See the detailed driving directions at the end of this hike description.

The Sterling Ridge Trail is well marked. The blazes are a blue dot on a white field, and you'll be following them for the entire hike. The trail is co-marked, for its entire length, as a section of the Highlands Trail (blue diamonds).

Soon after leaving the parking area and heading south, the Sterling Ridge Trail leaves a woods road and heads right (watch carefully for this turn—it's well marked but easy to overlook), uphill for a 100-foot climb. Soft moss covers the footway, indicating light use, which is surprising considering the quality of the hike. You now begin to get views down to Sterling Lake,

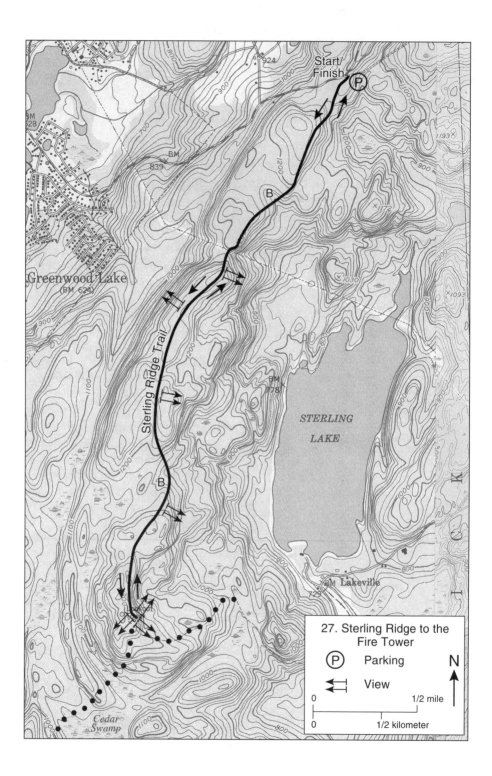

Start/
Finish

924

1000

900

1200

B

700

BM
828

BM
839

1000

1193

900

Greenwood Lake
(BM 620)

900

1030

1093

Sterling Ridge Trail

1200

1000

900

B

1100

1200

BM
778

STERLING
LAKE

900

1000

800

900

1000

1100

1000

900

900

800

BM Lakeville
729

800

COUNTY

1000

Cedar
Swamp

1000

1100

1000

900

**27. Sterling Ridge to the
Fire Tower**

Ⓟ   Parking   N

←⊏   View

0   1/2 mile

0   1/2 kilometer

which is scheduled to get a visitors center and become the hub of the new park.

After descending into a small notch with a seasonal spring, the trail climbs, levels off, then crosses under a major transmission line. After making a sharp left turn, the route climbs up to a rock prominence dotted with small cedars. With fine views, this area makes an excellent place for a break.

From here the trail continues on the ridge with several undulations and views. The large microwave tower seen to the east is in Harriman Park near Lake Welch. Some 45 minutes from the start, the footway enters a grove of mountain laurels. Should you be here in early June, you will be engulfed by large white and pink blossoms.

There are many rock outcroppings along the way. Many have stands of cedar, pitch pine, and/or balsam fir. One contorted cedar tree, complete with trail markers, is particularly attractive. Just beyond it is another lovely overlook with a full view of Sterling Lake.

In just more than an hour, a junction is reached with an unauthorized yellow-marked trail down to Greenwood Lake (markers may have been removed by park rangers). This herd path is the old Laurel Swamp Trail, which may be shown on older maps. Stay with the blue-dot trail. Some of the fir trees in this area show the harsh effects of the woolly adelgid (see the Introduction). Sterling Tower is reached after about 1.5 hours of hiking.

The tower is at an elevation of 1,380 feet and is periodically manned by volunteers or park personnel. At most times you can climb to the top of the stairs for a 360-degree view. Harriman Park spreads out to the east. To the west lies Greenwood Lake with Bellevale Mountain, the route of the Appalachian Trail, just beyond. The fire wardens have provided a nice picnic table for

public use. Retrace your steps to your car when you're ready.

OPTIONS

If you have placed a take-out car in Hewitt, New Jersey, you can continue on the Sterling Ridge Trail for an additional 5-plus miles for a total hike of 8.6 miles. The New Jersey section is parkland owned by Passaic County, which we hope will one day be merged into a Sterling Forest *Interstate* Park. The Sterling Ridge Trail undulates as it continues south but has no major climbs. There is a significant descent at the end before the trail passes the partially restored Long Pond Ironworks furnace and water-wheel (1766–1882) just before the trail emerges onto Greenwood Lake Turnpike.

The furnace area provides a fine ending to a long day. Partially restored and stabilized, the old stone walls, furnaces, and other remnants of the once industrious iron-working community now sit tranquilly next to the Wanaque River, and some interpretive signs have been installed.

The ironworks were founded in 1766 by German ironmaster Peter Hasenclever (Hike 21), who brought 500 ironworkers and their families from Germany to build a community: furnace, forge, houses, shops, and farms. A dam at "Long Pond" (now Greenwood Lake) provided the hydropower. Operations ceased in 1882 because of the industry-wide conversion to anthracite furnaces using Pennsylvania coal.

To place a car for the end-to-end hike: Drive on NY 17 to the junction with Sloatsburg Road (County Road [CR] 72). This junction is 3.6 miles north of the New York–New Jersey border and just south of Sloatsburg, New York. Take Sloatsburg Road about 5 miles into New Jersey, passing Ringwood State Park, and turn right onto to Margaret King Avenue. Proceed for 2 miles to a T-junction with CR 511 (Greenwood Lake Turnpike). Turn right, and continue for about 1 mile to a junction with East Shore/Awosting Roads. Park a car here in a large open area off the south side of CR 511. The Sterling Ridge Trail ends on the northeast side of this junction.

To drive to the start of the hike from here, go north onto East Shore Road. Avoid the Awosting Road turnoff at 2.5 miles, and pass the New York–New Jersey border at 4.4 miles. At 7.3 miles keep to the main road, avoiding Edgemere. At 8.4 miles you reach a well-marked junction with NY 17A. Turn right, and drive 1.6 miles to the trailhead parking on the right.

HNZ

28

Mount Peter to Arden on the Appalachian Trail

Total distance: 12.3 miles (or 8.7 miles)

Walking time: 6.5 hours (or 5 hours)

Vertical rise: 2,050 feet (or 1,450 feet)

Maps: USGS 7.5' Sloatsburg; Appalachian Trail Map Set (Hudson River to Greenwood Lake) #3

This arduous hike should not be attempted by anyone in poor physical condition or without motivation. It crosses several mountains with many false summits, includes some short sections of rock scrambling, and ends with a very steep descent down a precipitous hill, Agony Grind, that can be hard on tired knees. Fitzgerald Falls and Little Dam Lake are highlights of the trip, but some extremely beautiful sections, varied terrain, and vistas are also included. Navigation is not a problem because the hike follows the route of the Appalachian Trail (AT) throughout. Two cars are needed for a shuttle, and an option to shorten the hike is given.

Drive two (or more) cars north on NY 17 through Sloatsburg and Tuxedo. Turn right onto Arden Valley Road 5.5 miles north of the Tuxedo Railroad Station, and continue 0.3 mile to the ample parking at the "Elk Pen" on the right. Leave one car here. (During the early 1920s a herd of elk was indeed penned here. Transported from Yellowstone National Park, the animals didn't flourish, and the survivors were sold in 1942.)

Now drive south on NY 17 for 2.8 miles to the junction of NY 17A. Bear right at the light and right again at the stop sign at the end of the commuter lot. Turn right, and continue west along NY 17A. The hiker sign you may notice as you drive at about 5.5 miles is a sign for the Sterling Ridge Trail (Hike 27) and the Allis Trail. After 7.4 miles on NY 17A you'll reach a junction with NY 210. Bear right at the fork. Almost immedi-

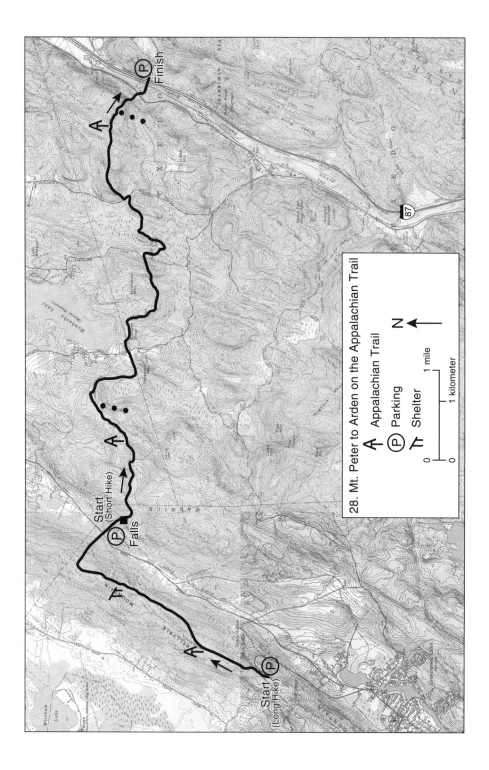

28. Mt. Peter to Arden on the Appalachian Trail

Appalachian Trail
Parking
Shelter

N

1 mile
0
0 1 kilometer

Finish

87

Start
(Short Hike)

Falls

Start
(Long Hike)

ately at another fork you must decide whether to walk the 12-mile hike or the 8-miler. For the longer hike, bear left, staying on NY 17A toward Warwick for almost 2 miles before making a sharp left turn at the crest of Mount Peter into Continental Road, where there's parking for six or seven cars.

For the shorter hike, take the right fork toward Monroe on Lakes Road (a.k.a. Mountain Lakes Road or Monroe Road). Continue straight ahead for 0.3 mile, paralleling part of Greenwood Lake on the right, to a stop sign. Drive straight ahead, now on Orange County Route 5, and proceed 3.7 miles to limited parking on the east side of the road close to a large power line stanchion. Walk east into the woods to reach Fitzgerald Falls, and pick up the directions for the longer hike from this point.

Starting on the full hike, walk back down NY 17A for about 150 feet, and enter the woods on the left. Almost immediately a blue-blazed trail enters from the left leading to the Hawk Watch platform used for monitoring spring and fall raptor migration.

A gentle uphill and short downhill through hemlock and laurel and across a gas line leads to the first rock jumble called the Eastern Pinnacles. Neither this scramble, nor the one following, is difficult, though both call for concentration and the use of hands as well as the need for secure footing. There are alternatives to following the AT up and over. A blue-blazed trail at the foot avoids the steep climb, and another, partway up the rocks, indicates an easier route across. We recommend following either the white AT or the second blue blazes because of the expansive views obtained from the top. Clambering over the rocks takes about 10 minutes, but walking around on the flat blue-blazed trail takes a little less time. On every rock scramble we advise keeping to the marked route, which is usually the easiest.

The AT now meanders gently downhill, crossing a brook on two logs before approaching Cat Rocks—another rock scramble, again offering expansive views from its flat top. Again another easier route is indicated by blue blazes.

A little less than an hour from the car a blue trail to the left leads to Wildcat Shelter. The AT now climbs over Bellvale Mountain. About 1 hour, 10 minutes into the hike watch carefully for a sharp 90-degree turn to the right, also signed with a Highlands Trail marker. Ignore any herd-path crossings and descend, gently at first but then more aggressively, to Lakes Road. Cross straight over. (The 8.7-mile hike begins here.)

Continue following the AT on a downward trend through an open area, under a power line, and across a wooden bridge over Trout Brook.

The stream crossings here can sometimes be difficult, but when the area is flooded, use the blue-blazed bypass trail that also leads to the base of Fitzgerald Falls. Water at the falls tumbles spectacularly 25 feet through a split in the jagged rocks, and we suggest a break here.

In the past, large amounts of garbage accumulated at this popular party spot, spoiling the beauty of the falls. During the fall of 1983 and the spring of 1984 an aggressive clean-up project was successfully spearheaded by the AT Management Committee of the New York–New Jersey Trail Conference (NY–NJTC). In addition, during the summer of 1984, the NY–NJTC hired local off-duty Warwick police to patrol the area during weekends and also worked with the local transportation department to post parking restrictions. This very successful project was a great example of teamwork that attacked a grievous problem head-on.

Follow the AT markers as the trail ascends steeply on the rocks to the right of

Fitzgerald Falls

the falls. At the top the trail first bears right, leading away from the stream through a luxuriant hemlock grove, until it descends to cross the main stream on stepping-stones. Cross a tributary and a gravel road, and begin the mostly steady ascent of Mombasha High Point. The many crumbling stone walls and the woods road underfoot are remnants of abandoned settlements. The stream to the right is calm in its upper reaches, and the area in spring is filled with wildflowers.

The junction with the blue-blazed Allis Trail and a register box is reached within 45 minutes from Fitzgerald Falls. There are two register boxes on this section of the AT. Please sign in as day hikers. The Allis Trail is named after a banker, J. Ashton Allis, who was an early treasurer of the Appalachian Trail Conference and a pioneer trail builder.

The summit of Mombasha High Point at an elevation of 1,280 feet is still about 1 mile distant. New York City is sometimes visible to the south, Schunemunk Mountain is to the northeast, and Harriman State Park to the east. Look west to see the route you traveled along the ridge of Bellvale Mountain. Mombasha High Point is almost the halfway point of the hike, but considerable work remains to be done.

The AT now takes the hiker through a different terrain of rock slabs and pitch pine, with views of West Mombasha Lake to the right. The trail switchbacks down, crosses woods roads, and undulates to a crossing of a small stream and a swampy area on puncheons. About 40 minutes from Mombasha High Point the trail passes close to a small unnamed pond, continues through a gap in an old stone wall, and uses almost continuous planking to cross an open field that is a designated butterfly refuge.

Emerge onto West Mombasha Road, walk straight over, cross the ditch on planks, and proceed ahead on what seems to be the top of an old rock wall. West Mombasha Lake can now be glimpsed through the trees to your left.

The trail now begins its climb to the first summit of Buchanan Mountain, which takes close to 30 minutes through a lovely section. After crossing a stream the trail dips into a valley lined with moss-covered rocks with streams, laurel, and hemlocks, looking much as we imagine a pixie grotto would look. This low-lying area is left behind as you climb the rocks on your left to the ridge. The trail follows the top of the ridge on a hog's back to the first summit of Buchanan Mountain with its lovely views and attractive rocks on which to perch for a break.

Continue to follow the AT blazes downhill, at first on a regular trail and then uphill on ominous-looking large rocks, to the true summit of Buchanan Mountain. Your route, now steeply downhill for 20 minutes, proceeds toward Little Dam Lake visible below.

Walk straight across East Mombasha Road, partway down the total descent, and continue on a winding woods road to the bridge over the inlet of Little Dam Lake--another pretty section with a resting spot on the banks of the lake. The AT follows the northern shore of the lake and proceeds over a ridge to emerge on Orange Turnpike.

Turn left onto Orange Turnpike for 250 feet, and reenter the woods on the right-hand side of the road just at the end of the guardrail. At the time of this writing the AT blazes were somewhat faded, but the trail is not difficult to follow. It now undulates over several shoulders of Arden Mountain, with the best views coming after the first rock climb. On the way there are two cairns and a register box, and just more than an hour from Orange Turnpike you'll see three blue blazes on the right. This new trail is a connector to the recently cut Indian Hill Trail (Hike 29).

Ten minutes more, and traffic noises intrude as you crest and begin the steep downhill of Agony Grind. The trail is routed through two rock gullies but has no exposure as trees cover the area. Fifteen minutes later, at the end of the descent, bear right and parallel NY 17 before emerging from the woods and crossing the road to walk the 0.3 mile on Arden Valley Road back to your car in the Elk Pen.

SJG

29

Indian Hill Loop

Total distance: 4.25 miles

Walking time: 3 hours

Vertical rise: 900 feet

Maps: USGS 7.5' Monroe; NY–NJTC Sterling Forest Trails #100; Sterling Forest Park map

Owned by Scenic Hudson and managed by the Palisades Interstate Park Commission, Indian Hill is now part of New York State's newest park, Sterling Forest. The remains of the historic Southfields iron furnace are situated at the edge of the Indian Hill property and are visited on this hike. The moderate hike, with one short steep descent, offers pleasant views of other sections of the Park, the Ramapo River Valley, and Harriman State Park.

The trails used on this hike were just recently scouted, built, and blazed by the New York–New Jersey Trail Conference (NY–NJTC). One very new section, a loop down to the furnace, has a short but quite steep downgrade to the furnace. Although well marked, the footway itself was not finished when this hike was written. Hunting is permitted in most of the Sterling Forest State Park (845-351-5910), including the Indian Hill section. A park information center is located on the west side of NY 17 immediately south of its junction with NY 17A.

From the south, take NY 17 north about 3.5 miles from Tuxedo. Just after passing the landmark Red Apple Rest, turn left onto County Road (CR) 19 (Orange Turnpike). If coming from the north, this junction is on the right, about 6 miles south of the New York State Thruway (I-87) exit 16, just past the Tuxedo Heights Condominiums and a deli.

Proceed up CR 19 for 1.3 miles, bearing right to avoid Bramertown Road, to a brown Indian Hill entrance sign and security gate. The seasonal "sand pit" parking area is 0.2

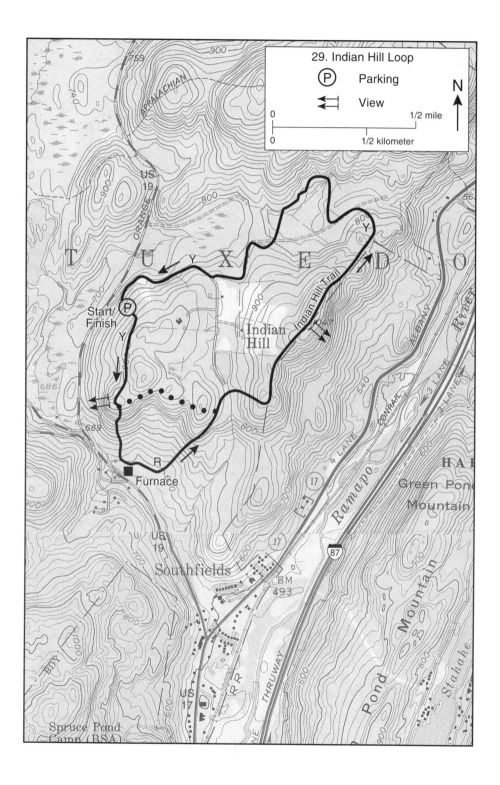

29. Indian Hill Loop

Ⓟ Parking

⮂ View

N

0 _____ 1/2 mile

0 _____ 1/2 kilometer

mile up the gravel entrance road. If the gate is closed, shoulder parking is available, but be careful not to block the gate.

The Indian Hill Trail is marked with yellow Scenic Hudson disks and starts behind the information kiosk, where a chemical toilet is available. As the trail is fairly new, some stretches of the footway may not be distinct, so be sure to keep an eye open, especially for the double markers that indicate turns.

The path, which begins as a narrow footway flanked by rocks, heads steeply uphill to the top of a viewless small hill. Mountain laurel abounds. After some ups and downs, the first viewpoint is reached in less than 20 minutes after a climb of only 200 feet. Although this is just a localized view over the hills to the south, much of what can be seen are the recently protected areas of Sterling Forest State Park. (Rock outcropping viewpoints dotted with pines and cedars are among our favorite places to pause.) Catch your breath, and enjoy this tranquil spot.

Immediately after the viewpoint, the red-marked Furnace Loop leaves to the right. Follow the trail down. The first quarter mile is steep, and the footway may not yet have been improved. If it's wet or icy or if you have small children along, this could be difficult. The entire section can be avoided by remaining on the yellow trail, but you'll miss seeing the furnace.

After the steep downhill, about 200 feet, you approach the massive Southfields Furnace, protected by a chain-link fence. Building began in 1804 and the furnace was "in blast" about a year later. By 1868 the Southfields Iron Works complex comprised not only a furnace but also a smith shop, stamping mill, sawmill, gristmill, wheelwright, branch rail line, and manor house, among other facilities. Although the loading ramp (supported by arches) and some of the walls of the casting room remain intact, the furnace has suffered decay from neglect and weathering. Its "last blast" was in the fall of 1887. Acquired by the Scenic Hudson Land Trust in 1997, emergency stabilization measures have now saved this remnant of our history. Tours may be offered from time to time. Check with the park office.

Some one hundred to two hundred years ago, iron was produced in stone furnaces, like Southfields, by mixing iron ore, charcoal, and limestone. Once a furnace was lit, the blast would run continuously, producing as much as 25 tons of pig iron a week. In those days, a furnace might have required cutting an acre of hardwood forest a day to be used in making the charcoal. Today, you would never know that almost the entire area of this hike had been clear-cut. Trees and other ground cover are again abundant. Nature has renewed and restored.

Continuing on red for a short distance along an old railbed (markers are scarce), be alert for a left turn in a cleared area. The pathway begins its climb, slowly at first, back up to the ridge. After a steeper ascent along a rock outcropping, the Furnace Loop Trail ends at a junction with the Indian Hill Loop, about 20 minutes from the furnace. For those who skipped the Furnace Loop, here is where they "rejoin" the hike.

The hike continues to the right, following the yellow blazes. However, it is worth taking a 3-minute detour left onto the yellow trail. Follow this trail until just before it makes a sharp left, and you'll see a pond through the woods ahead of you—another tranquil location worth a short visit. Return the way you came back to the red-yellow junction, and continue ahead, now following yellow markers as you will for the rest of the walk.

The view across the new Sterling Forest State Park

The yellow trail crosses the pond outlet stream and climbs up a hill, crossing some recent logging skid roads and skirting through a tangle of rocks. The ledges here offer nice views west into Harriman Park.

There are several short ups and downs and ample evidence of old farms. You may even notice the marked boundary between this new parkland and Harriman State Park, where hunting is not permitted.

Some 20 minutes from the pond, the trail approaches the edge of a ridge near a large cedar tree. Bushwhack right for a few yards to the edge of the ridge for a commanding view of the thruway, Ramapo River Valley, and Columbia University's Arden Conference Center on the hilltop beyond.

The trail swings off the ridge, switchbacks down about 120 feet, and parallels a stone wall. Now you've reached one of the area's mysteries.

The trail travels for some distance between two truly massive stone walls; some 6 feet high and as much as 8 feet wide, much wider and larger than walls encountered elsewhere. Why were they built? Did farmers just have lots and lots of rocks to clear? Did these walls have something to do with mining activity? So far no one has been able to offer more than conjecture. Scholars invited!

As you turn right through a gap in the walls, note the massive white oaks, reportedly more than a hundred years old. Soon you'll pass a junction with a blue-marked trail, an access path to the Appalachian Trail just to the north.

From here, the short half-hour journey back to the parking area crosses stone walls, traverses old woods roads, and passes old farmsteads; all offer a home for wildlife and opportunities for future off-trail exploration.

At 500 acres, Indian Hill is just one small part of the 17,000 acres of Sterling Forest State Park. How fortunate we are to now have this region protected and preserved for us and future generations.

HNZ

30

Summit of Schunemunk

Total distance: 7.5 miles

Walking time: 5 hours

Vertical rise: 1,600 feet

Maps: USGS 7.5' Cornwall; NY–NJTC West Hudson Trails #8

The full hike described follows part of the Long Path, some of the Jessup Trail, and the new Trestle Trail, and requires a short shuttle of about 5.5 miles. It begins with a quite demanding climb of about 1,000 feet elevation gain up to the ridge—some rock scrambling is needed—followed by an undulating ridge walk offering many viewpoints and, toward the end, a drop into the valley between the two ridges of Schunemunk. A short climb to the other ridge follows, and an easier walk takes you back to the second car. (If a second car is not available, it is still a splendid day's outing to walk to the summit and back; perhaps hike to the summit from the other direction at another time.)

Leave the New York State Thruway (I-87) at exit 16 (Harriman), and drive two cars north on NY 32 for 7.3 miles to the large black sign for the Black Rock Fish & Game Club. Turn left onto Pleasant Hill Road and left again onto Taylor Road. Taylor Road first crosses over Woodbury Creek, then over the thruway and passes a hikers' parking area on the right. The Jessup Trail is routed along Taylor Road, and as you drive you may notice the yellow-paint blazes. Turn left after 1.98 miles from NY 32 at the T-junction with Otterkill Road. Within 0.5 mile a massive railroad trestle can be seen. There is space for a few cars immediately below the trestle, but the official parking area and bulletin board is less than 0.2 mile farther down Otterkill Road on the right-hand side. Leave one car here.

Return in the second car to NY 32. Drive south for 3.3 miles, passing under the rail-

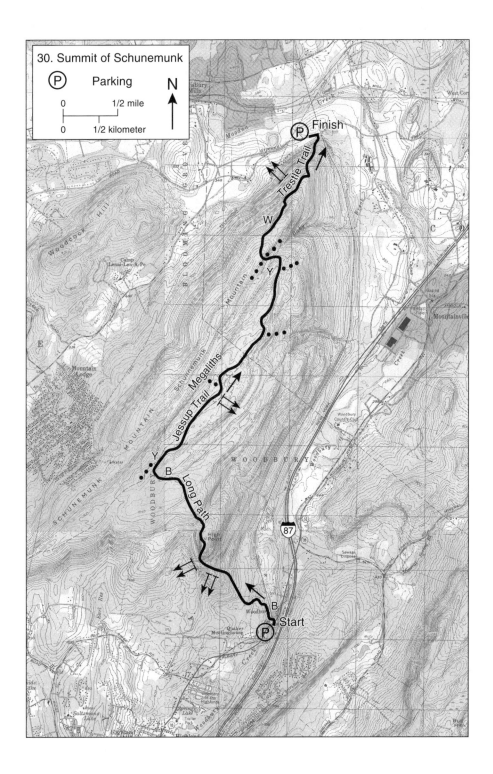

P   Parking

N

0   1/2 mile

0   1/2 kilometer

Finish

Trestle Trail

W

Y

Megaliths

Jessup Trail

Y

B

Long Path

High Point

87

B

Start

road trestle and continuing for another 0.2 mile. Park on the west side of the road close to the junction of NY 32 and Evans Road. (For those using one car and planning to walk to the summit and back, this parking area is 4 miles on NY 32 from the New York State Thruway [I-87] exit 16.)

Walk north on Route 32 toward the trestle, and just beyond the guard look to the left to see the turquoise-colored blazes of the Long Path on a tree at the entry of a dirt road. Scramble up the embankment, and turn left at the top of the first pitch to proceed under the trestle. Immediately turn right, and again scramble up a muddy slope to walk beside the trestle, now on your right-hand side. Turn left, and walk along the railroad tracks. Remember that the line is still active, and a bend in the track behind you would mask your presence from the sight of the train's engineer.

Walk along the tracks for about 10 minutes. Long Path blazes are few, but just as you approach the beginning of a chain-link fence on the right, find the Long Path blazes on the left, and walk into the woods. The trail makes a sharp left onto a woods road, and for a few minutes it parallels the tracks. Turn right uphill into the woods just before a stream crosses the woods road. The trail crosses an old stone wall and passes by a quarry on the left-hand side. At about 20 minutes from the car, just after crossing another broken-down stone wall, the trail brings you to a junction with a red-marked unofficial trail. Turn right to follow the Long Path blazes uphill.

The trail climbs consistently, and the Long Path soon bears right to a viewpoint and a scramble over Little Knob. Watch carefully to find this turn because at the time of this writing, there were insufficient blazes.

Still ascending, the route turns sharply to the right and takes you steeply up a rocky outcrop among pitch pine to the top of High Knob. This total ascent of approximately 1,000 feet in elevation gain from the car is the hardest of the day. The hiker is rewarded with a view of the Hudson River, Breakneck Ridge, Storm King to the left, Black Rock Forest in front, and below, the quarry you recently walked past and the thruway. It's a good place to take a breather.

Continue to follow the Long Path north along the ridge, which within a few minutes switches to the opposite side, giving a view in the opposite direction from the one you just left. Facing you is the main ridge of Schunemunk Mountain, along which runs the Jessup Trail (not the section to be used later on this hike).

Our trail, still rocky, descends and climbs back up for about 40 feet before flattening out to continue along the top of the ridge in a young hardwood forest. Ignore the cairn by the side of the footway that marks the unofficial trail to Dark Hollow Brook and any other red paint splotches. Forty minutes from High Knob the trail crosses a substantial stream—the upper reaches of Dark Hollow Brook. Shortly you arrive at the two cairns marking the Jessup Trail crossing. Leave the Long Path that continues straight ahead, and begin to follow yellow blazes up a large rock to the right. Here the diamond-shaped blue markers of the Highlands Trail commingle with the yellow blazes of the Jessup Trail. Do not be confused between the Highland Trail markers and the Long Path blazes—they are somewhat similar in color.

Climb the chunky rock to the right, and emerge into a large open area of slabs dotted with glacial erratics and pitch pines. The hike takes about two hours to this truly wonderful spot. Lingering here is well worthwhile.

The route onward is marked with cairns and leads to another upward scramble between huge boulders. You may think that the summit has been reached when you emerge into the open, but the true summit is still a little way off. The lengthy walk now traversed along the ridge undulates and changes between open areas of rock and groves of hardwood trees and laurel. After another 15 minutes the junction with the Western Ridge Trail is reached. This trail is marked with a blue dot on a white field, and the junction is additionally indicated with a large cairn in the footway.

Within another 10 minutes the summit of Schunemunk at 1,664 feet is reached. White paint underfoot indicates the site of a previous fire tower.

The Megaliths (Hike 31) can be reached by walking for a few minutes north on the Jessup Trail and watching for a sign on the ground pointing left in the direction of the Megaliths. The name is given to a group of enormous blocks split from the main bedrock. This spot is an excellent place for lunch. The Megaliths can afford much amusement by scrambling over, around, and beneath them. Those with less energy should take the opportunity to admire the view and pick out and identify other geographic points of interest.

The Megaliths and the summit are the high point of the hike and should be your turnaround point if you have been unable to spot a second car.

Continue north on the yellow-blazed Jessup Trail, dropping down almost immediately into a spectacular laurel grove that arches overhead. The junction with the white-blazed Dark Hollow Trail is reached within 10 minutes from the summit and the white-blazed Sweet Clover Trail in another 25 minutes.

The Sweet Clover and the Jessup Trails commingle, so the footway here is marked with both white and yellow blazes until the

Sweet Clover Trail departs to the left about 45 minutes from the summit, leaving only yellow blazes to direct you. The trail shortly breaks out to provide a view of the western ridge opposite. The Long Path is located along the top of that ridge, and on a clear day the Shawangunk Ridge and the Catskills can be seen beyond. The monument at High Point, New Jersey, can often be seen by following the Shawangunk Ridge south (left) with your eyes.

The Jessup Trail now descends steeply for about 300 feet to a woods road in the valley. Ignore the Jessup Trail that turns right and the red-marked Barton Swamp Trail going left. Cross Baby Brook on stepping-stones and begin a steep climb of about 250 feet, following red blazes. Straight at first, the trail turns left along a ledge with a drop-off to the left before continuing straight uphill to the junction with the recently built white-blazed Trestle Trail on the Western Ridge. Watch for the cairn. An excellent view of the ridge you have just left can be obtained by climbing to the crest of the high ground on the left when you reach this point.

Take the Trestle Trail north and downhill for about 45 minutes back to your car. The footing now is much more gentle, on soil rather than rock, at least for the first part of your journey. The trail pleasantly traverses a ridge and on the left in 20 minutes offers a view over the valley and of your ultimate destination: the trestle.

The official name for the trestle is the Moodna Viaduct. It was built about 1910 as part of a new freight bypass being constructed by the Erie Railroad. Until the 1980s the trestle was used only for freight. This rail section became a passenger line when the original line through Goshen and Middletown was abandoned, and it's now regarded as one of the most scenic on the rail route be-

Snow and ice on Schunemunk Mountain

cause it offers many outstanding views.

Thirty minutes' walking on the Trestle Trail affords an eye-level view of the trestle. Turn left when you arrive at a junction with the red-blazed trail encircling the mountain. The trail is now marked with red blazes as well as white ones and continues downhill quite steeply at times on a rocky road. This road runs almost underneath the trestle on your right-hand side before moving away from it. Otterkill Road is visible down to the right. At the time of this writing, the notice board erected by the Star Expansion Company is still in place to your left. Emerge onto Otterkill Road, turn left, and walk the short distance back to your car.

SJG

31

Schunemunk Loop

Total distance: 7.8 miles

Walking time: 5.5 hours

Vertical rise: 1,900 feet

Maps: USGS 7.5' Cornwall; NY–NJTC West Hudson Trails #8

Schunemunk, a mountain that sits in solitary splendor, is a hikers' favorite. The light sandstones, shales, and conglomerates that crown its summit provide a solid surface for a ridge walk replete with distinctive scenery, long views, gnarled trees, and uncommon rock formations.

This loop walk from the north will highlight the deep cleft that creases Schunemunk Mountain as well as take you to vantage points on both the long eastern and western faces.

To reach the trailhead, leave the New York State Thruway (I-87) at exit 16 (Harriman), and drive north on NY 32 for 7.3 miles to a sign for the Black Rock Fish & Game Club. Turn left and immediately left again onto Taylor Road, which crosses over the thruway. On the far side of the crossing, park at a designated area on the north side of the road. These lands are still privately owned, and hikers are warned that they enter at their own risk and cautioned that any use other than hiking is a trespass.

The yellow-blazed Jessup Trail has recently been relocated off Taylor Road. Only the most recent map will show the new route. Both the Jessup Trail and the white-blazed Sweet Clover Trail start across the road and travel along a paved private road past a barn. Turning west past a house, watch carefully for the well-marked division of the two trails (just after going through a gate). Stay with the yellow blazes as the Jessup heads toward and then parallels an active rail line. Follow the marked way and carefully cross the rail line and head into the woods, soon crossing the red-marked Otterkill Trail.

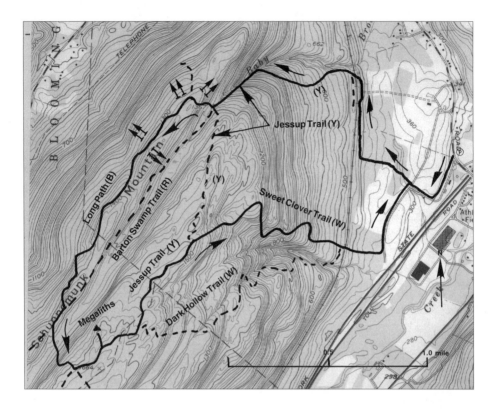

After not quite a mile, the trail begins to climb beside an old stone wall through mountain laurels. If your walk is taken in spring, wild oats, spring beauty, and trailing arbutus line the way. Farther along you join Baby Brook, where quartz crystals and conglomerates of rounded purple and green rocks brighten the streambed.

A climb of 700 feet brings you to an intersection. Here, an hour plus into the trip, the Barton Swamp Trail, marked with red dots on a white rectangle, forks right across Baby Brook to begin the climb of the western ridge. This scramble, over pinkish conglomerates, zigzags quickly uphill so that within a few minutes you enjoy views back over Storm King and Black Rock Forest. As you climb higher, the panorama of Beacon and Newburgh Bay on the Hudson

emerges. Near the top of the knifelike edge of the western ridge, views northwest to the Shawangunks and Catskills begin, and you have your first glimpse of the eastern ridge.

You pass a trail intersection with the new white-blazed Trestle Trail and soon come to a junction with the turquoise-blue blazes of the Long Path. Turn left and stay on the ridge following the Long Path, a 300-plus-mile route that runs north from New York City to just below Albany.

For about 45 minutes you can enjoy the openness of the walk, the views of the eastern ridge, and the occasional openings to the west. After nearly 2 miles along the ridge and after passing a junction with the white Sweet Clover Trail, the Long Path intersects the Western Ridge Trail, a 0.6-mile blue-dot-on-white crossover trail. Leave the Long

The West Hudson Hills

A hiker on the Long Path

Path, and follow the Western Ridge for its entire length. A brief descent brings you to the moist realm of the cleft, which you follow south briefly as your trail is co-aligned with a red-marked Barton Swamp Trail. The red trail continues south, but you want a blue-marked left fork, which shortly begins to climb the eastern ridge. This scramble will take 20 minutes and reach an intersection with the Jessup Trail (yellow markers).

Here turn left (north) to complete the loop. This part of the mountain is broader and more heavily wooded with fewer views, although from the peak at 1,664 feet you can see the northern end of Harriman State Park.

Just beyond the peak, arrows on rock slabs point you west to the Megaliths, columns of pink and white conglomerate split off from the ridge. Take the short detour left over to them. Besides the beauty of the area, your 3.5-hour walk to this point makes it a good lunch spot.

Returning to the main trail, a 15-minute walk north along the trail brings you to the spot where the Dark Hollow Trail forks right, showing white-with-black marks. You can take it down if you choose, for it intersects the way to be described near the base of the mountain. In fact, you may wish to return

another time to walk this alternate trail as well as others along Schunemunk's crest.

For now, continue on the yellow-marked trail along the ridge with its pink and purple conglomerate slabs, a color fantasy of gray-green lichens on mauve. The gleaming white-quartz pebbles shine like precious stones. You'll find two places with views in this just more than 1-mile-long portion of trail, which you can cover in less than 30 minutes. The next intersection brings you to a right fork onto the white-marked Sweet Clover Trail. Here a sign designates the distance south along the Jessup Trail but makes no mention of the 2-plus miles along which you'll follow this trail to your car.

The 40-minute descent on the Sweet Clover Trail is punctuated by tantalizing sounds of rushing water from the hemlock-concealed stream in a ravine, but there are no views into it. The trail emerges beside the railroad tracks, 50 yards north of the cairn that marks the end of the Dark Hollow Trail. Go straight across the tracks, and intersect a dirt road. The road leads you along the eastern edge of a field, then across it. You'll recognize the co-marked section on which you began the hike and soon emerge on Taylor Road opposite your car.

BMcM/HNZ

32

Mighty Storm King

Total distance: 7 miles

Walking time: 5.5 hours

Vertical rise: 1,200 feet

Maps: USGS 7.5' Cornwall, 7.5' West Point; NY–NJTC West Hudson Trails #7

NOTE: Storm King State Park experienced a major forest fire in the summer of 1999. To everyone's surprise, firefighters encountered explosions. (Fortunately, no one was hurt.) Long-forgotten unexploded shells, mostly from World War I, detonated under the intense heat. The park was closed, and a U.S. Army Corps of Engineers cleanup began in 2000. It is expected that at least the northern section of the park, including Storm King Mountain, will be opened for public use by 2003. However, before hiking, you are strongly advised to contact the Palisades Interstate Park Commission or New York–New Jersey Trail Conference for the latest information.

As a result of the closure, this section could not be fully field checked. However, we include this hike because we know the trails are well marked and maintained—and, more significantly, because Storm King is just a splendid hike.

"The Montaynes look as if some Metall or Minerall were in them. For the trees that grow on them were all blasted, and some of them barren with few or no trees on them." Thus did Robert Juet describe his view of the Hudson Highlands in September 1609 after his first trip up the Hudson in Henry Hudson's boat, anchored in what is now Newburgh Bay. The centuries have done little to alter the view.

The noble ring of hills through which the Hudson flows south of Newburgh is as impressive as any range in the state. Storm King guards the west bank, and Beacon, giving way to Breakneck Ridge and Taurus

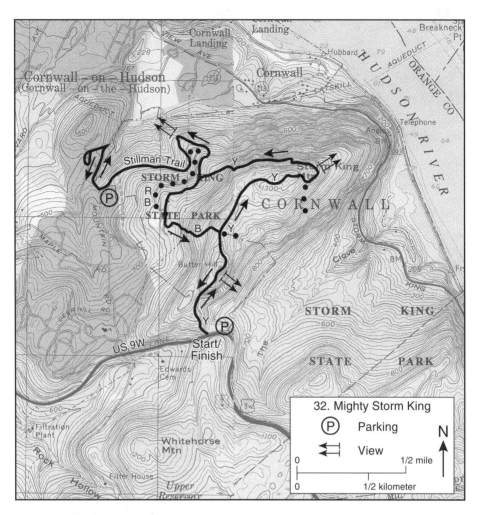

32. Mighty Storm King

(P) Parking

⇄ View

N

0   1/2 mile

0   1/2 kilometer

on the south, guards the eastern shores. They are all mountains you will want to climb again and again.

Storm King and Butter Hill form a semicircular crest that Benson Lossing believed the Dutch skippers thought of as a huge lump of butter, hence the original name Boterberg. Nathaniel Parker Willis, who settled at Idlewild at the foot of Storm King in present-day Cornwall, wrote weekly letters to the *Home Journal* in the 1850s, describing his bucolic surroundings. It was he who was able to change part of the mountain's name to the more romantic Storm King.

There are several ways to savor the walk on Storm King and Butter Hill. Sometimes the opportunity to get away for a short excursion makes the walk from US 9W across the vantages just west of Storm King's summit seem like a perfect outing. This is a round-trip walk of about 3 miles, with a climb of 350 feet, for a 3-hour excursion. The walk can be extended by a descent toward Cornwall and a visit to the Museum of the Hudson Highlands, with distance, time, and elevation as noted above.

Butter Hill and Storm King as seen across the Hudson

From the circle at the west end of the Bear Mountain Bridge, take US 9W north as it climbs the hills north and west of West Point. There is a large parking turnout at the height-of-land on Butter Hill 9.3 miles north of the bridge. Note that this parking area cannot be accessed from the southbound lane of US 9W.

From the north of the turnout, and quite close to the highway, the Stillman Trail, with its unsigned trailhead, begins its ascent. Yellow blazes appear on the open-rock crossings. The trail climbs the ridge near the road to a stone foundation, then winds into a stone-filled valley. A hard right across the draw at the head of the valley heads sharply up to the first knob with a narrow view of the river.

Notice all along the trail the signs of an older burn that swept this hilltop. Somehow the laurels and many of the oaks survive. A gentle walk to the next knob on Butter Hill yields views of Cold Spring and the quarry north of it on the slopes of Taurus. A few more minutes of walking brings you to the height-of-land on Butter Hill with its survey markers. This spot, only 30 minutes from the start, has views of the summits of Breakneck Ridge and Beacon.

Good views north and west accompany you as you walk north, especially when the leaves are down, permitting the range from Schunemunk to the Shawangunks to stand out in front of the distant blue hills of the Catskills. You'll pass by three junctions of recently opened (1998) trails. The first is the red-and-blue marked Bluebird Trail on the left and, just beyond, the blue-marked Howell Trail, which serves as a connector to the park's southern trail system. Just after the summit view, the white-marked By-Pass Trail diverges right and descends along the southern flanks of Storm King to intersect with the Howell Trail. This is an al-

Mighty Storm King

ternate return route, as an unmarked trail leads west along the flanks of Butter Hill back toward the parking turnout.

The walk on the northwestern flanks ends in a sharp right marked by yellow blazes as the trail reaches Storm King. The trail continues on the northern flanks of Storm King, with occasional viewing spots opening up en route. Stunted pines frame the vistas: the broad sweep of river, punctuated by Bannerman's (or Pollepel) Island, which lies 1,300 feet below your perch. This mysterious island has a strange tale. Jasper Dankers, a minister, recorded in 1680 that it was called Potlepels Eylant, Dutch for Potladle Island. General Henry Clinton fortified it in 1777 along with Constitution Island to the south. In the 1850s Benson Lossing reported that it was home to a solitary house that looked like a wren's nest, inhabited by a fisherman with an insane wife who thought herself to be the queen of England. Francis Bannerman bought the island to house his arsenal of secondhand military supplies, arms captured in the Spanish-American War. It was Bannerman who built the replica of a Scottish castle, whose remains you see. He had a thriving military-supply business until the U.S. government made it illegal for citizens to sell arms to foreign governments.

The trail continues, gradually descending, to a final opening overlooking the river east and southeast. It's delightful to picnic here and retrace your steps; but time permitting, you can continue along the trail for the steep descent, a real scramble at first, to the west.

The trail drops 700 feet in 0.5 mile. Along the way you'll notice the intersection with the Bluebird Trail (red and blue), one of your options for the return trip. You continue the zigzag route of the yellow-marked trail, coming out to a promontory with views north toward Beacon. After a distance of 100 feet, the trail reaches and follows a dirt roadway to Mountain Road. Turn right, then left to reach the Museum of the Hudson Highlands. Walk carefully along the narrow roads. The museum is open Tuesday through Sunday, noon to 5 pm and houses a natural-history collection highlighted by an assemblage of owls and snakes that live in these mountains but are rarely seen. You can enjoy a picnic beside a stream at the rear of the museum.

On the return, you have a choice. The preferred route follows the Stillman Trail from Mountain Road for 0.9 mile to a point where this trail turns sharply left and meets the lower end of the Bluebird Trail. From here, follow the red and blue marked Bluebird for its full length of 0.6 mile. Interestingly, the trail was not named for the bird. Before the route was marked, hikers used the acronym BLUBRD—bear left up, bear right down—to help them remember which way to go. It's easier now: Just follow the marked path as it ascends a rock-edged sidehill and a series of switchbacks to an intersection with the Stillman Trail. Turn right, following the yellow-blazed Stillman over Butter Hill, retracing your steps to your car.

An alternative route from Mountain Road, used more often before the Bluebird was established, stays on the abandoned roadway when the Stillman diverges left about 0.5 mile in. This road once led to a stone building constructed by Italian stonemasons before World War I. The ruins lie at the end of the roadway that zigzags up the mountain. It must have been a handsome place if the stonework along the road is any indication. Note the beautiful arch that carries the road over a small stream just before the Stillman Trail forks left. Notice, too, the huge grapevines curled around a nearby tree like a serpent in the Garden of Eden.

The road forks after a 20-minute walk; the foundations lie to the left. Walking through them to a stone stairway in a wall at the far end, you find the start of an unmarked path that bears right and contours around the slopes to intersect the Bluebird Trail. Turn right, and follow the blue-and-red blazes for a stiff 20-minute climb to the ridgeline and intersection with the Stillman Trail. Turn right, and retrace your steps to the parking turnout and your car.

BMcM/HNZ

33

Black Rock Forest—Northern Loop

Total distance: 5.5 miles

Walking time: 3.5 hours

Vertical rise: 600 feet

Map: USGS 7.5' Cornwall

There is a small trailhead for the trails in Black Rock Forest on its northwestern side that is ideal for this loop hike. Drive north on US 9W to Angola Road near Central Valley. Head southwest onto Angola Road for 1.6 miles, and then turn left on Mine Hill Road, and go 0.9 mile to the turnout. The Rich Mine in this vicinity was described in 1837 by Lewis C. Beck, a professor of chemistry at Rutgers. It was part of the Monroe Iron Works, owned by Hudson McFarlan, which produced quantities of nails and hoop iron dating back to 1808.

The trail begins opposite the uphill end of the turnout and is marked by three yellow diamonds. The faint beginning leads sharply uphill on a traverse that immediately offers views of Schunemunk Mountain and the Catskills. The trail is carefully marked, with double diamonds indicating switchbacks.

After a 10-minute climb, a triple marker alerts you to an intersection; the yellow-diamond-marked trail that forks right will be your return route. Take the left fork, marked with yellow circles, to a series of overlooks on open rock ledges. You continue on the ridge on high ground at the border of deeper forests and then descend slightly into them. Cross a small stream by hopping rocks, and walk through a wet area with trout lilies and violets. Beyond, a small rise leads to Hall Road, 1 mile from the start, but just before you reach it, the yellow-marked trail makes a sharp left. It's easy to miss the turn, but if you do, a left turn onto the road will do, for the yellow-marked trail reaches the road again in less than 200 yards.

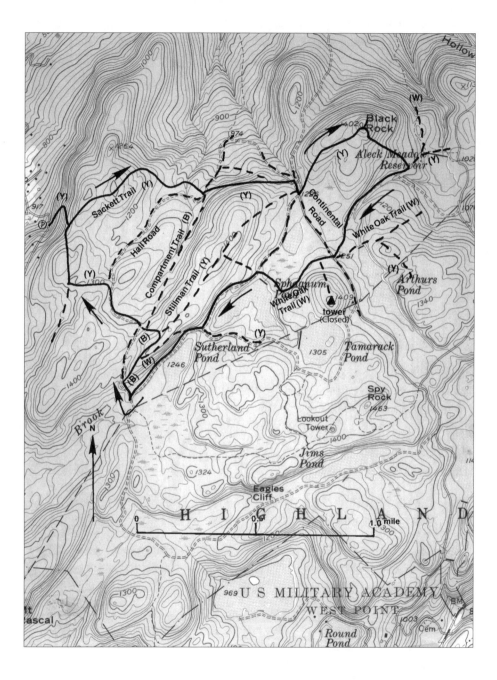

Continue on the roadway, which bears yellow markers, for 75 yards to a point where the road angles left and the yellow-marked trail takes off right, uphill.

Follow the trail as it traverses the mountain through a tall oak stand, with glimpses of the roadway below and left. Your route parallels the road somewhat, then climbs, crosses a bridge near a spring, and rejoins the road, which you follow for 200 feet to a road barrier. Continental and Hulse Roads intersect here, and the yellow-marked Stillman Trail goes through the intersection. Make a left turn onto the road across a bridge for 150 feet to a right fork. The spot is confusing! Immediately on leaving the road at this right fork, the yellow-marked trail makes a sharp left turn through a tall stand of laurel. A gentle climb continues on the right side of high ground, contouring the hill until you see a little rocky knob ahead through the trees—the summit of Black Rock at 1,042 feet and 2 miles from the start. You will want to pause here to enjoy the vista upriver. Yellow-painted footprints on the rock lead you to an opening in which Storm King is framed by Taurus and Beacon.

The continuing yellow-marked route from the summit is most eroded, attesting to the popularity of this section, in contrast to the faint trails you walk in the rest of the forest. You descend to White Oak Road in 10 minutes, and turn right onto it as it heads up the outlet of Arthurs Pond. A lovely swampy vista greets you as you cross a bridge; then head into a plantation of pines. A giant white oak marks the triangle intersection, where you turn left. Then in 100 feet you turn right onto the white-marked White Oak Trail into a spruce plantation.

Stay on the white-marked trail to pursue a varied nature exploration. This route leads you through a wet sphagnum area with typ-

ical bog plants. A large, grassy field off to your right is full of frog and bird sounds. The white-marked trail leads you to and along a small dam beside the very pretty impoundment of the Cornwall water system and Sphagnum Pond.

Beyond the pond the trail crosses Sutherland Road. A left on the road provides a pretty walk as it stays close to the shore of Sphagnum Pond. Stay straight ahead at the next road fork just beyond the pond. In a short distance, before the next pond, the road rises and curves. Watch for white blazes that direct you right and steeply uphill toward Split Rock. You can head up slope for a walk along the open escarpment on top of Split Rock, or continue on the road.

The road is close to the shore of Sutherland Pond; as it pulls away from the road, keep your eyes open for a small but obvious path that leads to a lakeside rock ledge and a lovely picnic spot. Sutherland is the only pond in Black Rock Forest where you can swim—the others are reservoirs for nearby towns. By the route outlined, this spot is 1.8 miles from the summit of Black Rock Mountain.

The jumble of rocks fallen from the escarpment below Split Rock should still intrigue you, so for a second route up, continue on the road for 0.2 mile to a fork, and turn right onto Hall Road. It is gated near the intersection; 75 feet beyond the gate a narrow blue-marked trail forks right, uphill, through laurel stands along the crest of the ridge. Within 5 minutes the trail splits. The way right is the other end of the white-marked Split Rock Trail; it soon leads to the open rock of the crest, past several vantage spots with views of Sutherland Pond and Black Rock tower. A yellow diamond beside one outcrop marks the place to turn left for 100 feet to again intersect

Sutherland Pond in Black Rock Forest

the blue-marked trail, near its intersection with the yellow-marked Stillman Trail, which comes in from the right.

From this apt-to-be-confusing intersection, you want the combined blue-and-yellow-marked trail for the walk downhill (west) to another peculiar intersection. Turn left, 50 feet to Hall Road. Turn right onto Hall Road for a 10-minute walk to a left fork where the yellow blazes of the Stillman Trail direct you on a narrow trail. In 5 minutes this trail, marked with yellow squares, reaches a three-way intersection. Go right, now on the Sackett Trail (yellow circles), and traverse the top of the ridgeline heading north, passing a western overlook. In 8 minutes the trail forks. You turn left, following yellow diamonds, for the sharp zigzag downhill to your car.

BMcM/HNZ

34

Black Rock Forest–Southern Ledges

Total distance: 9 miles

Walking time: 6.5 hours

Vertical rise: 1,300 feet

Maps: USGS 7.5' Cornwall; NY–NJTC West Hudson Trails #7; Black Rock Forest map

The hiking trails in Black Rock Forest are among the region's least used. They wind around and over a dozen peaks with elevations of more than 1,400 feet. But these peaks rise generally less than 400 feet from the high plateau that is a westward continuation of the Storm King intrusion of the Hudson Highlands. That plateau drops precipitously to the west and north, with the dark summit of Black Rock Mountain, namesake of the forest, standing out above the valley near Cornwall.

This hike will start at the forest's main public parking area and wind along the southern ledges that border on U.S. Military Academy posted lands.

From the traffic circle at the western side of the Bear Mountain Bridge, drive 9.8 miles north on US 9W, going over the shoulder of Storm King and then taking the first right onto Mountain Road at the STORM KING SCHOOL sign. Immediately turn right again, under the highway and onto a narrow road that leads to the well-signed parking area at the forest boundary.

From the map/information board, begin hiking on the new Duggan Trail (red marked), which gently descends for 0.5 mile to a stream bridge and a T-junction with the blue-marked Reservoir Trail. Note these junctions for your return trip. Turn left, now following blue blazes as the trail grinds uphill for about 15 minutes.

After gaining almost 400 feet of elevation, the blue trail ends at a junction with the yellow-marked Stillman Trail. Bear right onto the yellow trail, continuing uphill to a crossing of a dirt road. Again, look around and

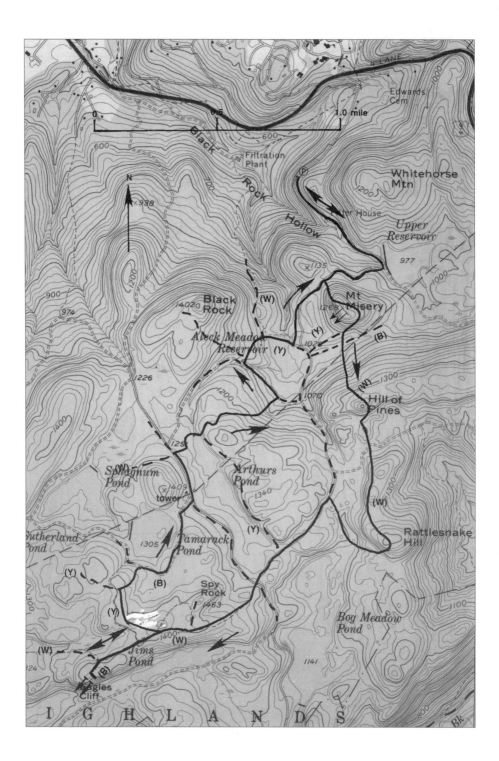

make a mental note of this trail-road intersection for the return trip.

Continue on the Stillman Trail across the road, and begin the climb up Mount Misery, elevation 1,268 feet. Now the hike begins to display the attractiveness of Black Rock Forest. The short 20-minute climb seems steeper than its 300-foot rise above the reservoir, but it yields views of Black Rock Mountain and Aleck Meadow Reservoir to the west. An equally steep descent follows, through rugged and boulder-strewn terrain. As the yellow-marked trail levels out, you see on the left the three white blazes of the Scenic Trail. Take the left onto the white-blazed trail, and in 100 feet or so you pass through a second intersection. Here, at 0.6 mile, you meet the blue-marked Swamp Trail, but continue straight ahead on the white-marked Scenic Trail.

The Scenic Trail begins another rough climb up the Hill of Pines (1,400 feet) and approaches an opening with a view below the summit. Double-white markers direct you up and left to the summit, with its view south-southwest over lakes and the fire-tower (closed) summit. The white-marked trail leads down through a narrow rock cleft to an open knob with views all around. Notice how flat and equal in height the summits of all the visible mountains seem.

The white-marked trail leads sharply right, down to a draw, then briefly up before the final descent to a dirt road. Turn right onto the road and then immediately left, essentially crossing it to begin climbing again. You quickly attain a ridge, then drop sharply down about 50 feet to walk on a relatively level high ledge near the southern boundary of the park. You can see one of the day's destinations, Spy Rock, ahead over ponds and lower hills. As you continue on the ledges, you look ahead to Eagle Cliff, also one of your destinations.

A steep descent follows, circling around and switchbacking down again near the park boundary. A double-white marker alerts you to a left turn along Bog Meadow Road. In 0.25 mile a yellow-marked trail forks right from your white-marked route toward Arthurs Pond and the fire tower, but you continue on the road, following the white markers to a T junction, where the marked trail reenters the woods.

After five minutes begin to watch carefully for a cairn—it will alert you to a blue-marked path on the right that leads 200 yards to a rock outcrop on Spy Rock. Here the Hudson Valley appears incongruously on your left as it bends into the Hudson Highlands. The view beyond the valley is toward the Shawangunks, with the Catskills beyond. South Beacon and Breakneck Ridge define the horizon on your right. At 1,461 feet this is the highest point in the western Hudson Highlands.

As you return to the Scenic Trail and continue quickly along it, watch carefully. In another 5 minutes, at about 200 yards, you should see three yellow blazes on a rock on the right side of the trail. Mark it well, for you'll retrace your steps to this spot after a visit to Eagle Cliff. Next, on the white-marked trail, you'll see on your left a yellow-marked trail to Jims Pond. Very shortly beyond, three blue markers direct you left to the knob of Eagle Cliff, 1,443 feet high, from which you can see the skyline of New York City beyond Anthony's Nose, Bear Mountain, Dunderberg Mountain, and the Timp. It takes a little more than 3 hours to reach this spot, about 4.5 miles from the beginning, which makes it ideal for a lunch break.

Return to the white-marked Scenic Trail, and retrace your steps to the three yellow blazes on the rock. A left turn puts you on a narrow path over a rise. A gentle descent

Tamarack Pond in Black Rock Forest

brings you in 0.2 mile to an intersection, where the yellow-marked trail makes a sharp left turn. You should turn right onto a blue-marked trail, which leads in 100 yards to Chatfield Road. Turn right onto it past Tamarack Pond, which you partly circle.

The next milestone on the road, near the intersection of Chatfield and Continental Roads, just more than 1 mile from Eagle Cliff, is an old stone building with a beehive oven. It is Chatfield House, built in 1834. The house was gutted by fire in 1908 and restored in 1932 by Dr. Stillman. The lands nearby were once pastures and orchard, and Tamarack Pond, originally called Orchard Pond, was used as a cranberry bog.

Turn left onto Continental Road and pass by Chatfield House. After 0.2 mile turn right onto the white-blazed White Oak Trail, passing opposite the foot of Arthurs Pond. Pass by the yellow-marked trail on the right, and continue on the white-marked trail on the left. This route takes you to a road beside Aleck Meadow Reservoir. Turn left toward Black Rock Mountain. One hundred feet past a stream, a yellow-marked trail makes a close pass by the road. Head right onto this trail, which shortly meets a white-marked trail. Continue on the yellow-marked trail to the right turn, and cross at the base of the reservoir's dam. Turn left onto the road below the dam, which takes you in 0.25 mile back to the point where you started climbing Mount Misery.

Here you have a choice. The best way is to turn left downhill on the yellow trail, and retrace your steps back to your car. Remember to leave the yellow trail near a stream, follow the blue markers downhill to the bridge, and then walk the red trail back 0.5 mile to the parking area.

Another way is to continue ahead on the road, passing the earthen dam of the Upper Reservoir toward the new Black Rock Science Center. Continue on the road past the center about 1 mile back to your car. Use care. While traffic is usually light, cars and trucks do use this road.

BMcM/HNZ

V. The Shawangunks

Introducing the Shawangunks

The Shawangunk Ridge (pronounced Shon-gum and commonly called "The Gunks") is a continuation of the northern end of the ridge that is called the Kitattinnies in New Jersey and the Blue Mountains in Pennsylvania. This long escarpment ridge of the Northern Shawangunks, edged with sparkling white cliffs, is visible to the west of I-87 and has been designated a "Last Great Place" by the Nature Conservancy. Mohonk Mountain House's Skytop Tower atop the ridge is a landmark seen from many miles away.

The Shawangunks are world famous for rock climbing. Oft-told legend has it that Fritz Wiessner—a celebrated and accomplished climber who had emigrated from Germany—became aware of these dazzling cliffs one afternoon in 1935 from across the Hudson while on Breakneck Ridge after a thunderstorm. Climbing at first at Sky Top, he and his friend Hans Kraus were responsible for many of the first climbs of the Shawangunk cliffs.

Recreation opportunities abound. Cross-country skiing and snowshoeing are popular in winter, when the high elevation of the ridge attracts snow that remains longer than in lower-lying communities. Mountain bikes are allowed on carriage roads in certain locations.

The picturesque 25,000-acre area is now controlled by four owners: Mohonk Preserve, Mohonk Mountain House, Minnewaska State Park, and the Sam's Point Dwarf Pine Ridge Preserve, each with its own trails, access points, and fee struc-tures. The area is a delight at every time of the year, with its combination of white rock slabs and cliffs, green pitch pines, blueberry bushes that turn bright red in the fall, sheep laurel, mountain laurel, and rhododendron blooming in June, and with luck a clear blue sky as a backdrop. The ridge contains five "sky lakes" and several major waterfalls.

There has long been a human presence on the Shawangunk Ridge. Arrowheads have been found, indicating use of caves and rock shelters by primitive peoples. Trees on the ridge were consumed for the production of charcoal, barrel hoops, and the tanning industry, and grist millstones were hammered out from bedrock. Probably the best-known group heard about today are the berry pickers, whose shacks and discarded vehicles can still be seen on the Smiley Road, which runs 7 miles from Ellenville to Lake Awosting. Berry pickers invaded the area each summer from as early as 1862. Their practice of setting fires to handicap the growth of competing vegetation resulted in improved berry crops for them and the development of a pygmy pine forest probably unique in the world.

The Shawangunks owe their first development to the vision of Alfred Smiley, who first saw the Shawangunk escarpment in 1869. Alfred later developed the Minnewaska resort. His twin brother, Albert, purchased his first 280 acres for $28,000 and began the development of the hotel and grounds. At Albert's death in 1912, the property had grown through more than a hundred purchases to encompass 5,000 acres. The brothers transformed a boulder-strewn land into a premier resort by the systematic construction of carriage roads and walking paths.

Environmentalists and land protection agencies are constantly working to extend ownership of lands on the Shawangunk Ridge into the public domain.

THE MOHONK PRESERVE

845-255-0910 (Hikes 38, 39, and 40)
The Mohonk Preserve is New York State's largest privately owned nonprofit nature sanctuary. Its lands are open to the public for recreational activities compatible with preservation. Hikers on Mohonk Preserve lands need to be either Mohonk Preserve members or to have purchased a day pass, which they may be required to show to a ranger. The day fee is $7 on weekends and $5 on weekdays. Day passes, memberships, and trail maps are available for purchase at the Trapps Gateway Center (visitors center) and cost $1 for nonmembers, free to members. To find the Trapps Gateway Center—well worth a visit—drive west on NY 299 from the town of New Paltz, turn right at the junction with US 44/NY 55, and within 0.5 mile turn right again into the facility. Inside the center is a small gift shop and much information on the natural history of the area. Outside there are nature trails to be walked.

MOHONK MOUNTAIN HOUSE

845-255-1000 (Hike 40)
This elegant building is a private hotel that reflects the leisure and elegance of Victorian vacations. The trails and walks that circle the building were laid out with the same 19th-century attitude that fostered the resort. Today these walks are a marvel of rock climbs, lover's lanes, deep-woods walks, and vantage points that reflect their

builders' humor. Every spot is named, every path has often been walked, and many folk have rested at the summerhouses—but the fun and sense of discovery are still there. A Mohonk Preserve annual or day pass is honored on Mountain House lands, but day visitors are not allowed inside the hotel.

You may easily become infatuated with the area and wish to return to the Mountain House. Fabulous meals are provided for overnight guests and for those reserving in advance. In addition to a day pass, it is possible to purchase "A Day at Mohonk" that covers meals and entry to the hotel. Call for information on a shuttle bus from the main parking lot to the interior as well as for rates.

MINNEWASKA STATE PARK PRESERVE

845-255-0752 (Hikes 37 and 38)
This spectacular state park preserve owes its existence to a chain of events beginning in 1879 when Alfred Smiley opened the first of two hotels overlooking Lake Minnewaska, following the example set at Mohonk by his twin brother. Many carriage roads for horse-and-buggy travel (now referred to as carriageways) were constructed in addition to walking trails. In the 1950s the Smileys' general manager bought the property and endeavored to update the facilities by adding a golf course and a downhill ski slope. However, financial difficulties forced the sale of part of the acreage, including Lake Awosting, to New York State for a park. Continuing financial problems and a proposal by the Marriott Corporation to build condominiums, a 450-room hotel, a golf course, and other amenities resulted in a long legal battle. In 1987 the property was added to one of New York State's most beautiful parks, administered by the Palisades Interstate Park Commission.

Lake Awosting and Lake Minnewaska

within the park are renowned for their aquamarine color and exceptionally clear water. During the summer, scuba diving is allowed in Lake Minnewaska by permit. Swimming is allowed in restricted areas in both lakes. Cross-country skiing is a favorite winter occupation. Bicycle and horse riding is permitted only on specified carriageways. Entry fees and hours vary according to the season.

SAM'S POINT DWARF PINE RIDGE PRESERVE
516-272-0195 (Hike 36)
During the late sixties the village of Ellenville leased Sam's Point and the area around Lake Maratanza to a commercial organization that developed a tourist attraction called Ice Caves Mountain, installing lighting, stairways, and paths through a crevice on the cliff edge. At the time of this writing, the facility is closed to the public. Many others have cast their eyes on the area. A wind farm was once mooted, and trial gas drilling wells were sunk. In 1996 the Open Space Institute purchased the tract from the village. Now managed by the Nature Conservancy, low-impact access is permitted to this spectacular area. An improved visitors center and additional hiking trails are proposed in the master plan now being developed. A parking fee of $5 is charged.

35

Shawangunk Ridge

Total distance: 6.15 miles

Walking time: 3.25 hours

Vertical rise: 1,100 feet

Maps: USGS 7.5' Wurtsboro; NY–NJTC Long Path Guidebook, fourth edition, 1996, Section 11

The Shawangunk Ridge hike described is particularly special because this section of the Long Path was temporarily closed for several years while the Open Space Institute negotiated the purchase of the tract from private owners. The ridge called Shawangunk is part of the same ridge that in New Jersey is called the Kitattinny Ridge. This route for the Long Path was created as a more natural alternative to the suburban lowland route through Orange County. During the trip from NY 52 to Ferguson Road (formerly Roosa Gap Summitville Road), the hiker often walks on Shawangunk slabs above the scrub oak, blueberry, and pitch pine so prevalent on the ridge and is thus afforded many good views. In addition, the trail passes an attractive cascade and some fascinating free-standing rocks, inviting the walker to spend time scrambling among them.

A car shuttle is needed. Leave the New York State Thruway (I-87) at exit 16, Harriman, and drive two cars on NY 17 (the Quickway) 29 miles west to exit 114, Wurtsboro, Highview. Exit 114 is only available going westbound. Turn right at the end of the exit ramp onto Old Route 17 (County Road 171), and drive 0.5 mile. Turn left onto Shawanga Lodge Road, and follow it for approximately 3 miles to a stop sign at Pickles Road. Almost immediately turn left onto Ferguson Road, continue 0.6 mile downhill, and watch carefully for the blazes that indicate that the Long Path crosses the road here. Leave one car on the side of the road where there is space for several cars.

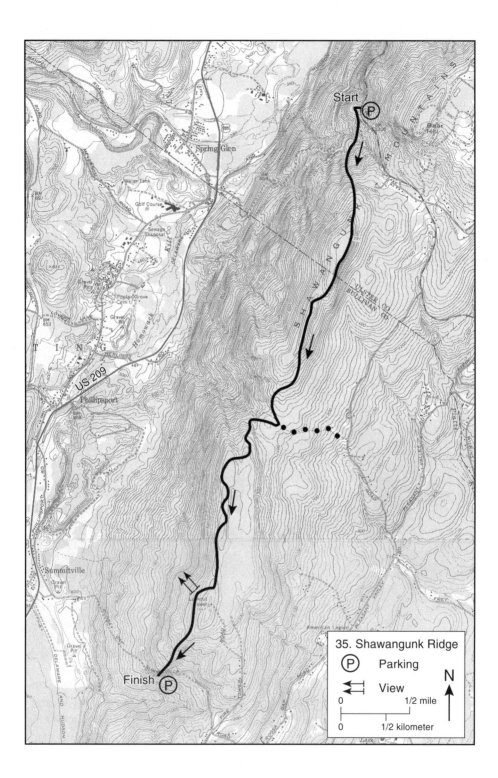

Start

Spring Glen

Water Tank

Golf Course

Sewage Disposal

US 209

Phillipsport

Summitville

Finish

35. Shawangunk Ridge

Ⓟ Parking

◄━ View

N

0   1/2 mile

0   1/2 kilometer

Drive the second car back to the stop sign at the end of Ferguson Road, and proceed straight across and downhill on Pickles Road. After 0.7 mile turn left at the stop sign at the end of Pickles Road onto unsigned Burlingham Road. (Pickles Road changes its name to Ski Run Road on the other side of Burlingham Road.) Drive 2 miles on Burlingham Road to a stop sign at Frey Road, bear left over a bridge onto Pleasant Valley Road, then left again after 0.2 mile at another stop sign onto Cox Road. Drive another 2 miles, and turn left onto NY 52, pass the turning on the right to Cragsmoor, and park on the roadside after 1.7 miles, at the large overlook on the left. The overlook is at the crest of a hill, so take care when driving across NY 52 to park.

Walk toward the southeast on NY 52, back the way you have just driven, and turn right uphill into the woods at the end of the guardrail where you see the turquoise blazes of the Long Path. Views of the valley can be seen on the right when there are no leaves on the trees. After the first short climb, the Long Path descends quite steeply on an easy footway to cross an often-dry watercourse. Within 10 minutes from NY 52, jog a little bit to the right onto a woods road, and continue downhill to a magnificent cascading stream. Cross the slabs cautiously because they are often slippery, and once on the other side, turn sharply left, paralleling the stream uphill.

The trail approaches a wet dip and another woods road, where again it jogs a little to the right to reenter the woods at a cairn. In this section there is a limited view of the valley to the right and of Bear Cliff behind as the trail ascends on a rockier path to emerge onto larger Shawangunk slabs. During the climb the hardwoods gradually diminish in size, and small stunted pitch pines make their appearance.

The Long Path is routed along the top of an escarpment after a little more than an hour's walking. Down to the left are tall rock pinnacles, and the Long Path remains in this area of large rock piles even when the trail switches to the other side of the ridge. Although it is still early in the hike, this place is good for a break and perhaps some rock scrambling.

The Long Path descends slightly and winds its way through a hardwood forest mixed with laurel stands. After about two hours from the start, the trail reaches the boundary of the small Department of Environmental Conservation (DEC) Roosa Gap parcel, which is marked with an orange blaze on a tree to the right of the trail. The turquoise paint blazes now change to round blue DEC disks.

After the boundary the trail crosses a lovely old rock wall and passes through a damp area. Here are many very wide rock walls, evidence of how many rocks the farmers were forced to dig out. The trail is routed beside a couple of these walls, and after walking with one on your right, the Long Path makes a sharp left just before approaching a mix of walls that look as though they border a woods road. Be careful here because at the time of this writing, there was no left-turn blaze.

Pass to the right through a gap in a wall, and cross straight over a woods road. (This woods road leads to Cox Road.) The trail now bears right and follows the base of a rock escarpment on the left. After passing an interestingly curved stone wall protecting a spring, the trail turns left up an easy route to the top of the rock wall—another pleasant place to take a break.

Very soon the trail arrives at another boundary of the DEC parcel, and the blue DEC disks change back to turquoise paint blazes. Shortly after the boundary, the trail

Old stone walls close to Cox Road on the Long Path between Route 52 and Roosa Gap

makes a 90-degree turn to the left and climbs slightly. Look back to see the microwave towers at Lake Maratanza, Sam's Point, and Gertrude's Nose. Carry on down and back up a minor knoll to reach a large rock, commonly known as Jack's Rock, where there's a wonderful view. For about 20 minutes you walk high on the escarpment. The song of the rufous-sided towhee is almost always heard along here, blueberries abound in season, and there's often a good breeze. There's also an intriguing tree to the right of the trail with hunter's spikes embedded in the trunk. The maintainer from the New York–New Jersey Trail Conference has been unable to remove these. Ignore the distinct herd path that leaves to the left of the main footpath, and continue downhill to reach the Jack Hennessey Memorial sign. Mr. Hennessey is remembered as a dedicated volunteer trail maintainer of this section whose excellent trail work continues to inspire others.

While undulating along the top of the ridge with a downhill bias, stop a moment to view the Wurtsboro Airport just below with the Bashakill in the distance, and on a clear day, High Point in New Jersey. Take a break to watch the gliders usually active at the airport.

Now begins a serious descent on slabs until Ferguson Road becomes visible below. The Long Path continues across this road, but turn right to find your car.

SJG

36

Verkeerder Kill Falls Loop

Total distance: 9 miles

Walking time: 4.5 hours

Vertical rise: 900 feet

Maps: USGS 7.5' Ellenville; USGS 7.5' Napanoch; NY–NJTC Shawangunk Trails #9

The described hike is very much out in the open with little protection from the sun until Verkeerder Kill Falls is reached when there is a canopy. We advise taking plenty of water. This loop hike uses an abandoned paved vehicle road, the High Point Carriageway, the red-blazed High Point Trail, and the turquoise-blazed Long Path back to the paved road. The high points of the hike are Sam's Point and the magnificent falls, where the somewhat shallow Verkeerder Kill Falls drops from the plateau to a pool beneath. At certain times of the day a rainbow can be seen, and the falls are spectacular when frozen.

Entry to Sam's Point Dwarf Pine Ridge Preserve is from the village of Cragsmoor. From the junction of NY 302 and NY 52 in Pine Bush, drive northwest for 7.25 miles through Walker Valley, passing the boundary of the town of Wawarsing, and turn right at the sign for Cragsmoor. (Alternatively, drive 3 miles on NY 52 from the village of Ellenville and turn left for Cragsmoor.) Pass the historical society building and the Cragsmoor Free Library on the left, and after driving 1.5 miles from NY 52, turn right at the Cragsmoor post office, where there's a sign for Sam's Point Preserve. The road becomes rough shortly after passing the firehouse on the right, but continues to Sams' Point parking 2.75 miles from NY 52. The parking fee is $5 (an honesty box is provided). The visitors center to the right of the gated entry to the property is normally open on Saturday, Sunday, and holidays 10–6 during the summer. Any questions re-

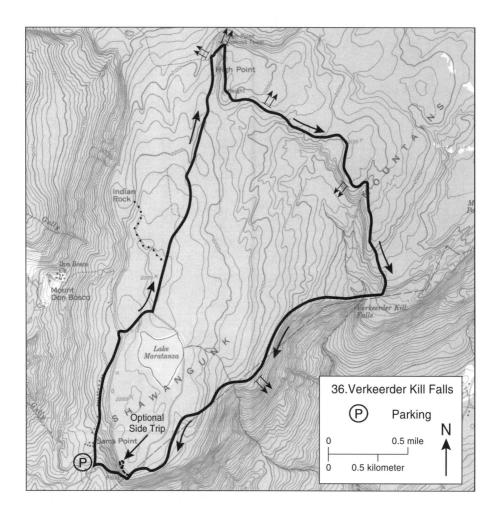

36. Verkeerder Kill Falls

(P) Parking

0 ——————— 0.5 mile

0 ——————— 0.5 kilometer

N

garding fees or visitors center hours should be addressed to: The Nature Conservancy, 251 River Street, Troy, NY 12180 (518-272-0195).

After parking, squeeze through the space between the gate and the wall. Just beyond the bulletin board are two directional signs. Don't choose the road to Sam's Point on the right, but take the left-hand fork, walking uphill on a once-paved road leading to the High Point Carriageway. These two roads were once part of a one-way auto route. After an old quarry is passed on the left, the road levels out and passes several old berry-picker shacks, also on the left. Ignore the service road on the left leading to the radio antennaes reached within 20 minutes, and continue to a sign. Lake Maratanza glistens on the right, and the residue from when the town of Ellenville dredged the lake is visible as piles of sand at the far end. Turn left for High Point and the Indian Rock Trail junction about 1 mile down the road. If your energy level is high, walking out to Indian Rock is a 1.5-mile round trip blazed in yellow—and well worth it

Glacial erratics above Verkeerder Kill Falls

Stella Green

to see the impressive rock and the tremendous view obtained by climbing the rock.

High Point Carriageway becomes a little narrower and grassier as you continue. On the right can be seen periodic reminders of the now defunct wind-farm project in the form of roads and circular concrete objects. The exposed top of High Point comes into sight within about an hour. High Point at 2,246 feet is at almost at the same elevation as Lake Maratanza (2,242 feet) and was once the site of a fire tower.

Turn right at the sign for High Point, and climb steeply for about 100 feet, following red-paint blazes. Stringers at the beginning correct the wetness that sometimes pervades here, but the route to High Point is mostly rocky. Ignore another rocky road entering on the right just before the summit.

Slide Mountain (highest peak in the Catskills), Wittenberg Mountain, and Cornell Mountain are visible across the valley.

Farther right is the Devil's Path (Hunter, Plateau, Sugarloaf, Twin, and Indian Head Mountains in the Catskills), and over to the left, the radio antennaes passed on the way to High Point are distinct. The rusty post is the remains of a support carrying a telephone line to the fire tower.

Follow the red turn signal to the right, passed on the approach to High Point, onto a narrow footway. The trail is easy to follow because pitch pine, blueberries, sheep laurel, and ferns grow very densely close to the footway. Where the trail emerges onto slabs of Shawangunk grit, the path is marked by cairns and with red (and occasional blue) blazes mostly placed underfoot on rock. At times the trail maintainer has placed rows of smaller rocks to keep the walker on track.

Elevation is gained, and Storm King, Breakneck Ridge, and the gap between that contains the Hudson River can be seen (in good conditions) toward the left. Look also for Sky Top (Mohonk Mountain House) and Gertrude's Nose (Minnewaska State Park). Leaving this high slab behind, the trail descends off the rock and back down onto lower ground into a pitch-pine forest. Some of these pitch pines, from which the preserve takes its name, are thought to be hundreds of years old. Growth is stunted by the wind and rain and by the thin and unfertile soil.

The cliffs seen ahead are those along which the trail is routed, and the depression just below is the route of the Verkeerder Kill. Along the way you may find a couple of clear streams that in the Shawangunks do not run for long after rain has ceased. Occasionally the trail continues over rock slabs showing large polished areas that are a result of the glacier that passed this way. The trail ascends onto the cliffs observed previously and undulates closer to the gap where the falls tumble down. Walkers should remain on hard surfaces, thereby protecting the islands of soil and fragile vegetation that surround these rocks.

The High Point Trail ends within about 1.5 hours at the junction with the Long Path marked in turquoise. The Long Path is a long-distance trail beginning at the George Washington Bridge. Once ending at Windham in the Catskills, the Long Path is being extended toward the Adirondacks and can already be walked as far as the Mohawk River. The Long Path once continued east from the junction with the High Point Trail into Minnewaska State Park at Mud Pond, but this section has recently been closed at the request of the private-property owner.

Turn right onto the Long Path following the turquoise blazes. Very soon on the right there are two large boulders on a slab to the right above the trail. It's well worth the extra few minutes to climb up to see where you've been and where you're going. The

dip immediately in front of you carries the Verkeerder Kill to the falls, the hill in front of you is the route back to your car, and the tip of one of the towers protrudes on the horizon. Some 15 minutes, beginning with a steep descent, brings you to Verkeerder Kill Falls, still in the hands of a private landowner. Sitting on one of the several vantage points to watch the water falling 100 feet to the splash pool below is a joy at any time of the year. The best time to visit is after a heavy rain; during times of drought the falls are reduced to a trickle. They're particularly fascinating in winter when ice forms on the cliff.

Bear right, and cross the Verkeerder Kill. (Continuing upstream accesses a swimming hole that is popular in hot weather.) The Long Path now heads uphill into an area of oak, birch, and maple interspersed with rhododendron—the first tall trees seen all day. The trail levels out and reaches a sign requesting that walkers stay on the designated trail that now makes a 90-degree turn to the left. The brushed-in trail to the right should be ignored as it is now abandoned.

The trail from Verkeerder Kill Falls steadily gains elevation and takes about an hour to walk. Favorite spots on the journey include several large boulders close to the trail and an area of hardwoods with a seasonal stream. Views behind you as the terrain becomes more open include Castle Point, Hamilton Point, Gertrude's Nose, Mud Pond, and Lake Awosting.

This part of the Long Path ends at a gravel road. Turn right slightly uphill to a T junction, and then walk left. A sign confirms that you're headed toward the Interpretive Center and Sam's Point.

Walk back on a deteriorating paved road, and in 7 or 8 minutes turn right into a wide parking lot to visit Sam's Point, a large open rock slab with protective artificial rock walls overlooking the parking lot and the road back to your car.

Sam's Point was at one time called the Big Nose of Aioskawasting. The legend surrounding the current name of this magnificent promontory is that Samuel Gonsalus, a famous local hunter and scout constantly at odds with his Native American neighbors, was one day alone at the summit of the mountain and was surprised by a group who started in pursuit as Sam ran away. Sam, a big man and always a good runner, outpaced his enemies and flung himself from the brink to land in a clump of bushes that broke his fall. His enemies retreated, assuming Sam was dead.

Retrace your footsteps across the Sam's Point parking lot, and turn right to walk back down the road. A hotel once existed beneath these impressive cliffs. Pictures indicate that although the front facade was straight, the rooms were misshapen to follow the shape of the cliff. The road switchbacks downhill, taking you back to your car.

SJG

37

Minnewaska Loop

Total distance: 9.75 miles

Walking time: 5 hours

Vertical rise: 1,000 feet

Maps: USGS 7.5' Gardiner; USGS 7.5' Napanoch; NY–NJTC Shawangunk Trails #9

In an effort to avoid walking the carriageways that are often crowded with bike riders, the hike described does not include a visit to either Lake Minnewaska or Lake Awosting. Other special places, such as the sparkling Peters Kill as it tumbles over rocks and Rainbow Falls, are included to make up a peaceful and rewarding hike in Minnewaska's backcountry.

Leave the New York Sate Thruway (I-87) at exit 18, New Paltz, and drive west on NY 299 through town, crossing the green steel bridge over the Wallkill River. Continue on NY 299 toward the cliffs of the Shawangunks visible ahead. The tower on the cliff to the right is the Albert K. Smiley Memorial Tower above Mohonk Mountain House. Pass Humpo Marsh with its birdhouses and at 5.5 miles from the bridge turn right at the junction with US 44/NY 55. Pass the new Mohonk Preserve Visitor Center on the right, switchback up the mountain, continue under the steel Trapps Bridge, ignore the Mohonk Preserve Trapps Entry parking on the right, and turn left into Minnewaska State Park, about 10 miles from the crossing of the Wallkill River. Stop at the fee-collection booth, and make a note of the park closing time, which is closely adhered to. On a fine weekend it's advisable to arrive early because the lot has been known to fill up and close by 10:00 AM. Turn right immediately after the tollbooth, not uphill on the paved auto road but along a dirt road to the Awosting parking lot.

Walk through the gate on the left at the back of the parking lot, and within a few

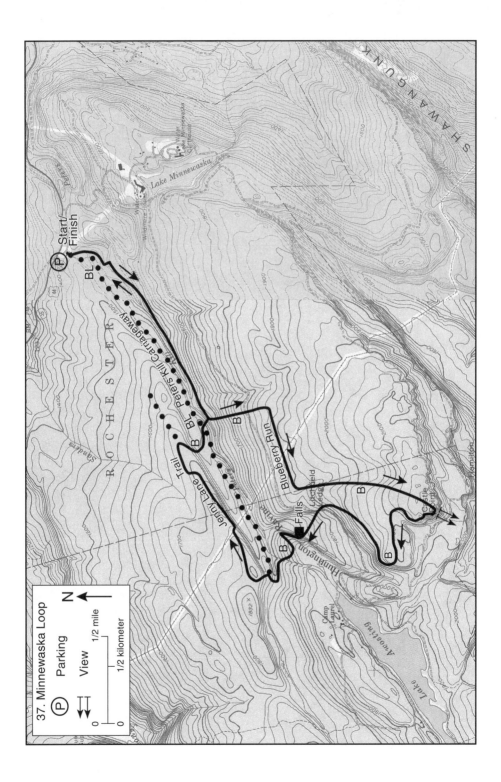

37. Minnewaska Loop

Ⓟ Parking

View

N ←

0 ——— 1/2 mile
0 ——— 1/2 kilometer

Start/
Finish

Ⓟ BL

Lake Minnewaska

S H A W A N G U N K

R O C H E S T E R

Peters Kill Carriageway

Trail

Jenny Lane

BL

B BL

B

Blueberry-Run

B

Litchfield
Ledge

B

Castle
Point

B

Falls

Huntington

B

Camp
Laurel

Awosting

Lake

Rainbow Falls

yards take the Mossy Glen Trail on the left marked with yellow-paint blazes. The three yellow blazes in a triangular pattern with the single blaze uppermost indicate the beginning of a trail. (Reversed, with the solo blaze below the other two, the pattern indicates the end of a trail.) The Mossy Glen Trail is a recent addition to the Minnewaska trail system. Ignore the occasional side trails down to the Peters Kill and out to the Peters Kill Carriageway, and walk straight ahead through mountain laurel and a mixture of hardwood and evergreen trees. Fifteen minutes brings you to the newly constructed bridge over the Peters Kill. The trail and the bridge over the Peters Kill were built by volunteers from the New York–New Jersey Trail Conference and opened on National Trails Day in June 1999.

The Mossy Glen Trail parallels the Peters Kill, which is tinged with brown from tannic acid in the trees. The Peters Kill rushes along through chutes, in cascades and falls, often slowing into deep, inviting swimming holes. After a rain this trail may be wet, though in the Shawangunks this dampness doesn't last long. However, the polished slabs, smoothed from glacier travel, can be very slippery, so care should be used if they are wet.

Within 45 minutes the Mossy Glen Trail ends, indicated by the three yellow blazes on a tree to the left. A cairn in front and blue markers indicate the junction with the Blueberry Run Trail. Turn right to spend a moment on the slabs by the Peters Kill, close to the Blueberry Run Bridge. This bridge was built in the early 1980s by a park-led summer youth group funded by *Reader's Digest* and has stood the ravages of time well.

Retrace your footsteps to the end of the Mossy Glen Trail, and walk uphill on the Blueberry Run Trail, at first on slabs and then back into the laurel-blueberry forest,

noting how the sound of the Peters Kill recedes. After an hour from the start, the Blueberry Run Trail crosses the Awosting Lake Carriageway. Stay with the blue blazes that are sometimes a little sparse in this section. Voices can sometimes be heard drifting up from the carriageway that the trail parallels. Cross the power line after 10 minutes from the Awosting Lake Carriageway, and walk back into the woods. To the right can be seen the foothills of the Catskills and the Rondout Reservoir, one of New York City's water supply chain.

The Blueberry Run Trail now swings away from the Awosting Lake Carriageway, emerging onto glacially scoured slabs. Cairns and blue blazes underfoot mark the route, with the occasional row of small rocks indicating the way. Soon the trail dips down into a very special section: a deep, dark hollow with towering trees protected on the right by a tall cliff. Imagine Snow White discovering this place. Climbing up to more rock slabs, the trail opens up and is even more spectacular in autumn when the blueberries turn fiery red, complementing the views to the Devil's Path in the Catskills.

Almost two hours into the hike, a carriageway comes into view on the left. There are at least two USGS benchmarks here, indicating arrival at Castle Point. The end of the Blueberry Run Trail is indicated by three blazes on the edge of a rock. Walk over to the edge of the cliff to take in the view. Nearby Lake Awosting can be seen, and the Catskills are still in view. On a good day High Point Tower, New Jersey, can be seen immediately ahead; the Lake Maratanza radio antennae stand out; and over to the left is the gorge of the Hudson between Breakneck Ridge and Storm King, as well as the whole stretch of Harriman–Bear Mountain State Park, Sterling Forest, and the New York–New Jersey Highlands. Look down at your feet to see where the Long Path drops off the side of the cliff.

With your back to the view, notice that carriageways are going in both directions. Walk left, past the ending of the Blueberry Run Trail on the right, and follow the turquoise blazes of the Long Path downhill on the Castle Point Carriageway. Long Path markers are slightly larger than those you have followed on the previous trails. Ignore the large blue square-metal markers used by cross-country skiers and be aware that mountain bicyclists often come up very fast and silently behind you. Occasionally the Long Path blazes leave the carriageway to detour toward the cliff edge, but these excursions are only minor. Stay on the Castle Point Carriageway until it makes almost a 360-degree turn. A couple of minutes after the start of that swing to the left, watch carefully on the right for a couple of rock steps going up into the woods just before another bend in the carriageway. The turn signal is fairly well marked on a tree to the left of the carriageway, but look closely to find a blaze on the rock step. This turn should be reached roughly in 8 or 9 minutes from Castle Point.

Walk up the two rock steps and follow the trail as it bears left and continues on the top of a low cliff. Descend to the left—the first drop reached is probably the easiest—and walk alternately on slabs and through tunnels of rhododendron bushes. This section of the Long Path is on Litchfield Ledge, and after about an hour from Castle Point the trail turns left downhill to reach the Awosting Lake Carriageway.

Go straight across the carriageway, and continue steeply down on a rocky trail in a stand of hardwood and large hemlocks toward Rainbow Falls, reached within 5 minutes. Cross a couple of water courses, bear right across the runoff from the falls, and work your way up the jumble of rocks to get a superior view (and probably also a wetting). Be careful here because wet rocks are usually slippery rocks. Continue away from the falls, and within about 3 minutes begin a steep rock scramble up to where the Long Path turns left at the top. (The unmarked herd path ahead leads out to a viewpoint.) The falls can be heard when they are in full spate, but not seen as you emerge onto a slab above them. The Long Path now returns into the laurel-hemlock and hardwood forest and makes a quick climb up a rock to the right onto an open area. From this point there's a view of almost all the Catskill High Peaks and the Hudson River valley over to the right.

The Long Path now begins a gentle descent on rock slabs interrupted once by an occasionally tricky stream crossing and a short ascent before reaching the Peters Kill Carriageway. Turn right, and cross over the Peters Kill on an earthen berm above the stream. Do not continue down this carriageway to the right unless you are very fatigued and wish to return directly to your car.

The hike continues by turning left onto an open roadway. At the end of the open space look for the Long Path blaze and turn right uphill. Just ahead, before the right turn, is a pleasant resting spot by Fly Brook.

The Long Path now follows an old woods road that flattens out quickly and reaches a power line. Cross under, turn right, and parallel the power line to the next pylon, where the trail turns left into the woods just before the power line continues to descend.

Finding the place where the Blueberry Run Trail intersects the Long Path is imperative. Walking is easy for about 10 minutes from the power line and follows fairly closely along the edge of a cliff marking the Peters Kill valley, eventually moving away and going a little faster downhill. In another 10 minutes watch for a broken sign on a tree facing you on the left, and look right to see the beginning of the Blueberry Run Trail. Just past this junction there's a severely bent pitch pine tree on the Long Path that might alert you to the new direction you must take.

The Blueberry Run Trail, marked in blue, descends steeply for a few minutes before swinging left, flattening out, and entering a hemlock grove that can sometimes be wet underfoot. Cross a stream on stepping-stones, and emerge after about 5 minutes on the Blueberry Run Trail onto the Peters Kill Carriageway. Cross straight over, passing a sign BLUEBERRY RUN PATH, and descend on rock steps to the bridge over the Peters Kill that you probably visited earlier. Cross the bridge, and walk up the slabs on the other side to the cairn and the three yellow markers where you previously exited the Mossy Glen Trail.

Retrace your footsteps along the Mossy Glen Trail to your car.

SJG

38

The Trapps to Gertrude's Nose

Total distance: 9.15 miles

Walking time: 6 hours

Vertical Rise: 800 feet

Maps: USGS 7.5' Gardiner; USGS 7.5' Napanoch; NY–NJTC Shawangunk Trails #9; Mohonk Preserve Trail Map Northern Section

For a special look at this geologically intriguing area known as the Gunks, try the hike along the Trapps to Gertrude's Nose. The hike uses trails on the escarpment edge as well as some easy walking on carriage roads, ending with a stroll through deeply forested areas. The route includes a visit to spectacular Millbrook Mountain and Gertrude's Nose. The beauty of the Shawangunks lies in the way the views continuously unfold, enlivening every few feet of each walk.

Millbrook Mountain has lately attracted high flyers as well as hikers. Peregrine falcons returned to nest here in 1998 for the first time after an absence of 40 years. They failed to rear any chicks that year but were successful in rearing one female chick in 1999 and another in 2000. It is hoped that these females will return with a male peregrine falcon in subsequent years. The Millbrook Ridge Trail is closed at certain times to protect the falcon's privacy, and before starting out it is advised that you check at the Trapps Entry Visitor Center (see the section introduction) to make sure the trail is open to hikers.

Drive west from the New York State Thruway (I-87) exit 18 through New Paltz on NY 299 to the junction with US 44/NY 55. Turn right, uphill, passing the Trapps Gateway Center on the right (see the section introduction). Continue around the "hairpin bend," driving underneath the Trapps Bridge to the Trapps Bridge entry. This parking area is on the north side of US 44/NY 55 approximately 1 mile from the junction with NY 299.

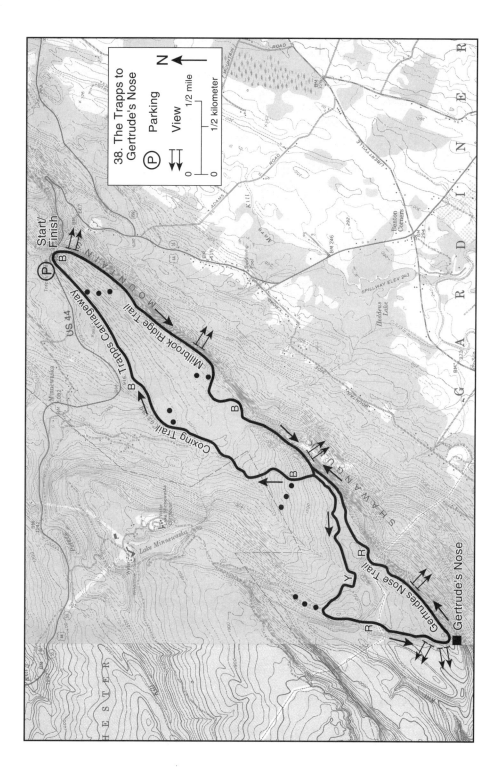

38. The Trapps to Gertrude's Nose

Ⓟ Parking

⬆⬇ View

0   1/2 kilometer

0   1/2 mile

N

Start/Finish

Ⓟ

US 44

Trapps Carriageway

Millbrook Ridge Trail

Coxing Trail

Lake Minnewaska

Gertrudes Nose Trail

Gertrude's Nose

The hike begins on lands that belong to the Mohonk Preserve, using the Millbrook Ridge Trail, which follows the cliff tops southwesterly on a trip that for a non-rock climber is as much of a thrill as the climbers get from these famous cliffs.

Walk to the far (northeast) corner of the parking lot on a shaled path. After 5 minutes ignore the red-blazed Shongum Path leading to Split Rock entering from the left and the entry on the right to US 44/NY 55 through an arch. Porta Potties are available on the left. Climb the steep rock steps to the steel Trapps Bridge, and turn right across it, continuing straight ahead on the Trapps Road. Note that this carriageway is used for the return to your car.

It is the rock and its history that is so impressive. The Shawangunks were formed about 450 million years ago, first as sedimentary deposits worn from an even older mountain range. The sediments that form the shining white conglomerates were once deposited along the shores of an inland sea, whose waters tumbled and smoothed the quartz pebbles that were later embedded in these gleaming white rocks. These sediments were shaped by heat and pressure, faulted and bent, and uplifted about 280 million years ago to form the magnificent cliffs of the Shawangunks' southwestern face, where the horizontal layers of deposits are worn away. The dip to the northwest produces the long slopes so characteristic of the area. The age of the uplift makes the Shawangunks one of the youngest formations in the east.

So let's begin the walk along the straight, thin ridges of the sloping face of the Shawangunks' geological history. Scrub oak and pitch pine are your companions, opening up to offer a series of beautiful vistas along the way.

Approximately 100 yards down Trapps Road from the steel bridge watch for the Millbrook Ridge Trail on the left. The entry is marked with three blue blazes, and the trail immediately climbs steeply on large slabs to arrive at the site of the annual Hawk Watch, organized by the Mohonk Preserve to evaluate the migrating raptors. After about 25 minutes from the car, you deserve to take a break here to look down on the uplifted rocks with the Undercliff Carriage Road behind the climber's parking lot, and backward to Dickie Barre. The roof of the new visitors center peeks out from the trees below to the right.

Almost immediately the cleft in the Shawangunk ridge becomes apparent. The eastern ridge meets the western one near Minnewaska, a resort whose lands once encompassed most of the central Shawangunks. The cliffs and tower of Mohonk—a hotel whose grounds, together with Mohonk Preserve lands, make up the northern Shawangunks—are visible as you climb the trail. These cliffs and Sky Top Tower frame the high peaks of the central Catskill range—a view that reappears many times during this walk.

Follow the blue blazes of the Millbrook Ridge Trail as it undulates along the top of the ridge, alternating between rock slabs and soft pine-needle-covered paths. Ignore the many herd paths going out to viewpoints as the trail descends into a little draw, climbs again—this time more sharply—turns left, and returns to the exposed slopes of the surprisingly narrow ridge. The trail is routed along bare rock as much as possible, minimizing erosion of the fragile crannies of blueberries and laurels, as it zigzags across the ridge to take advantage of the rock walkways and the views. The lack of a defined foot tread means you need to watch carefully for the trail blazes because it's easy to wander off the trail when eyes are diverted to distant views.

Your first objective is Millbrook Mountain, and on the way two red-blazed trails enter from the right. The first one, Bayards Path, appears after about 40 minutes into the hike, and the Millbrook Cross Path comes in after approximately another 40 minutes. Here the Millbrook Ridge Trail makes a 90-degree turn to the left. Here are numerous underfoot examples of glacial erosion where many of the exposed surfaces of the pebbles in the slabs have been smoothed down.

A section of tall trees with few views is followed by a deeper valley. Climbing again with Millbrook Mountain looming ahead like the Rock of Gibraltar, the trail passes a big rock slab, cantilevered to create a shelter. Then after walking through another protected area of large hemlocks and over a stream, scramble left up rocks to circle to the edge of the cliffs once more. The Millbrook Mountain Trail traverses a hog's back 1,200 feet above the Coxing Kill Valley to the right and the Wallkill Valley to the left. Reddens Lake, whose position marks your progress through this part of the walk, is seen below. The view south down the Hudson Highlands reveals Breakneck Ridge and Storm King, and toward the north the Catskills are framed by the cliffs just scaled. Observe how the Minnewaska Ridge to the northwest grows closer as it connects with the Trapps Ridge you're traversing. Their joint thrust forms the prong of Gertrude's Nose, your ultimate destination.

Close to the high point that is Millbrook Mountain, observe the three red blazes on a rock and a sign announcing the entry of the Millbrook Mountain Trail on the right. Note this junction very well because this trail will be your route back. Coming from Millbrook Mountain, the sign is easily missed because on the return journey it faces away from you. Within a couple of minutes three blue blazes indicate the end of the Millbrook

Ridge Trail, and other blazes draw attention to the beginning of the red-blazed Gertrude's Nose Trail. The loop of the Millbrook Carriageway is visible down to the right. Be cautious because it's easy to confuse one red-blazed trail with the other.

The Millbrook Ridge Trail is 3 miles in length, and after about 2 hours you arrive at Millbrook Mountain—an excellent place for a prolonged stop. Take care as you peer over the edge to get a better glimpse of the talus below.

With your back to the view, walk down the slabs to the loop of the Millbrook Carriageway, and turn left. It's easy walking, a bit dull, but the quickest way to make a loop walk around Gertrude's Nose. The carriage roads are the marvel of Mohonk and Minnewaska—miles and miles of graded pathways that today make for superb walking. They all are paved with the Martinsburg shale, a 2,000-foot layer of which underlies the Shawangunks. The shale weathers to a dense but surprisingly soft and smooth walking surface. Except on the trails, the shale is unnoticeable, for it is almost everywhere, topped with the white icing of the conglomerate. You may encounter mountain bikers along this road. The yellow diamond markers are for cross-country skiers in the winter. After a gentle downhill, the Millbrook Carriageway makes a determined bend to the right before ascending slightly and then resuming its downhill trend. It takes just more than 30 minutes to cover the 1 mile to the signed intersection of the Gertrude's Nose Trail, blazed in red which leaves the carriage road on the left. Yellow flags also draw attention to the trail as well as two red blazes on a rock.

Follow the Gertrude's Nose Trail as it descends toward Palmaghatt Ravine, the deep cleft between the trail you are following and the Hamilton Point Road. The ravine

The Millbrook Ridge Trail

was once the site of a "salted" gold mine scam, which deceived several investors nearly a century ago.

For a time the trail is along the edge of hemlock-covered ledges, sometimes on the white sloping slabs of the cliff tops, yielding views ahead to Gertrude's Nose. In places the trail is routed into the woods away from the cliff edge to protect the islands of fragile plants growing on the rock slabs. After a 20-minute walk, the trail descends steeply through deep and shady hemlock woods to an opening under a power line, then crosses a little stream where there's almost always cool, refreshing water (but remember to always treat water before drinking). This part of the trail is badly eroded, and there are plans to reroute it. Highbush blueberries can be found in abundance by the stream in season.

Head out to the white slabs, and stop to admire some of the glacial-erratic boulders

that dot the cliff tops. Observe also the deep clefts that fissure the cliffs, created as the soft shale foundations weathered and became displaced. Admire the wind-sculpted rock wonders as you walk the 40 minutes it may take to cover the mile from the carriage road to the Nose. Here the evidence of another geological force is clear: the glaciers that once covered the Shawangunks to a depth of 4,000 to 5,000 feet. As the ice mass moved along the northwestern slopes, the rocks it pushed along scraped the conglomerate, leaving striations—long, thin scratch marks—that can be seen occasionally. The smooth polish of many surfaces is also the work of the glaciers, achieved as the ice mass moved over a layer of mud.

Pause at the promontory of Gertrude's Nose for another break, and enjoy the views to the east. Take note of two new signs along the way, emphasizing that the area is ecologically sensitive and requesting that walkers remain on the marked trail and tread only on bare rock surfaces. Look around and wonder at the large tumbled rocks, the many cracks and crevices, free-standing boulders, and smooth slabs that make Gertrude's Nose such a special place.

Gertrude's Nose is the main focus of this hike, so after lingering a while, begin the return journey by continuing to follow the red blazes around the point to the left along the ridge. The route is close enough to the escarpment edge to give several good views east and north and even on toward Millbrook Mountain. In little more than 30 minutes the trail again crosses on rocks underneath the power lines. Just as the trail begins to climb after the power lines, look for a herd path to the right that will take you to a deep hole in the rocks. Stand here for a few moments to feel the cold air escaping upward before returning to the trail, which now climbs along ledges amid stunted trees and rocks that form a landscape reminiscent of windswept tropical islands.

As you approach Millbrook Mountain the trail is routed quite close to the Millbrook Carriageway, seen below to the left.

From Millbrook Mountain find the blue blazes that led you here earlier, and follow them for a short distance to the junction with the Millbrook Mountain Trail. Remember to watch carefully for the sign, and head downhill following red blazes on a rocky path for about 5 minutes to the junction with the Coxing Trail. This junction has a sign and three blue blazes. Leave the red-blazed Millbrook Mountain Trail, and turn right onto the Coxing Trail, following it downhill at first on slabs and then through hemlocks and laurel. Walking here is very different from the preceding ridge traverse and is a peaceful end to an exhilarating outing. After strolling through a wet area, watch for an attractive spring to the west (left) of the trail.

The spring, bordered and protected by a rock wall, is called the James Van Leuven Spring, after one of the early settlers of the land. Old maps dated 1865 indicate that part of the Coxing Trail was once a public road and that the James Van Leuven cabin was probably located on the hump above the spring. There appears to have been no cellar, so probably the house was a log cabin.

Cross the outlet of the spring on stepping-stones and the subsequent swampy area on planks. The Coxing Trail becomes wider, and the rock walls that can be seen show where the land was once cleared and farmed. There are muddy sections. Blazes are few, but the area is quiet and serene and the footway easily followed. This old road you are following runs parallel to the Millbrook Ridge Trail and passes by the two red-blazed connectors seen earlier, the Millbrook Cross Trail and the Bayards Trail.

Walking the Coxing Trail takes about an hour before the Trapps Road is reached. Turn right, and be aware that mountain bikers use the Trapps Road. After a while you may notice traffic on NY 44/55 down to the left. Pass the entry point of the Millbrook Ridge Trail used earlier to arrive at the steel bridge from which you wend your way back to your car.

SJG

39

Trapps Gateway Center Loop

Total distance: 5.75 miles

Walking time: 2.5 hours

Vertical rise: 500 feet

Maps: USGS 7.5' Gardiner; USGS 7.5' Mohonk Lake; NY–NJTC Northern Shawangunk Trails #10; Mohonk Preserve Trail Map Southern Section

The hike begins from the newly constructed Trapps Gateway Center of the Mohonk Preserve (see section introduction).

Most of this hike is mellow, with almost unnoticeable elevation gain while on the carriage roads, but it starts out with a short, sharp ascent using the same route for the return journey. The two carriage roads used, Undercliff and Overcliff, loop around spectacular cliffs of Shawangunk Conglomerate and offer views to the south from the Undercliff carriage road, and less obstructed views to the north from the Overcliff carriage road. Undercliff was built in 1903 by the Mohonk Mountain House and is part of the carriage-road system linking the lands of the Mohonk Preserve, the Mountain House, and Minnewaska State Park Preserve. This particular carriageway is remarkable because of its route across the boulder rubble at the base of the Trapps.

The southern aspects of the cliffs are world famous for their rock-climbing reputation. The rock resembles that in the Dolomites, and the Gunks were allegedly discovered as a rock-climbing area in the 1930s by Fritz Wiessner (see section introduction). Climbing the cliffs remains popular to this day, and while walking you'll probably see climbers above you—fascinating to watch. Every route up the cliffs is named and allocated a number indicating its degree of difficulty.

Walk up the rock steps from the preserve parking lot to the Trapps Gateway Center, turn left in front of the main door,

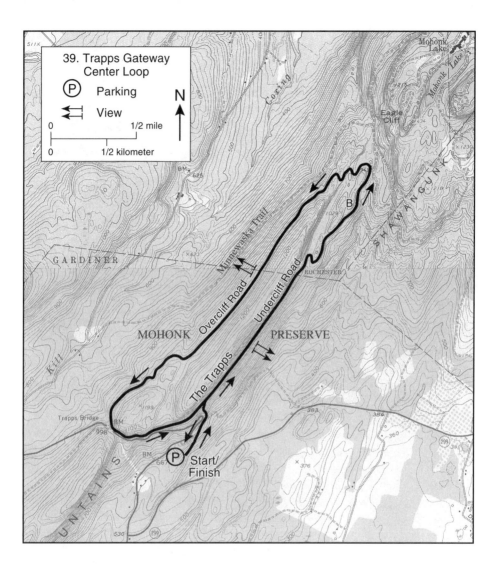

and walk straight ahead to a sign: EAST TRAPPS CONNECTOR TRAIL. The trail emerges onto the overflow parking lot and continues for a short distance down the gravel service road before turning left steeply uphill into the woods. Turn right when the trail emerges onto a private road, and walk to the end of the small parking lot. Note the cautionary sign ROUGH PATH AHEAD, and walk up the wooden staircase on the left. The

trail is unmarked but easy to follow on 240 well-constructed rock steps. It crosses a pseudowooden bridge and flattens out for a while immediately below the hairpin turn on the auto road. The trail turns left partway up to continue beneath a rock cliff, then makes a couple of turns between boulders before emerging in about 15 minutes onto the Undercliff Carriage Road. The climb is a little more than 300 feet vertical gain.

Near the steel bridge in Mohonk Preserve

Turn right onto Undercliff Carriage Road. Look around so that on your return you'll recognize the turn down to your car. (There is a sign, but if you should overlook it, you may walk the circuit forever.) Be aware that bicycles are permitted on these carriage roads. The yellow-blazed trails you may notice that leave the carriage road to the left are access routes for climbers. This carriage road, completed by the Smileys in 1903, follows the cliff line. We are constantly amazed to think of the energy expended by the workers who built such a substantial road with only hand tools.

The tower seen on the cliffs is Sky Top on the grounds of the Mohonk Mountain House. The sign for the Sleepy Hollow Trail remains on the left just before the Undercliff Carriage Road begins the first curve of an S bend. The Sleepy Hollow Trail was recently closed and will probably remain so because it traversed a very swampy area used for

breeding by a rare salamander. You then arrive at Rhododendron Bridge, where several carriage roads converge in an H formation. Walking from the upper end of the East Trapps Connector Trail to Rhododendron Bridge takes about 40 minutes on a very slightly uphill gradient.

Neither cross Rhododendron Bridge nor go straight ahead on Laurel Ledge Carriage Road, but turn left onto Overcliff Carriage Road. (For a short distance Laurel Ledge can be seen below, and the short connector trail soon joins Overcliff Carriage Road from the right.)

The northern end of the Sleepy Hollow Trail connects here from the left just as the Overcliff Carriage Road makes a nearly 180-degree turn to the right. Look up now to the right as the road climbs gently up through a notch to the splendid cliffs decorated with pitch pine. The views from the Overcliff Carriage Road are more open than those from the Undercliff Carriage Road.

There are many fine slabs enhanced with sparse foliage on both sides. The Coxing Valley is underneath, with Dickie Barr and Lost City on the horizon.

Overcliff Carriage Road curves more than Undercliff Carriage Road and imperceptibly climbs and dips once before it reaches the junction with the Undercliff Carriage Road. Trapps Bridge to your right, which crosses over US 44/NY 55, is commonly called "the steel bridge" because it's the only carriage road bridge converted from wood to steel. An honesty box is placed at the kiosk, as well as a box containing cards for a raffle drawn at the end of every month—the prize is an annual membership to the Mohonk Preserve.

Walking from Rhododendron Bridge takes almost an hour.

Turn left onto Undercliff Carriage Road between two massive boulders. You pass another kiosk within 10 minutes from the steel bridge and a Porta Potti just a few minutes later. Watch now for the sign for the East Trapps Connector Trail, and walk back down to your car. In wet weather these rock steps may be slippery.

The Mohonk Preserve has constructed several nature and sensory trails below the Trapps Gateway Center that would be a pleasant addition to the walk you have just completed. An interpretive brochure is available from the visitors center.

SJG

40

Duck Pond Scramble in Mohonk

Total distance: 7 miles

Walking time: 4 hours

Vertical rise: 1,000 feet

Maps: USGS 7.5' Mohonk Lake; NY–NJTC Shawangunk Trails #10 and #10A; "A Hiker's Map of the Mohonk Lake Region in the Shawangunk Mountains" (Mohonk Mountain House Map available at the Gatehouse); Mohonk Preserve Trail Map (Northern Section)

This hike begins on land owned by the Mohonk Preserve and continues onto Mohonk Mountain House property (see section introduction). Highlights of this hike are a lake and a high point visible from miles away. It also includes some simple walking on carriage roads and some serious rock scrambling requiring the use of hands as well as feet to negotiate large boulders. Such scrambling might be unsuitable for those with acrophobia.

Sometimes the maze of carriage roads is confusing, and it's often useful to consult both the New York–New Jersey Trail Conference maps and one of the preserve maps.

Exit the New York State Thruway (I-87) at exit 18, New Paltz. Drive west on NY 299 through town, and cross the Wallkill River on a green-steel bridge. Proceed along NY 299 for approximately 1.25 miles from the bridge, and turn right onto Gatehouse Road. Bear right, and avoid the gatehouse entry road. Within 0.7 mile from NY 299 a T junction is reached with a directional sign for Mohonk. Turn right onto Butterfield Road, then almost immediately left onto Pine Road, and drive 0.8 mile toward Sky Top, now looming immediately above you. Continue straight ahead past a private house on the right, cross a bridge, and climb on a dirt road to a small parking area with space for five or six cars. Please do not trespass on the private road ahead nor block the gate.

Walk left through a gate, continuing on the dirt road you've just driven. In a tunnel just above this road to the right is the

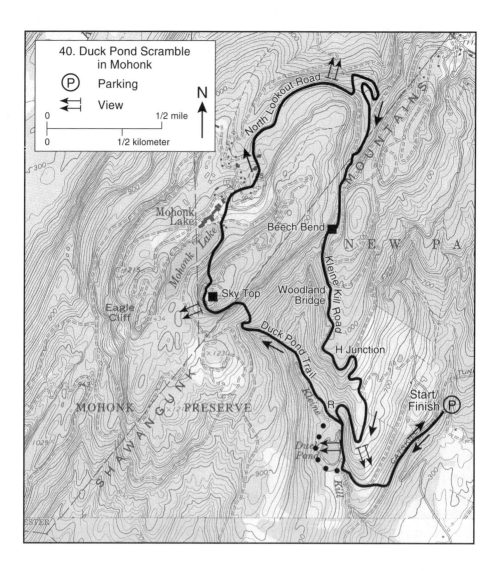

40. Duck Pond Scramble
in Mohonk

P   Parking

    View

N

0   1/2 mile

0   1/2 kilometer

Catskills–New York Aqueduct. Within a few minutes our route takes us up a ramp onto the aqueduct itself. The road ahead is Lenape Lane. Cross over, and turn left onto the aqueduct through a gate. Leave the aqueduct after 6 minutes of brisk walking, turning right onto the Glory Hill Trail marked with three blue markers on a tree to the left of the trail. Follow blue blazes looking down onto the aqueduct, and make a right turn

within 2 or 3 minutes, climbing slightly and emerging onto an old woods road, where the trail makes a left turn through a wire-cabled gate. Continue to follow the blue blazes uphill, ignoring the woods road entering on the right, until you reach Duck Pond. Originally called Kleinekill Lake, Duck Pond was constructed in 1908. There are views of Sky Top across Duck Pond, and a couple of benches to rest if needed. If you are fortunate you may glimpse the huge snapping turtle that lives in Duck Pond. A nature trail has been created around the north side of Duck Pond, but our route skirts the right-hand side past the Kleine Kill Farm Road entering on the right.

After about 17 minutes from the beginning of the hike, watch on the left for the beginning of the Duck Pond Trail marked in red. Take this trail, and walk slightly downhill to a plank bridge crossing a marsh. (The planks to the left are those that connect with the Nature Trail and should not be taken.) Your route now roughly follows the Kleine Kill, eventually climbing above it on a rocky trail before emerging onto Oakwood Drive with a sign indicating you have just left Mohonk Preserve property. The Duck Pond Trail crosses straight over Oakwood Drive and continues to climb more steeply up to a summerhouse on Forest Drive.

With your back to the summerhouse look slightly left for a red arrow on a rock indicating the beginning of the Birchen Trail. This arrow may be a little confusing because it points in both directions. Follow the red markers to the right, mostly on rocks rather than on trees, to the base of the cliff where there's a wooden sign indicating that the Birchen Trail turns left and that you have come from Forest Drive. Walking time so far is approximately 40 minutes.

Turn left onto the Birchen Trail (the trail to the right is the closed portion of the Birchen Trail). Scramble now over and under large boulders—there is a ladder to help climbers over a particularly difficult spot. About 15 minutes into this adventure, ignore a trail entering from the left. Continue toward the Crevice. As you approach, the markers indicate a route up and over a large boulder that hikers with short legs might find difficult to negotiate. There's another route to be found by climbing toward the

left and back to the right behind the obstacle. At this point the Spring Trail down to the Mohonk Spring enters from the left, and there is a good view of Eagle Cliff.

The Crevice is a deep, narrow cleft naturally formed when the cliff beneath Sky Top split. The footing is rough, and sometimes slippery, but clambering through is a real adventure, though not meant for the fainthearted. It takes about 10 minutes to negotiate the Crevice and a few minutes for your eyes to become accustomed to the low light. The first aid to the climb is another ladder, the second a staircase that may be more easily negotiated without your day pack. (Push it ahead or drag it behind.) The last narrow scramble is up onto a large open rock slab. Stop to wonder how Victorian women in long skirts managed to clamber through this passage and to admire the view. Once you have taken a breath, face the view and move right to cross a small bridge, and immediately on your right climb up a crack in the cliff to emerge on another viewpoint that looks down onto the slab you have just left. Look to the left from this vantage point, climb a few rocks to a staircase, and emerge onto Sky Top Carriage Road with the Smiley tower above. This viewpoint is dedicated to the poet John Greenleaf Whittier. Turn right onto the carriage road, take the herd path to the left, and jog a little more to the left to find the tower entrance.

The Albert K. Smiley Memorial Tower was "erected in grateful memory of a man whose exalted character and useful life stand as a beautiful example to mankind." Albert Smiley lived to be 84 years old, and the cornerstone for the tower was laid nine years after his death in 1912. Climb the 102 steps to the top of the tower to admire the 360- degree view that includes Duck Pond, Lake Mohonk and the Mountain

Mohonk Mountain House from Sky Top Path

Stella Green

House, the Sky Top Reservoir just below, the Catskills in the background, and, on a clear day, parts of six states. From this vantage point we once saw an eagle fly by. The elevation of the tower is 1,542 feet, and most of your climbing for the day is now behind you. This stone tower is the third to be built on what was once called Paltz Point. The previous towers were made of wood and were used for fire spotting.

With your back to the tower entrance turn right toward a bulletin board to find Sky Top Path immediately on your left, starting downhill on about a dozen rock steps and a few wooden ones to Sky Top Carriage Road. (This carriage road encircles the top of the mountain.) From here Sky Top Path switchbacks downhill, and within a couple of minutes the rough path to the Labyrinth, Spring Path, and Lake Shore Road enters from the left. Continue straight ahead, admiring the views of Mohonk Mountain

House as you walk. On the way, several attractive summerhouses are passed, and by taking a short side trail on the left via a wooden staircase and rock slabs, extra-special views may be obtained. Continue downhill on Sky Top Path, ignoring the Reservoir Trail that leaves to the right. The children's playground and the green-roofed conference center are also on the right as you reach the flat ground by the lake in front of the Mohonk Mountain House. Day hikers are not permitted inside the hotel, but the gardens to the right are delightful to explore at any time of the year.

Take the Grove Path to the left behind the putting green and toward the greenhouse. In a few minutes the paved entry road is crossed, signs to the Fern and the Mossy Brook Trails can be seen, and the greenhouse is visible. Turning left, leave the greenhouse on your right, and then turn right to the Picnic Lodge, also known as the

Day Visitor Center. The Picnic Lodge is open at certain times in both winter and summer, often selling beverages and lunch items.

Face the Picnic Lodge, and look for a shaled path going off to the left, indicating a route to North Lookout Road and the Gatehouse. Almost immediately a right turn takes you past the side of the Picnic Lodge and a sign behind the lodge indicates WALKERS TO THE GATE with an arrow. When this small path reaches the North Lookout Carriage Road, continue by walking at the base of a stupendous cliff. Hemlock Lane leaves the North Lookout Carriage Road to the right within about 0.75 mile. North Lookout Carriage Road is built on a cliff line with tremendous views of the Devil's Path, traversing Hunter, Plateau, Sugarloaf, Twin, and Indian Head Mountains in the Catskills. Here the North Lookout summerhouse provides a wonderful rest spot. Continuing along North Lookout Carriage Road for about 5 minutes, watch carefully to the left to find a sign for Rock Rift Crevices. You are now reentering Mohonk Preserve lands. Rock Rift Path, marked with red blazes, switchbacks left, right, then left again, descending steeply. Five minutes' descent brings you out on Rock Rift Road. Walk straight across to Rock Rift Crevices, signed as a rock scramble.

Rock Rift is blazed with red paint and is entered on the right. The first obstacle is encountered at the beginning: a hemlock growing in the crevice that must be pushed past, making the hiker wonder how soon this tree may completely block the route. After one small ladder the adventurer imagines he is finished, but there's more as the blazes lead right and you reenter the rock fissures, requiring scrambling and crawling. As you walk, notice the malformed roots and tree branches as they struggle toward the light. One tree in particular has been contorted almost into a circle. Water runs into the crevice just before the end, sometimes gathering on the floor. The whole trip probably takes about 30 minutes. Turn right when you emerge into the open, and walk down to Old Glen Anna Carriage Road. Just facing you is a beautiful tributary that eventually runs into Mossy Brook. Turn right onto Old Glen Anna Carriage Road, walking slightly uphill to the junction with Bonticou Road. At this junction admire the extensive rock wall supporting the carriage road.

Turn right onto Bonticou Road. Within a couple of minutes look for a sign, and turn left onto North Lookout Road (there is a bike route at this junction on the right). Walking is hard for a few minutes because large lumps of shale have been deposited in an effort to improve the surface.

Continue ahead on the North Lookout Carriage Road to arrive in a few minutes at a junction for the Whitney Road returning to the Gatehouse and a path to the right for the Picnic Lodge. (Here is another boundary between the Mohonk Preserve and the Mohonk Mountain House.) North Lookout Carriage Road makes a 180-degree bend to the right called Beech Bend, and at just past the 90-degree mark the Glen Anna Path (not to be confused with Old Glen Anna Carriage Road) heads southwest. The Glen Anna Path is quite short, ends in a staircase, and emerges onto the paved auto road between the Gatehouse and the Mountain House.

Cross straight over the paved road, ignoring Huguenot Drive to the right, and turn left to Woodland Bridge, where there are two carriage roads. Take the closest one called Bridge Road toward Rock Spring Bridge and Forest Drive. The DO NOT ENTER signs at Woodland Bridge are for motorists, not pedestrians. Forest Drive is reached within 5 minutes (Rock Spring Bridge is off to the right). Watch your trail maps here, and be careful to walk left onto Forest Drive to make the right turn onto Kleine Kill Road, which begins the descent needed to reach your car.

Shortly a complicated H-formation junction with Oakwood Drive is reached. Bear right and then left onto Duck Pond Road. Duck Pond Road descends and makes a determined bend to the right, giving great views of the valley through the trees. The road swings back to the left with views of the Gatehouse passed earlier and Humpo Marsh on US 44/NY 55 that was not seen on the drive in.

Down to the left Duck Pond can be seen. Pass by the red Duck Pond Trail used earlier, and walk down Kleine Kill Farm Road, leaving Duck Pond on the right and following the blue-blazed trail used before. Don't forget that after the cable gate the trail moves off the woods road and makes a sharp right turn into the woods. Remember also that when you come to the metal gate, you need to cross over the aqueduct and bear right, then left to reach your car.

SJG

VI. The North Country

Introducing the North Country

A term usually more aptly applied to New York's great Adirondack Forest Preserve, we use the term as a catchall for those hikes that don't quite fit any of the other sections in this book. Our "north country" is a large geographic expanse that includes some state parks, small semipublic preserves, a historic site, a very remote ridge, and a taste of the wilderness of the Catskill Forest Preserve.

These ten hikes provide genuine diversity: the widest geographic expanse, the most remote peak, the highest summit, the most spectacular gorge, and the "top" ridge walk.

We hope they just whet your appetite for the many additional offerings available "up north."

41

Mills-Norrie State Parks

Total distance: 5 miles

Walking time: 3 hours

Vertical rise: Minimal

Maps: Available from Taconic State Park Region Headquarters, Mills-Norrie State Parks, Staatsburg; USGS 7.5' Hyde Park

The east shore of the Hudson River between New York and Albany was settled by holders of large patents and purchases. Portions of a few of these magnificent holdings survive as modern parks. In the mid-Hudson Valley, the most beautiful of these parks are the great homes and estates built in the 19th century. Some, like the Vanderbilt Mansion and the Mills Estate, were the homes of industrial and financial leaders of the time. Clermont, the home of many generations of Livingstons—a family that includes notable statesmen—dates to the 18th century. Frederic Edwin Church, the Hudson River School painter, designed the grounds of his Persian-influenced castle, Olana, to frame the vistas of the distant Catskills.

Each of these parks has walks laid out by the original owners. Most walks are short and take the hiker through manicured grounds. The walks along the Hudson at the Mills-Norrie State Parks are special: They are longer, offering a half day of outdoor activity, and a portion go directly along the river because the railroad, which closely follows the eastern shore through most of the valley, lies inland here.

The Mills Estate was built by a great-great-granddaughter of Robert R. Livingston, Ruth Livingston Mills, and her husband, Ogden Mills, a wealthy financier. The Greek-Revival mansion, which was designed by the firm of McKim, Mead, and White, was completed in 1896. The Louis XV and Louis XVI rooms were richly furnished with art from Europe, ancient Greece, and the Orient.

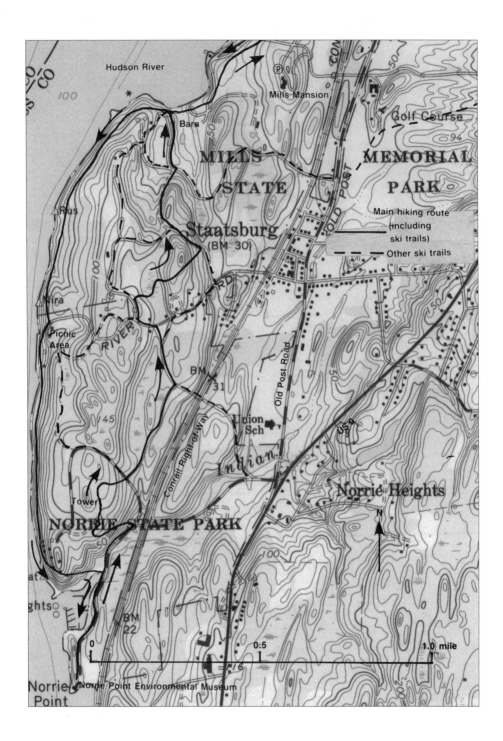

Hudson River

Mills Mansion

Golf Course

94

MILLS

STATE

MEMORIAL

PARK

Barn

50

Rus

Staatsburg
(BM 30)

Main hiking route
(including
ski trails)

Other ski trails

Nina

RD

50

Picnic
Area

RIVER

BM
31

45

Conrail Right-of-Way

Old Post Road

Union
Sch

US 9

Indian

Norrie Heights

Tower

N

NORRIE STATE PARK

100

at

50

ghts

100

200

BM
22

0   0.5   1.0 mile

1 / 6

Norrie
Point

Norrie Point Environmental Museum

Maple-bordered roadways at the beginning of the Mills Estate walk

Barbara McMartin

The estate's formal sweep of lawn and its tree-covered roadway offer a charming beginning to the trails that lead south to the adjacent Margaret Lewis Norrie State Park. To reach the Mills Estate, turn onto Old Post Road, which loops west from US 9 around the village of Staatsburg. You'll want to stop at the park offices in the mansion and get a map, although the ski-touring map available there does not show the shore-hugging route that's the centerpiece of this walk. You can follow its red-, blue-, and green-marked trails on your own.

Walk west from the estate on the blue-marked trail, following the roadway toward the waterfront boathouse, enjoying views of the Catskills on the way. The boathouse, architecturally interesting in itself, is a barrel-vaulted stone structure. The roadway curves around the cove beyond; watch for the white-marked trail that forks right to

hug the shoreline. Along it, hemlocks shade the small shale cliffs bordering the river with its shingle beach. The narrow trail follows the top of moss-covered ledges while you have lovely views of water and gnarled cedars. Only an occasional old stone wall will make you believe that this land has ever been disturbed by humans.

A 40-minute walk brings you to a picnic area, which also can be reached by a roadway from Norrie State Park. The white-marked route continues on the far (south) side of the parking area but farther inland, leading through a camping area to a roadway. Follow that roadway out until it intersects another park road, not far from the railroad. South on the park road, in about an hour's total walk, you reach the Dutchess Community College's Norrie Point Environmental Center, open Saturdays from 11 AM to 5 PM and Sundays from 1 PM to 5 PM.

You may want to see its exhibits of the plants and animals of this portion of the Hudson shoreline.

As you return north along the road, watch for an underpass below the railroad. Opposite, a red post along the road alerts you to an abandoned roadway that serves as one of the park's unmarked trails. Follow this road to the left as it curves back and then almost disappears on the summit of a small hill with a stone water tower. There are a multitude of such walkways in the park, some of which shortly will be marked as nature trails.

Following the roadway, you intersect one of the park roads (blue marked) that has been identified as a ski-touring route. Your route back north to the Mills Estate can take any one of the intersecting segments of the ski trails, most of which follow abandoned roadways, but for now follow the blue-marked trail to a T intersection, where you turn left on the red-marked trail.

Your detour through the woods takes you past a marsh, through beautiful forests, and to a memorial pylon noting that this land was given to the people of Staatsburg in memory of Lewis Gordon Norrie, 1901–1923. Just beyond the pylon turn left, following the ski-touring signs. As the park map indicates, these trails all lead back to the large barn near the point where the white-marked trail headed along the shore. To extend your walk, you may wish to choose different segments of the loop; they are clearly marked and easy to follow. A most delightful way to end the day is with a picnic on the lawn in front of the mansion.

BMcM

42

Black Creek Forest Preserve

Total distance: 2.5 miles

Walking time: 1 hour

Vertical rise: 300 feet

Maps: USGS 7.5' Hyde Park; Black Creek Forest Preserve Trail Map

The nonprofit organization Scenic Hudson was formed in 1963 to spearhead and coordinate environmental organizations to fight the plan by Consolidated Edison to build a stored energy facility on Storm King Mountain. The Con Ed scheme included the building of a large reservoir within Black Rock Forest, a pumping station at the base of the mountain, and tall transmission towers crossing the Hudson River into Putnam County. Controversy continued for 17 years until the utility company, under unrelenting pressure, dropped its plans for the project. Since that date, Scenic Hudson has been responsible for the protection of many thousands of acres in the Hudson Valley. The Black Creek Forest Preserve is just one of these areas.

Although comparatively short in a park that is relatively small, the hike described has much of interest. The breeze from the Hudson and the tree canopy on a hot summer's day when energy levels are low is very welcome. Prior land use by man is evident along the way, mostly in the form of stone walls. The trails to be used are the Black Creek, the Vernal Pool, the Hudson River Trails, and the Old Farm Road.

Drive north on US 9W, 5.5 miles from the intersection with NY 299. Turn right at a large sign WINDING BROOK ACRES ON THE HUDSON (Hudson River Front Efficiency Cottages) and a small sign BLACK CREEK ROAD. The Black Creek Forest Preserve bulletin board can be seen from this junction when leaves are down from the trees. Drive down the short distance to the bulletin board, and park.

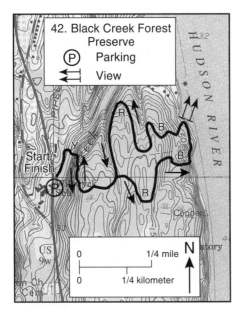

42. Black Creek Forest Preserve

Ⓟ Parking

⇄ View

0 — 1/4 mile
0 — 1/4 kilometer

N

Alternatively, from the Port Ewen traffic light in the center of town, head south on US 9W, pass the Shaupeneak Ridge Cooperative Recreation Area on the right, and after 6.1 miles turn left into the Black Creek Forest Preserve at the signs indicated above.

With your back to the bulletin board, walk down the gravel path and across the black-topped road to find the three yellow Scenic Hudson markers on a tree opposite. Continue gently downhill toward the Black Creek on a dirt path over a small wood bridge. Within 2 minutes walk across the huge 120-foot suspension bridge built by Scenic Hudson in 1999 for walkers to cross the Black Creek.

Black Creek gets its name from the dark color of its water caused by tannic acid from hemlocks. The creek flows north for almost 20 miles from its source at Sunset Lake, passing through Chodikee Lake on its way to the Hudson River.

On the other side of the bridge the Black

Creek Trail, marked in yellow, starts immediately uphill, bearing right through a mixed forest. Switchbacks are in place, as are rock and wood steps that prevent erosion and ease the steep ascent of some 160 feet. The 5- or 6-minute climb brings you to an interesting kiosk, where exhibits are changed periodically. The bench provided at this location is one made in several different designs scattered along the trails provided by Scenic Hudson.

The marked trail now turns left, and although the footway may not have had sufficient use to make it distinct, logs have been placed to both sides of the path to indicate the route. Within 10 minutes the trail passes the first vernal pool, known as Hemlock Pool, over to the right. The trail bears left across a footbridge over a small stream and almost immediately reaches the junction with the red-blazed Vernal Pool Trail. Turn right at the sign indicating the way to the Hudson River, and note that the route back is along the road ahead.

In this section, at about 25 minutes into the hike, several vernal pools appear. The trail then turns left along the side of a stone wall, still in excellent condition, swings through a gap in the wall, and parallels its right-hand side. When you arrive at the sign indicating that the Red/Blue Crossover Trail turns left, follow the red markers and turn right onto the Hudson River Trail. Walk steeply downhill following blue blazes, catching an occasional glimpse of the Hudson River through the trees. Just as the trail starts to climb after a sharp descent, look for logs marking the side of the trail, and turn left up a herd path to a (winter) viewpoint—a pleasant place for a short break.

Continue downhill, curving toward the water and walking below the recent rock overlook to reach the river level after 35 minutes walking. Jog down to the river at

Pitch Pine Overlook on the Hudson River

the first reasonable place. At low tide here it is possible to explore and to examine the crumbling slate rocks. The trail parallels the river, passing a bench on the right-hand side, and within a few minutes brings the walker to another pleasant resting spot with an attractive pitch pine growing on the water's edge. Ahead is private property, with a small swimming beach not open to the public. Across the river are the Mills-Norrie State Parks (Hike 41).

Leave this pleasant spot and begin the climb back, at first within sight of the way down but later bending farther from the river. Honor the signs indicating that the herd paths on the right are private, and continue walking the switchbacks to the junction with the Red/Blue Crossover Trail. Turn right onto the Vernal Pool Trail marked in red. A few minutes from the junction, stop to admire an imaginative piece of trail work: a large flat slab of rock, crossing what would be a stream after rainfall. The trail crests and continues through a group of tall red pines with the river and the private home visible to the right.

Fifteen minutes from the river, the trail passes a deep pit with an old piece of machinery sitting on the lip. Walk left down to Old Farm Road, and again turn left. A gate to the right indicates private property, and ahead, when the leaves are off the trees, can be seen a swampy area and the Black Creek. Old Farm Road, now to be followed, has a slightly uphill gradient with an interesting raised wood erection on the right, assumed to be a high-water route.

Within 25 minutes the Vernal Pool Trail enters on the left. You may recognize this junction as the one you did not take when you passed this way earlier. Continue straight ahead on the yellow-marked Black Creek Trail, and retrace your footsteps to the car.

SJG

43

Shaupeneak Ridge

Total distance: 5.25 miles

Walking time: 2.5 hours

Vertical rise: 1,350 feet

Maps: USGS 7.5' Hyde Park; USGS 7.5' Rosendale; Shaupeneak Ridge Trail Map

The Shaupeneak Ridge is an area administered jointly by the Scenic Hudson Land Trust and the New York State Department of Environmental Conservation (DEC). Farmers traditionally used this area to cut wood. These old wood lots were assembled by a developer over the years by purchase at tax sales, then bought from the developer at the end of the 1880s when property values fell. The property was acquired by Scenic Hudson, and the tract eventually opened in 1996 as the Shaupeneak Ridge Cooperative Recreation Area.

Shaupeneak Ridge is part of the Marlboro Mountains, a discontinuous ridge extending from Kingston to Marlboro along the western side of the Hudson River. The terrain is quite rugged and includes streams, a waterfall, and a lake, all of which are visited on this hike. The hike includes many short sharp climbs of about 50 feet elevation gain, and it begins and ends with a substantial ascent and descent on the White Trail. The hike described uses the White, Yellow, Violet, Red, and Blue Trails. There are a number of rock walls and old woods roads in the area. It's sometimes easy to be led astray by following one of these woods roads, so watch carefully for marked turns in the trail. If you're walking but not seeing markers, backtrack to the last one seen, and try again.

Bicycle riding is permitted. You may notice an orange-blazed trail at the northwestern end of the tract that has been built by mountain bikers and is mostly used by them. Fishing for pickerel in Louisa Pond re-

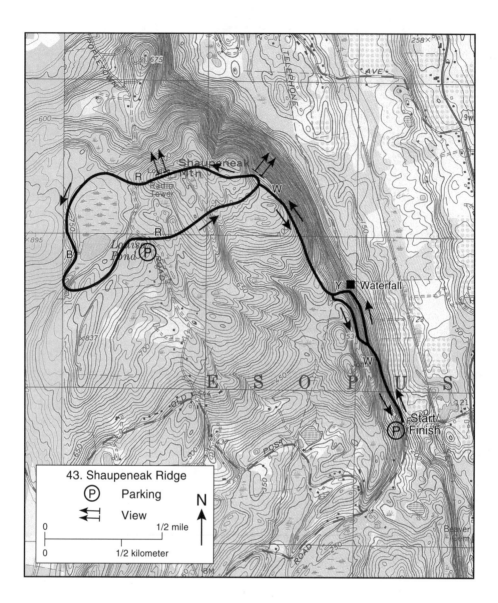

quires a DEC license. Information on obtaining hunting permits is available at the information kiosks.

To reach the starting point, drive north for almost 6 miles on US 9W from the junction with NY 299, or south on US 9W for a similar distance from the traffic light in Port Ewen. Turn west onto County Road 16 (Old Post Road), cross both an active railroad track and a pond fed by a spur of Black Creek, and turn right into the parking provided for visitors to the Shaupeneak Ridge Cooperative Recreation Area.

Walk up the gravel path to the information kiosk, where maps are usually available, and continue walking to the left. The area is open here, with evidence of fill removal at one side. Follow the white disks embossed in black with either the Scenic Hudson or Shaupeneak Ridge Cooperative Recreation Area name. The trail is flat at first, routed along the base of high ground and skirting a private home uphill on the left.

Ten minutes from the car the White Trail bears left and starts uphill. Turn right onto the Yellow Trail that joins the White Trail only a short way ahead, and after a short distance, watch for the junction with the Violet Trail leading to the waterfall. The junction is about 50 yards from where the Yellow Trail starts its steep climb. The waterfall is on an unnamed stream in a mossy grotto and runs except in drought conditions. At the time of this writing a large number of blowdowns are close to the cascades, but these are slated for removal. Purple trillium bloom here in the spring.

The Violet Trail is a spur trail, so stay long enough to enjoy the falls, and then retrace your footsteps to the Yellow Trail and turn right, uphill. The Yellow Trail snakes its way uphill by the side of a pretty stream that cascades down on moss-covered rocks to feed the main falls below. When you reach the junction with the White Trail, turn right, cross the stream, and continue uphill, passing a vernal pool on the right.

The White Trail ends, and the Red Trail begins about 30 minutes' walking from leaving the waterfall. Follow the red markers to the right, perhaps resting awhile at the view of the Hudson River. The castlelike building below is Mount St. Alphonsus, one of the many monasteries in the Hudson Valley.

The Red Trail undulates along the ridge and bypasses private property on the right-hand side until it crosses paved Poppletown Road. Louisa Pond can be seen through the trees to the left. The pond was created in a glacially carved bowl by a com-bination of man-made and beaver-created dams, and on this side it's partly emergent marsh and partly floating bog. The area is sensitive to human intrusion and should not be disturbed.

Cross over Poppletown Road, and continue for a couple of minutes to the end of the Red Trail, where it meets the circular Blue Trail. Follow the Blue Trail to the right. (Take the Blue Trail to the left back to the Louisa Pond parking area if you need to cut short your hike, and follow directions from there.)

The Blue Trail parallels the paved road for a short distance before making a turn to the left away from it on a once-graveled woods road. You may encounter some wet patches here, but the trail soon moves away from the lake through a wonderfully dense hemlock grove—one of the best we have seen recently.

The Blue Trail circles the lake, but this hike only uses about three-quarters of its length. At times the trail rises high above lake level, but eventually it drops down to cross the Louisa Pond outlet on stepping-stones, about 30 minutes after leaving Poppletown Road, close to a large beaver dam. Dutchman's breeches and the white and lavender round-lobed hepatica bloom here in early spring, making a remarkable display of color.

The Blue Trail climbs away from the outlet and continues at first across a pleasant grassy opening before using a gravel path to arrive at the Louisa Pond parking area. There is another information kiosk here, a park sign, and space for about six or seven cars. The two benches provided offer an attractive spot overlooking Louisa Pond for the weary hiker to rest.

Cross over Poppletown Road, and look for the three red markers of the Red Trail that begins with a short eroded ascent fol-

Hepatica

lowed by a comparable descent. The microwave towers visible recently across Louisa Pond are now located on private ground on the left-hand side of the trail. The junction with the White Trail is reached after a 15-minute journey on the Red Trail.

Turn right onto the White Trail, and stay on it all the way back to your car. It takes about 15 minutes to reach and pass the upper junction with the Yellow Trail, and another 5 minutes of steep descent brings you to the lower Yellow Trail junction.

A short distance south on the east side of US 9W is the Black Creek Forest Preserve (Hike 42) that could be successfully combined with this hike if time permits.

SJG

44

Stissing Mountain

Total distance: 4 miles

Walking time: 4 hours

Vertical rise: 950 feet

Maps: USGS 7.5' Pine Plains

Stissing Mountain's long profile so dominates the surrounding flattened fields that it appears taller than its 1,403-foot height would indicate. The fields, remnants of a glacial lake, encircle this Precambrian gneiss, enhancing the mountain's scale. A pair of trails leads to the restored fire-tower summit, making a loop walk possible, although views are limited to openings in the forest cover. A companion walk around Thompson Pond, to the west below the mountain, makes this a lovely, short day's excursion. The pond is part of a kettle lake, formed with Stissing and Mud Ponds to the north by the melting of glacial blocks. Now the resulting bog pond, filling with grasses and cattails, is home to many birds. From the path that winds along its shores, you can not only watch those birds, but you'll also be treated to views of Stissing across the marshes as the mountain rises steeply from the level of the lakebed.

The mountain is unusual in that its Precambrian mass was thrust on much-younger sandstones and shales that form the surrounding valley, completely isolating it from similar landforms that make up the Ramapos and the Hudson Highlands. Its strong profile, which dominates the countryside, is the result of resistance of the Precambrian rocks to erosion.

The pond and 300 acres are managed as a preserve by the Nature Conservancy. The area is home to many mammals, migrating warblers, and marsh birds, plus a rich variety of plants that find their niches in areas as varied as the pond and the adja-

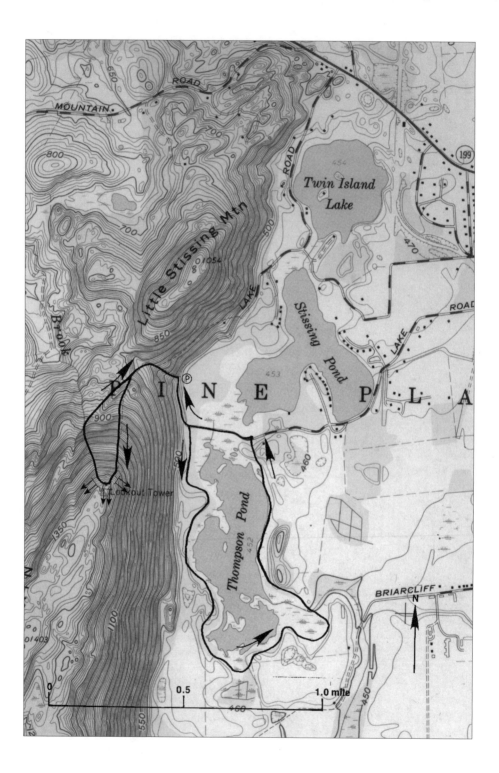

cent wooded slopes of Stissing Mountain.

To reach the trailhead, start at the intersection of NY 82 and NY 199 in Pine Plains, and drive south for 0.4 mile on NY 82. A right turn onto Lake Road takes you out of the village, along a lovely stretch of maple-lined road, and across a causeway, 1.6 miles to the Thompson Pond Sanctuary entrance on the left. The trailhead for Stissing Mountain is unmarked and 0.2 mile farther, near a bend in the road where the shoulder is wide enough for parking.

There is little or no marking of the trail, but it's easy to follow. The 950-foot climb should take you less than 40 minutes. It begins steeply up a narrow path that intersects an abandoned roadway, which you'll meet after a 5-minute climb. Another 5-minute walk brings you to a fork. The way right follows the old roadway and streambed. It's the much more obvious choice. You'll return that way.

Take the left turn up a fairly steep path. Stones heaped beside the trail indicate that this, too, was once a cleared way, but it's now rubble filled and eroded. You can see Stissing Pond occasionally through the scrub oaks and birches, tantalizing glimpses that finally open up, after a 30-minute walk, to reveal the northern hills. The summit is overgrown; however, the views from the fire tower are almost unobstructed. The tower was recently adopted and restored by the Friends of Stissing Landmarks, and now you can climb up.

You are now just above the treeline. From here you will see a spectacular view of the Catskills to the west. Stissing Pond, Twin Island Lake, and Massachusetts are visible to the northeast. Thompson Pond and Connecticut lie to the east. Portions of the southern end of the Shawangunks are visible to the southeast. The foundations of a cabin lie below the tower on the narrow summit ridge.

Walk beside the tower, heading south on a faint path. The descent is simple if you keep bearing right; left always leads to private lands. The first choice of paths is within 100 yards of the tower, and the way right is steeply down to intersect an abandoned roadway in another 100 yards. At this point a right turn continues downhill, following the roadway past some handsome rock ledges. Below the ledges and after another right fork, you can see Little Stissing Mountain through the trees. Thirty-five minutes of walking and a few more right turns bring you back to the fork you passed on the ascent. Retrace your steps for the 10-minute walk to your car, completing the 1.5-mile circuit.

OPTIONS

To add to the excursion, walk along the road to the Thompson Pond Sanctuary entrance. An old road leads you south into the sanctuary, and 200 yards from the road is a registration booth and a map of the sanctuary. You scarcely need a map for the counterclockwise walk around Thompson Pond. There's a short loop to the pond from the registration booth, marked with blue arrows. The main trail around the pond, marked with yellow, continues on an abandoned roadway. The only time you might have trouble is at the far southern end, where the trail leads briefly to a weed-filled field. Head left along the fence, and the way will soon become obvious again. The trail continues near the sanctuary border, heading down into a swamp toward a decrepit boardwalk. The swamp, outlet of Thompson Pond, marks the headwaters of Wappingers Creek. Lovely views of Stissing follow, and then the trail cuts again to the border fence circling around another swampy area, taking you briefly to the edge of a barnyard. The trail then heads back closer to the pond for the rest of the return to Lake Road. An hour or so will take you around the 2.5-mile circuit. With binoculars you'll surely want to take longer. There's also a rich variety of ground cover to examine and a series of framed views of marsh and mountain to enjoy.

BMcM/HNZ

45

A Taste of the Catskills—An Ascent of Slide Mountain

Toal distance: 6.5 miles

Walking time: 5 hours

Vertical rise: 1,800 feet

Maps: USGS 7.5' Shandaken; USGS 7.5' Peekamoose; NY–NJTC Southern Catskill Trails Map #43

This hike in the Catskill Forest Preserve is offered to whet hikers' appetites for more exploration of this much-beloved area. Hiking in the Catskills is much more rugged than in areas farther south, and weather conditions are usually more inclement, so it's important to include additional clothing and extra snacks in your day pack and wear sturdy boots, should you hike there.

The Catskill Park is defined by a "blue line" on official New York State maps and the entire park covers 705,000 acres. Responsibility for the state-owned lands in the Catskill Park is in the hands of the New York State Department of Environmental Conservation (Region 3 telephone: 845-256-3000), and under the State Forest Preserve Act of 1885 it has been designated "forever wild."

Naturalist John Burroughs and painter Thomas Cole among others have made the Catskills the focus of their artistry, and legends such as Washington Irving's story of Rip Van Winkle delight many folk even today.

Walking to the summit of Slide Mountain is very popular, and on fine days the summit can become crowded, so an early start is advised. Ascending by foot to the top of the Catskills' highest peak is most rewarding and leaves the hiker with a great feeling of accomplishment. The view from the top is becoming more limited as the trees grow in, but many other vistas can be seen on the way. It was once claimed that all the other Catskill Mountains higher than 3,500 feet can be seen from viewpoints on or near

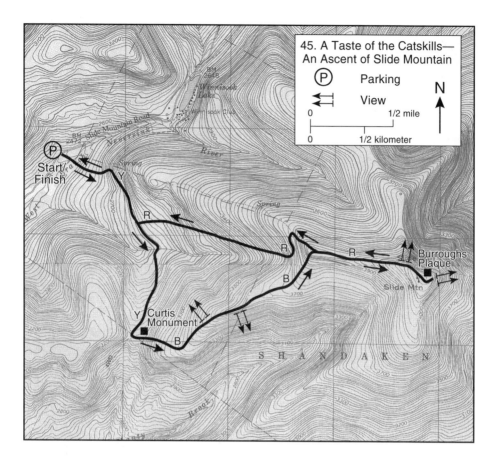

45. A Taste of the Catskills—
An Ascent of Slide Mountain

(P) Parking

View

N

0   1/2 mile

0   1/2 kilometer

Slide Mountain summit. This hike uses part of the Phoenicia–East Branch Trail, it ascends on the Curtis-Ormsbee Trail, and returns on the Wittenberg-Cornell-Slide Trail, also known as the Burroughs Range Trail.

To reach Slide Mountain parking, leave the New York State Thruway (I-87) at exit 19, and head west on NY 28 for approximately 30 miles to the small town of Big Indian. Turn left (south) onto County Road 47 (Slide Mountain Road). The road is winding, so special care should be taken. The drive over the pass begins after 7 miles, at a hairpin bend. Pass Winnisook Lake on the left, and then turn left into the Slide Mountain Trailhead parking lot, 2 miles from

the hairpin bend. The lot contains a nicely maintained outhouse.

Please sign in the register (and sign out when you return). Signing in not only helps to monitor trail use, it could be useful should you have a problem while on the trail.

The Catskill Mountains are our region's most popular backpacking area. However, neither open fires nor camping is permitted above 3,500 feet throughout the year, although camping is allowed above that elevation during winter months from December 21 to March 21.

Your trip begins on the Phoenicia–East Branch Trail marked with Department of Environmental Conservation yellow "foot-trail" disks. The trail is rocky and begins to climb almost immediately, crossing three streams on stepping-stones. After a 360-foot climb, the trail ascends a few wooden steps to emerge onto an old carriage road, a remnant of the time in the 1880s when city folk were transported to the summit as part of a day in the country. Turn right, your direction confirmed by a yellow arrow on a tree immediately facing you. Continue ahead on the Phoenicia–East Branch Trail for 0.7 mile from the parking lot, watching for a piped spring on the left-hand side of the trail, which comes immediately before the red-marked trail that joins from the left. Note this junction because your return route emerges here. Continue straight ahead following yellow blazes toward Denning for another 0.8 mile.

The Phoenicia–East Branch Trail shortly crosses on a three-log bridge over an unnamed feeder tributary of the West Branch of the Neversink River and ascends very gently. In this section the trail is often wet because water from the mountain discharges across the road on its way downhill.

Turn left at the next junction onto the blue-marked Curtis-Ormsbee Trail for the 2.25-mile climb of 1,100 feet to your goal. The stone monument at the side of the trail commemorates William "Father Bill" Curtis, a sports writer and an official of the Fresh Air Club of New York, and Allan Ormsbee, who it is believed were responsible for the route of this trail—one of the most picturesque in the Catskills. They died in a sudden Mount Washington, New Hampshire, snowstorm on June 30, 1900, on their way to an Appalachian Mountain Club meeting at the summit.

This delightful trail soon rises sharply through a section of large rocks and continues to ascend steadily through other rocky

sections of typical Catskill scenery interspersed with flatter sections. On your way up, look for a viewpoint to the left of the trail, and another to the right 4 or 5 minutes after the NO CAMPING sign at the top of a short rock face at 3,500 feet. The 20-yard unmarked trail leads to a grand overlook and is an excellent place to take a break. Immediately ahead is the unmistakable flat top of Table Mountain, Van Wyck Mountain is to the right, Lone Mountain and the smaller bump of Rocky Mountain to the left. Appearances can be deceptive, and strangely enough Rocky's elevation is lower than where you are now standing. Immediately below is the valley of Deer Shanty Brook and over the ridge behind, the valley of the East Branch of the Neversink.

Continue upward through one of the loveliest parts of the trip as the trail proceeds through a quiet and peaceful stand of balsam fir until the junction with the Wittenberg-Cornell-Slide Trail is reached. Your target is very close now, with only 0.65 mile of gentle walking to the summit. On the way a short step to the left offers another tremendous panorama from a rock overlook—one of the best to be seen. Particularly impressive is the view of Panther Mountain and Giant Ledge, apparently only a stone's throw down to the left. Wittenberg and Cornell Mountains are below and beyond, with Hunter Mountain and the Devil's Path to the right, and the Blackhead Range is on the horizon. The Ashokan Reservoir, also visible from this viewpoint, is clearer than from the summit rock. We suggest making the short walk to the actual summit of Slide Mountain and then returning to this viewpoint for an extended break.

At 4,180 feet Slide Mountain is the highest and most prominent peak in the Catskills, its height established in the early

Icicles along the Curtis-Ormsbee Trail

1880s when Arnold Guyot surveyed the area. Now trees partially obscure the view at the summit rock. Most visible is the 12-mile-long Ashokan Reservoir. Completed in 1915, the reservoir displaced several hamlets and farms from the Esopus Valley and was the first in a series of other reservoirs built to supply New York City with water. Amazingly, water is gravity fed down underground tunnels to supply the populated city far to the south.

Between 1927 and 1976, before the no-camping rule was established, a lean-to was in place at the summit, with water available from a spring reached by an unmarked side trail a short way farther down the Wittenberg-Cornell-Slide Trail. If you are short on water and replenish at the spring, be sure to treat it before drinking. Just below the summit slab is a slate plaque erected by the Winnisook Club in 1923, commemorating John Burroughs's work. Slide Mountain was one of Burroughs's favorite places. He visited many times, and one of his most widely read essays is entitled *In the Heart of the Catskill Mountains*. This famous writer, who died in 1921 at the age of 84, had a multifaceted career. A farmer's son, he taught school in his youth, became a journalist in New York City, a treasury clerk in Washington, D.C., and a bank examiner.

When you are finally ready to leave this high point, walk back to the junction with the Curtis-Ormsbee Trail, but now continue straight ahead on the red-marked Wittenberg-Cornell-Slide Trail. Continue downhill about 1.5 miles on this wide and sometimes rocky path until you reach the junction with the Phoenicia–East Branch Trail where you were earlier in the hike. Turn right at this junction, and retrace your footsteps back to your car, taking care not to miss the left turn from the woods road.

Today the Catskill region is increasingly popular for recreational opportunities of many kinds. If after this hike you find yourself interested in scaling the summits of other peaks in the Catskills and need information regarding membership in the Catskill 3500 Club, write to: The Catskill 3500 Club, 755 Anderson Avenue, Apt. 4J, Cliffside Park, NJ 07010. This club was formed in 1962, and regular membership requires climbing all 35 peaks in the Catskills plus an ascent of four specified peaks in winter. Winter membership is granted after the hiker has climbed to the summit and back of all the 35 peaks between December 21 and March 31. Patches and certificates are awarded to successful aspirants; contact www.catskill-3500-club.org.

SJG

46

Olana

Total distance: 7 miles

Walking time: 3 hours

Vertical rise: 300 feet

Maps: Park map available at ticket office at Olana

Just as the romanticism of 19th-century Hudson River School painting is exemplified in the works of Frederic Edwin Church (1826–1900), the belief that nature could be manipulated to express that romanticism is summarized in Church's home, Olana. The Olana State Historic Site near Hudson preserves the grounds that Church designed and the Moorish castle he built that surveys the Catskills and a bend in the Hudson River. Now, a century later, a walk through the grounds and a tour of the castle summarize those romantic notions of nature as eloquently as any river site or any painting.

Olana is on NY 9G, 1 mile south of the entrance to the Rip Van Winkle Bridge between Hudson and Catskill. The park grounds are open year-round from dawn to dusk. Tours of the castle are offered Wednesday through Sunday 10–4 from the first week in April through the last Sunday in October. There is a fee of $3 for the tour, and advance reservation is possible. Group tours are by advance reservation at all times. There are also guided tours of the grounds available outside of the regular tour. Call for information: 518-828-0135.

Frederic Edwin Church studied with Thomas Cole and painted Hudson River and Catskill scenes throughout his career. For two decades he traveled throughout the east coast of the U.S., to Newfoundland, and to South America. In 1867 he and his wife traveled to Europe and the Near East. The Eastern cultures, along with those of Greece and Rome, had profound effects on

The North Country

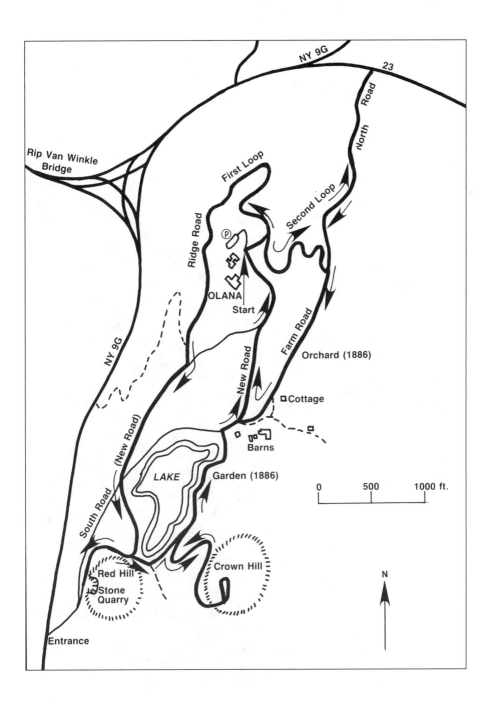

NY 9G

23

Rip Van Winkle
Bridge

North Road

First Loop

Second Loop

Ridge Road

P

OLANA

Start

New Road

Farm Road

Orchard (1886)

NY 9G

Cottage

(New Road)

Barns

South Road

LAKE

Garden (1886)

0   500   1000 ft.

Crown Hill

Red Hill

Stone
Quarry

N

Entrance

A view of Olana, home of Frederick Edwin Church

both travelers. The architectural styles of the ancient and eastern worlds inspired the stone castlelike residence they later named Olana, a Latin interpretation of a Syrian word meaning "our place on high."

Olana sits on a narrow ridge 500 feet above the Hudson, a site that inspired Church to write, "About one hour this side of Albany is the center of the world—I own it." The magnificent trees that now edge the sweeping lawn have grown to full maturity, as have the oaks and maples that shade the carriage roads making up the park's trails. From the castle, the view southwest encompasses the northern escarpment of the Catskills, the bend in the Hudson, and a lake Church had constructed as a necessary artistic counterpoint to complete the dramatic view. The castle's windows were designed to frame portions of that view, enabling its owners to command in nature a view as awe inspiring as Church's painted scenes.

A walk on portions of the 7.5 miles of trails and carriage roads is more of an elegant stroll than a hike, but you can extend it through two lovely loops. A trail enters the woods just below and east of the road to the visitors' parking area. A left fork near the beginning takes you onto Ridge Road, which winds to the north and then below the castle with one vista of the river and the Rip Van Winkle Bridge. Follow Ridge Road, marked with yellow disks, as it circles to the park entrance road (South Road),

which you follow downhill (south) toward the lake. Turn left from South Road along the lake. The first right from this trail leads to the southern park boundary. This route continues on private lands along a very narrow ridge that affords glimpses of the Hudson.

Returning to the lake trail, continue north along the lake, enjoying occasional glimpses of the hilltop castle. The next right turn, red marked, leads to a circle on the summit of Crown Hill, where a cut in the forest reveals the castle again. The entire park is full of such surprising, yet planned, vistas. The lake trail ends at a roadway (marked New Road on the map), along which you can make your way north to the castle.

A second loop also begins near the parking area but goes to the right (south) down through a deep ravine of stately trees to the North Road. Follow this north to the park boundary and back to enjoy more of the noble forest. Retracing the route south to continue on Farm Road, you remain on the ridge overlooking the old orchards. You may wish to turn west from the roads and wind generally west and uphill through the fields toward the castle. If you do, be wary of the poison ivy patches. Near the intersection of the two paved park roads, a pathway circles below the castle and leads gently up to it via a small but charming Victorian garden that's tucked just below the castle garden wall.

BMcM

47

Huntersfield State Forest

Total distance: 4+ miles

Walking time: 2.5 hours

Vertical rise: 1,000 feet

Maps: USGS 7.5' Ashland; NYS DEC Booklet "Mount Pisgah State Forests"

The Huntersfield Reforestation Area is part of the Mount Pisgah State Forest Unit, totaling just less than 4,300 acres. In 1928 the state legislature authorized the Conservation Department (predecessor of today's Department of Environmental Conservation) to buy marginal and abandoned farmland and restore it to productive use. Open areas were replanted with spruce and pine, with more than 600,000 acres eventually purchased. Most of this unit was purchased in the 1930s and is managed for timber production, recreation, wildlife habitat, and watershed protection.

A section of the 330-plus-mile Long Path, a major hiking trail from northern New Jersey that eventually will reach the Adirondacks, traverses the ridges of this area. Huntersfield Mountain, at 3,428 feet, is the highest point on the Long Path outside the Catskill Forest Preserve. If it was only 72 feet higher, it would be a major destination of hikers "bagging" area peaks higher than 3,500 feet. Its lack of those 72 feet virtually ensures that you'll find considerable solitude on your hike.

To reach the trailhead, leave the New York State Thruway (I-87) at exit 21 (Catskill). Follow the signs (left and then soon right) to NY 23 west. Take this highway for 30 miles to Mail Route Road (County Road [CR] 5), just past Ashland. Turn right, and proceed 2.4 miles. Then go left onto CR 10 and quickly right onto Schrader Road. Follow Schrader for 1.3 miles, and then turn right onto Albert Slater Road (also known as Tompkins Road). After

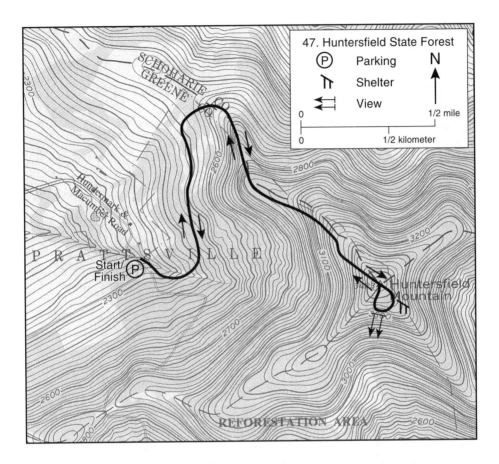

another 1.4 miles, make another right onto Marvin Rion Road (CR 11). Another 0.4 mile brings you to a right turn onto Huntersfield Road (a.k.a. Huntersmark-Macumber Road). Follow this for 1.1 miles (turns to dirt after 0.9 mile), parking on the right at a logging road intersection. Do not block the road or park on private property at the end of the paved road. The dirt road isn't maintained in winter. Total distance from I-87 is 37 miles.

Cross to the left side of the main road, and enter the woods following the turquoise blazes of the Long Path. The trail parallels the stream and is rocky and muddy and not heavily used, so be sure to follow the blazes when a clear footway isn't evident. Ten minutes along the trail joins a major logging road as it travels through a forest of planted pines with a good supply of blackberry bushes thrown in. Note the red clay in the soil. Farming must have indeed been hard in this area.

Be observant of the blazes along the road as the trail turns off to the right in 15 to 20 minutes. The route now becomes steep, but after only 5 minutes it levels off as it joins an older rocky trail. This is the boundary between state and private land with the trail route available with the kind permission of the landowner.

The path now begins a typical Catskill

A view from the loop

ridge walk: stretches of relatively easy walking interspersed with steep climbs onto rock outcrops and ledges. One section, soon after passing the yellow-paint blazes that indicate the state-land boundary, has an obviously cut viewpoint just a few yards off the trail to the right.

Somewhat more than an hour's hiking brings you near to the summit of Huntersfield. Here the state built a yellow-blazed loop trail to several viewpoints and a lean-to. Take the yellow trail right just before reaching the summit (which is marked with a USGS survey marker on a rock). The yellow trail goes steeply down more than 100 feet to a fine viewpoint complete with bench.

The view west is out to the Schoharie Reservoir, a major part of the New York City water supply system. This reservoir, built between 1919 and 1927, forced 350 residents of the community to relocate to Gilboa and neighboring communities. Water from the Schoharie is sent through the Shandaken Tunnel, an 18-mile-long conduit that leads under a mountain to the Esopus Creek and then eastward to the massive Ashokan Reservoir. The combined waters reach the city's distribution system through the 92-mile-long Catskill Aqueduct that consists of deep-rock tunnels, steel pipe siphons, and buried conduits snaking beneath mountains, valleys, and rivers. The aqueduct burrows 1,114 feet beneath the Hudson River between Storm King and Breakneck Mountains near Cornwall. The whole system is certainly an engineering wonder.

Continue along the yellow loop, crossing a service logging road and then steeply up to a lean-to. This hefty structure, complete with fireplace and table, was built in 1999 with labor from residents of a nearby youth correctional facility. The lack of a water source, however, makes it a less-than-ideal camping stop.

The loop continues past another view (again with bench) and circles up to the summit rejoining the Long Path. Cross over the summit, pass the yellow trail's beginning where you first began the loop, and retrace your steps back to your car.

HNZ

48

South Taconic Trail

Total distance: 9.4 miles

Walking time: 7 hours

Vertical rise: 2,000+ feet

Maps: USGS 7.5' Copake (NY/MA), 7.5' Bash Bish Falls, NY–NJTC South Taconic Trails #14

A sentinel line of hills forms the border between New York State and Massachusetts and Connecticut. A 15-mile range trail follows the crest, paralleling the border, much of the time in New York State. This most eastern of New York's great trails is a relative newcomer, built between 1972 and 1976 by Bob Redington and Frank Cary, both residents of Connecticut. This hike takes you on the best portion of that trail system, from the Whitehouse Road in the south to NY 344 in the north. The route encompasses a chain of vantages that will inspire any hiker and make light the rigors of the long walk with its many climbs.

The Taconics are remnants of a thrust mass of mostly unmetamorphosed shales ranging from Cambrian to Middle Ordovician in age. The ancestral Taconics, products of violent upheavals known as the Taconic orogeny, eroded away; sands and gravels from the mountains were washed west into a sea whose waves deposited a thick layer of the quartz-pebble conglomerate; its later upthrust became the Shawangunks. By Late Silurian times only the eroded vestiges of the original Taconic Mountains remained, and fine muds and limestones again accumulated in a shallow sea, forming the bed of Upper Silurian limestone near Pine Plains and beneath Stissing Mountain. From overlooks on the Taconic Ridge, this quiet plain contrasts vividly with the forces that created the mountains on which you'll walk.

Because of the length of the walk and the advantages of staying on the ridge, a two-

Bash Bish Falls

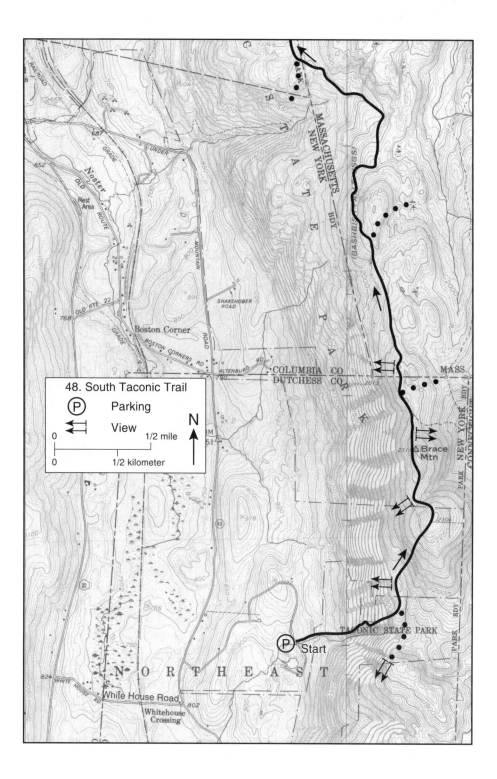

48. South Taconic Trail

Ⓟ Parking

⟵⟵ View

N

0 ──────── 1/2 mile
0 ──────── 1/2 kilometer

Ⓟ Start

RAILROAD

Noster
Rest
Area

OLD ROUTE 22

GRADE

MOUNTAIN ROAD

SHAKSHOBER ROAD

Boston Corner

BOSTON CORNERS RD

ALTENBURG RD

OLD RTE 22

GRADE

COLUMBIA CO
DUTCHESS CO

MASSACHUSETTS
NEW YORK

STATE

PARK

(BASH BISH)

MASS.

△ Brace
Mtn

NEW YORK
CONNECTICUT

PARK BDY

PARK BDY

TACONIC STATE PARK

N O R T H E A S T

White House Road

WHITE HOUSE RD

Whitehouse
Crossing

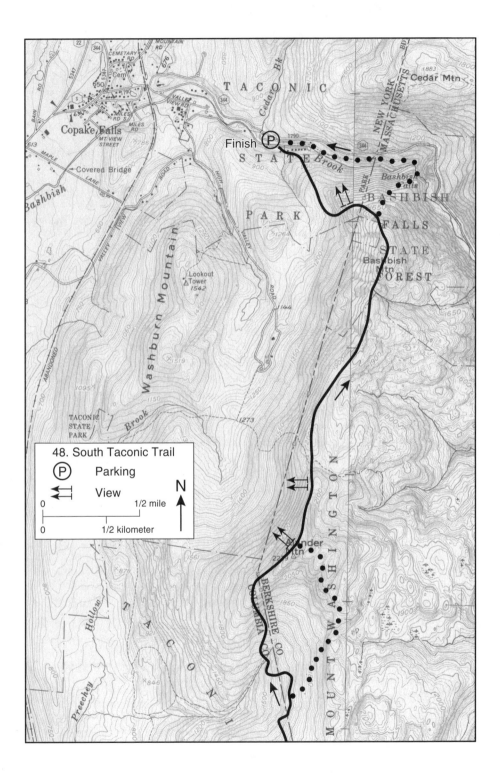

48. South Taconic Trail

Ⓟ Parking

⟵ View

N

0 _____ 1/2 mile

0 _____ 1/2 kilometer

car trip is best. To spot one car at the north, turn east from NY 22 at Copake Falls onto NY 344, and drive through Bash Bish Falls State Park to a parking area on the south side of the road, 1.4 miles from NY 22.

Leave one car, and return in the other to NY 22. Drive south on NY 22 for 7 miles, turn left onto Whitehouse Road, and turn left again in 0.7 mile onto Under Mountain Road. A right turn in 0.3 mile onto Deer Run leads in 0.9 mile to a small parking turnout on the left. Three white blazes denote the southern terminus of the South Taconic Trail, which begins by following the edge of the field. You'll be following these white blazes for the entire hike. The gentle uphill toward the looming mountain quickly ends in 0.4 mile in a scramble beside a small stream. In 0.5 mile the trail reaches a tall but scanty waterfall. The trail then turns and zigzags up the steep face, yielding views along the northern escarpment of the Taconics and south to Stissing Mountain, with the Shawangunks and Beacon beyond.

Within 30 minutes the scrambling ends, and you reach a sign pointing 0.7 mile back the way you just climbed and 1.24 miles ahead to Brace Mountain.

There will be views all day, but from here you can take a short 0.18 mile detour to the right to a lookout. This detour uses a faintly marked (and unmaintained) red trail that leads to private land. If the route is posted against trespass, avoid it.

Continue north on the South Taconic Trail, past a couple of nice openings with pretty views. Then as the trail turns again to the mountain, you climb a pair of ledges to reach South Brace and a vantage point with views south over Riga Lake and South Pond beyond. A 1.4 miles, a turquoise-marked trail forks back to Riga, but this goes over private property and should not be used.

About an hour and a quarter from the start, you reach the summit of South Brace (2,304 feet), with its superb views. Beyond, the summit continues open with small birches and oaks. You drop into a saddle, then climb to a huge cairn monument on the summit of Brace (2,311 feet), from which there is a 360-degree view. From this point, nearly 2 miles from the start, you see Bear Mountain, and the highest summit in Connecticut, to the east; Mount Frissell in Massachusetts is to the northeast. The split summit of Mount Adams is on the horizon ahead.

Continuing north, the trail descends about 350 yards to intersect a woods road. The way right leads into Connecticut; your trail continues north, joining the old, shingle-filled road, which follows along the narrow ridge to a signpost pointing to Mount Frissell and the tristate marker. From this point it is 3.71 miles to Alander Mountain.

Continuing along, you'll pass a red-marked trail, 2 miles from the summit of Brace, denoting a trail joining from Robert Brook to the west. The South Taconic Trail continues for about a 10-minute, 0.5-mile walk to a fork where a blue-marked unmaintained trail turns right toward the summit of Alander Mountain. You can gain the summit by this blue-marked route, but we suggest continuing on the trail you've been following.

Some 0.2 mile later you'll come to an intersection with yet another blue-blazed trail. Make a sharp right, and continue to follow the white blazes as you climb steeply up to the summit of Alander Mountain, again disregarding an additional blue-blazed intersection.

From the summit itself (2,238 feet), you view the hemlock-rimmed valley of Alander Brook. West of the summit there is a point from which the capitol in Albany appears against the skyline—at least on a clear day.

The South Taconic Trail continues north along the precipitous northeast ridge of Alander. The descent is fairly steep as it follows the narrow ridge, crossing to the west to overlook a bucolic scene of farm fields and little ponds.

The path stays high on the ridgeline, descending slightly, occasionally climbing little knobs, punctuated with many lovely view spots. After more than an hour of winding across the ridge, you reach an intersection. Choose carefully here.

We discourage you from taking the right fork, an unmaintained blue trail. If chosen, you'll have to ford (walk across through a foot or more of cold water) Bash Bish Brook, and this is often difficult, sometimes dangerous. If you get to the crossing and change your mind, it's a long steep climb back up to the junction.

The route left on the South Taconic Trail avoids fording the brook. After about 45 minutes it leads you to a bridge over the brook and back to your car. You should not, however, miss seeing Bash Bish Falls. There is a well-signed connecting trail from the parking area, or you can drive east on NY 344, for about a mile, into Massachusetts. There is a parking area on the right and a short path down to the falls.

BMcM/HNZ

49

Vroman's Nose

Total distance: 2 miles

Walking time: 1 hour

Vertical rise: 760 feet

Map: USGS 7.5' Middleburgh

The Nose is a trip you save for a lazy afternoon when you'd rather watch than walk. From this geologically unique cliff, 600 feet above the Schoharie Valley, there are fine views of the lowlands and the long ridge of the northern Catskills.

You won't have to work too hard to visit Vroman's Nose, and the hike itself is very easy. It may be harder to find the trailhead, though the trail itself is well marked. Vroman's Nose is west of Middleburgh, which is about half an hour southwest of the Albany-Schenectady area, at the intersection of NY 30 and NY 145.

Just south of Middleburgh on NY 30, at 0.6 mile on the right, is Middleburgh Road, which runs into West Middleburgh. Vroman's Nose is obvious; its vertical cliffs rise above NY 30 in front of you. The trail starts north of the hill, to your right as you look south at the Nose. Turn right onto Middleburgh Road, and go 0.6 mile to a point where Line Creek crosses the road (the town line between Middleburgh and Fulton). A few hundred feet beyond the bridge, park on your left, where you notice a rough parking area with room for several cars.

A wagon road runs south through a hay field from here, into a forest of large pine and hemlock, turning right as it leaves the field. This trail has recently been improved with water bars and grading. Turquoise Long Path markers appear, but there are no state trail signs, as this is private property belonging to the Vroman's Nose Preservation Corporation (VNPC). The goal of VNPC is to keep the area forever wild and

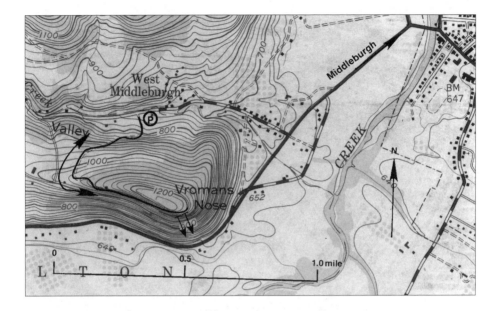

open to the public. The path is self-guiding, and a steady climb over easy terrain (steep in places) takes you through a hardwood forest to the "summit." You actually can cover the distance in 20 minutes, but take your time to enjoy the views of the Catskills that will open up toward the south. The overlook, a long and dangerous cliff, is located approximately 50 feet southeast of the summit, a wooded plateau of roughly 10 acres. The area of flat stone near the precipice is known as the Dance Floor, for dances were actually held there in the early 1900s during Prohibition.

The heavily scored summit of Hamilton sandstone shows evidence of its past in scratches (striae) and chatter marks of an advancing glacier, which moved from the northeast about 50,000 years ago, forming the present topography of the Schoharie Valley. The cliff is heavily engraved with initials and ugly painted graffiti, to such a point that it has had an erosive effect. Several concrete fireplaces have been built to help

prevent the assembling of fire rings by visitors. Fortunately, there is very little litter surrounding the few crude fireplaces people have assembled nearby.

Trees such as oak, hickory, pine, and cedar thrive on the plateau, which is covered in bearberry (called kinnikinnick by Native Americans). The early-spring flower, fringed polygala, also appears.

Dr. Vincent J. Schaefer noted the presence of fossil brachiopods, pelecypods, and trilobites that characterize the Middle Devonian–period thin sheets of Hamilton sandstone. Flagstones from Vroman's Nose were used for sidewalks in cities such as Troy, Albany, and Schenectady. Early in 1942 Dr. Schaefer visited the Nose with an employee of the General Electric Research Laboratory to photograph the testing of artificial fog generators, ultimately used for the screening of ships, personnel, and cities from air attack during World War II. He pointed out a curious atmospheric phenomenon that generates a strong thermal up-

---

Vroman's Nose

Vroman's Nose

draft against the cliff: "The dark-colored rocks of the cliffs of Hamilton shale and sandstone become quite warm whenever the sun is shining on them. This produces a massive upcurrent of heated air. Light objects such as grass, small twigs, and similar objects when thrown away from the cliff edge are carried upward and toward the north."

You may notice birds, notably turkey buzzards, taking advantage of this free ride. This presents an opportunity to get some good pictures of them as they circle lazily with no wing movement.

The long, open fields of farmland to the north, east, and south of Vroman's Nose were settled originally by Native Americans, who left evidence of campfires under its thin soils. It was a Schenectady farmer, Adam Vroman, who established the first farm here in 1713. He was followed by German Palatines who originally settled in the lower Hudson River Valley. Crops common to the valley today are corn and carrots. In the past, hops were grown successfully in the alluvial flats along the Schoharie Creek.

Dr. Schaefer originally conceived of the Long Path in 1931, then planned to cross Vroman's Nose. The path's purpose is the same today as then: to link the outstanding scenic, geologic, prehistoric, and historic features of the area traversed. Dr. Schaefer died in the summer of 1993. He will miss the completion of the Long Path as it forges its way north to the Adirondacks, but his memory is inextricably bound to it and to those who use the trail. The section that crosses the Nose was dedicated in October 1993.

Beginning at the George Washington Bridge in New York City and (ultimately) ending in the northern Adirondacks at Whiteface Mountain, the Long Path comes up from Gilboa, following old roads on the valley's east side. From Keyser Kill Falls, through Panther Creek to Brouck Falls, and into the high country beyond Fultonham and Watsonville, the Long Path follows hill roads near Patria and then descends the ridge to Vroman's Nose. From there it drops down to cross the Schoharie at Middleburgh, goes east through the village, follows a woods road to the top of a rocky cliff east of town, and heads for Dutch Billy's Hill in the Helderbergs.

Although its founders originally intended to construct Adirondack-type lean-to shelters a day's hike apart along the Long Path, these ambitious plans were interrupted by World War II. The Long Path still has its enthusiasts, however, whose mission it is to maintain and continue the trail to its planned destination.

Those who have walked sections of the Long Path may have been frustrated by the sparingly applied turquoise blazes that designate it. Unlike present hiking trails, the trail originally was meant to be unmarked except on topographic maps. "Thus," to quote Dr. Schaefer, "a hiker must know how to read a topographic map. Such a route eliminates most of the difficulties of trail maintenance and marking, overuse, litter, and the host of other problems that are inherent in the present trail systems. The Schoharie Valley and especially the Vroman's Nose area is a perfect example of the Long Path idea."

Looking south, you'll have fine views of Windham High Peak and the Blackhead Range, beyond long esplanades of furrowed ground, a geographical contrast that is as unique as Vroman's Nose itself. (For more information, write to Vroman's Nose Preservation Corporation, 34 Davis Lane, Cobleskill, NY 12043.)

BMcM

50

Thatcher Park and Indian Ladder

Total distance: 0.5 mile

Walking time: 45 minutes

Vertical rise: Insignificant

Map: USGS 7.5' Altamont

Indian Ladder is a short walk, best enjoyed along with a picnic to John Boyd Thatcher State Park and strolls through its lovely grounds, which cap the Helderberg Escarpment. The trail, less than 0.5 mile long, explores one of the state's most striking geological formations; here is a wonderful place to view the accumulations of sand and limestone mud that have been compressed into rock, uplifted, and eroded to form the mountain bastions bordering the plains that much later became the site of the sea of Albany. These light-colored ramparts derive their name from the Dutch *helder*, meaning bright or light, and *berg*, meaning mountain.

The uplift of these mountains in the Early Tertiary period and later glacial actions expose a long segment of the earth's history, so a trip to study these formations makes an informative outing. Combine it with the view from the amphitheater formed by the cliffs or a picnic beneath the shade trees of the Paint Mine or Indian Ladder picnic areas, and you have a day in a pastoral setting unlike any that exists in the lowlands arrayed before you.

This is a nice getaway spot for a lazy summer afternoon when you are not quite up to a strenuous hike. Be warned, though, that weekends here can be very crowded. The park is easily reached from the capital district. Coming west from Albany from NY 20, take NY 146 into Altamont where NY 156 branches to the right. Follow NY 156 to the junction of NY 157 and a sign pointing left to the park, 5 miles distant. There is plenty of parking. You will find good directions to the trailhead, whose starting point is just north of the Indian Ladder picnic area, behind the park's administration building. A comfort station is also located here. With some allowances made for conditions, the Indian Ladder Trail is open from May 1 through November 15. Numerous hiking trails exist south of Route 157, and the entire escarpment can be walked on the informal Cliff Trail, which runs from Hale's Cave Picnic Area to Stone Lot Picnic Area.

Verplanck Colvin, the surveyor who mapped the wilderness areas of northern New York, wrote about the Helderbergs in 1869, shedding some light on the origin of the name Indian Ladder:

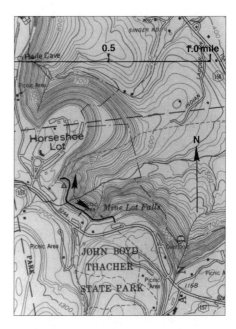

What is this Indian Ladder so often mentioned? In 1710 this Helderberg region was a wilderness; nay all westward of the Hudson River settlement was unknown. Albany was a frontier town, a trading post, a place where annuities were paid, and blankets exchanged with Indians for beaver pelts. From Albany over the sand plains . . . "Schenectada" (pine barrens) of the Indians . . . led an Indian trail westward. Straight as the wild bee or the crow the wild Indian made his course from the white man's settlement to his own home in the beauteous Schoharie Valley. The stern cliffs of these hills opposed his progress; his hatchet fells a tree against them, the stumps of the branches which he trimmed away formed the round of the Indian Ladder.

While it may be that an old Indian Ladder once leaned against this cliff, heavy steel staircases now serve a curious public. This first section of trail follows what was origi-

nally the Indian Ladder Road, constructed in 1828 from Albany and westward into the Schoharie Valley.

The upper layers of rock are the youngest, known to geologists as the Coeymans limestone. That formation takes its name from the nearby town where it is well exposed. Of the two limestone formations in Thatcher Park, the Coeymans (pronounced *kwee-mans*) is the thickest, averaging 50 feet from top to bottom. Look closely here and you may find the preserved remains of small sea creatures. These hard-shelled fossils of *Sieberella Coeymanensis* and other invertebrates date from the Late Silurian and Lower Devonian periods, about 415 million years ago.

Continuing down the trail, you notice thin layers (2 to 3 inches) of alternating light and dark beds of a "ribbon limestone," which is softer than the Coeymans and recedes beneath it as a result of erosion. This is Manlius

---

Thatcher Park and Indian Ladder   275

Indian Ladder Trail

limestone, a formation used extensively in the manufacture of cement at Manlius near Syracuse. Those thin limestone ribbons form a 50-foot-thick layer that also contains the preserved remains of invertebrate sea creatures and algae. Part of the formation also contains a 2- to 3-inch layer of water lime, which has been used for making the Portland cement that will set up underwater. This forms a ledge known in the park as the Upper Bear Path. At the base of the Manlius formation is limey mud rock known as Rondout Formation. It is a water lime that is well exposed near the Ulster County town of Rondout. It was used to produce Rosendale, or natural cement. This formation is less resistant to erosion, though it has eroded back to form the Lower Bear Path, the ledge you are standing on.

The presence of limestones in Thatcher Park and their characteristic ability to dissolve in rainwater has caused such phenomena as disappearing streams, sinkholes, caves, and underground streams. Underground erosion can create caves, which occasionally collapse to form surface depressions called sinkholes. The Karst topography is named after its frequent appearance in the Karst region of the Dalmatian Alps. Nearby Thompson's Lake is a sinkhole, which drains through a subterranean cave at its south end.

Once in the large amphitheater, which is called Indian Ladder Gulf, you will see Outley and Minelot Creeks. Together they have been responsible for the erosion of this impressive embayment. When the water table is high, these two creeks form spectacular falls that you can walk behind on the trail. The talus slope beneath the cliff consists of rock that has been broken off and fallen from the cliff face. Along the Indian Ladder Walk, watch for small limestone-loving ferns, such as cliffbrakes and spleenworts.

The view from the cliff top encompasses the Adirondack foothills, Vermont's Green Mountains, the Berkshires of western Massachusetts, and the Taconics. There are paths at cliff top with views or shaded paths behind that you can follow to extend the 45-minute walk along the Indian Ladder into a fair day's outing.

The park welcomes groups, and facilities include picnic areas with covered pavilions, fireplaces, water fountains, and modern comfort stations. There are also refreshment stands, swimming pools, baseball diamonds, and areas set aside for paddle tennis, handball, and basketball. Pets on leashes are permitted. Rock climbing is not allowed.

Winter activities include cross-country and downhill skiing (no lift), snowshoeing, tobogganing, and snowmobiling. There is a vehicle entrance fee. For information call the John Boyd Thatcher State Park office at 518-872-1237.

BMcM

Glossary

balloon hike: Out and back on the same trails with a loop in the middle.

benchmark: A permanent metal disk at a known elevation used for surveying.

blaze: A trail marking that can be either a painted symbol on a tree, a sign, or a rock cairn.

bushwhack: Walking off trail to reach a goal.

cairn: A pile of stones to indicate a trail junction or the route of a trail.

carriageways: Formerly called carriage roads. Long-established horse and carriage routes. Most often found on old estates.

cart track: A farmer's road used by farm equipment—usually between fields.

col: A pass between two peaks or a gap in a ridge line.

erratic: Large boulder assumed to have been left by a retreating glacier and usually of a different rock type from that in its vicinity.

footway: The surface of a trail.

herd path: An unmarked footway (see *bushwhack*).

lean-to: A three-sided shelter used for overnight stays, sometimes near a water source.

marker: A metal or plastic disk nailed to a tree to indicate the route of a trail.

ravine: A deep narrow cleft in the earth's surface usually caused by runoff.

saddle: A ridge between two peaks.

scree slope: A slope covered with small rocks and gravel that have broken away from the cliffs above.

stile: A structure built over a fence or wall that allows hikers to cross without having to deal with a gate. Common in Great Britain.

stringers/bog bridges/puncheons: Logs laid lengthwise over fragile terrain that is often wet.

switchback: A trail that zigzags on the side of a steep ridge, hill, or mountain, which allows for a more gradual and less strenuous ascent or descent, thus preventing erosion.

talus slope: Talus slopes are more angled than scree slopes. Talus is also larger than scree, and the rocks have sharper edges, all of which makes a talus slope far more dangerous to cross and more difficult to scramble up or down.

thru-hiker: A hiker attempting to hike an entire long-distance trail from end to end in one continuous journey.

trailhead: The beginning/end of a trail.

woods road: Old dirt road formerly used for farming, logging, or mining activities.

vernal pools: Small ponds that form in the spring and that dry up later in the year. Breeding grounds for frogs and salamanders.

Bibliography

Anderson, Scott Edward. *Walks in Nature's Empire: Exploring The Nature Conservancy's Preserves in New York State.* Woodstock, Vt.: Countryman Press, 1995.

Appalachian Trail Guide to New York–New Jersey, 14th edition. Harpers Ferry, W.V.: Appalachian Trail Conference, 1998.

Binnewies, Robert O. *Palisades: 100,000 Acres in 100 Years.* New York: Fordham University Press & Palisades Interstate Park Commission, 2001.

Bird, Christiane. *New York State Handbook*, 2nd edition. Emeryville, Calif.: Moon Handbook/Avalon Travel Publishing, 2000.

Buff, Sheila. *Nature Walks in and around New York City.* Boston: Appalachian Mountain Club Books, 1996.

Burgess, Larry E. *Mohonk, Its People and Spirit: A History of One Hundred Years of Growth and Service*, revised edition. Fleischmanns, N.Y.: Purple Mountain Press, 1993.

_____. *Daniel Smiley of Mohonk: A Naturalist's Life.* Fleischmanns, N.Y.: Purple Mountain Press, 1997.

Clyne, Patricia Edwards. *Caves for Kids in Historic New York.* Monroe, N.Y.: Library Research Associates, reprinted 1992.

_____. *Hudson Valley Tales and Trails.* New York: Overlook Press, reprinted 1997.

Dunwell, Frances. F. *Hudson River Highlands.* New York: Columbia University Press, 1992.

Fagan, Jack. *Scenes and Walks in the Northern Shawangunks*, 2nd edition. Mahwah, N. J.: New York–New Jersey Trail Conference, 1999.

Fried, Marc. *Tales from the Shawangunk Mountains. A Naturalist's Musings–A Bushwhacker's Guide,* revised edition. Geneva, N.Y.: W. F. Humphrey Press, 1981.

_____. *The Huckleberry Pickers. A Raucous History of the Shawangunk Mountains.* Hensonville, N.Y.: Black Dome Press, 1995.

_____. *Shawangunk: Adventure, Exploration, History and Epiphany from a Mountain Wilderness.* Gardiner, N.Y.: M. B. Fried, 1998.

Guide to the Long Path, 5th edition. Mahawah, N.J.: New York–New Jersey Trail Conference, 2002.

Harrison, Marina, with Lucy D. Rosenfeld. *A Walker's Guidebook: Serendipitous Outings near New York City, Including a section for Birders.* New York: Michael Kesend Publishing, 1996.

Henry, Edward G. *Catskill Trails: A Ranger's Guide to the High Peaks. Book One: The Northern Catskills.* Hensonville, N.Y.: Black Dome Press, 2000.

_____. *Catskill Trails: A Ranger's Guide to the High Peaks. Book Two: The Central Catskills.* Hensonville, N.Y.: Black Dome Press, 2000.

Hopkins, E. M. *The Sunk Mine.* May 1887. Copied by Olive Adams, Nelsonville, N.Y., June 1957; papers in the library of the Putnam County Historical Society.

Kiviat, Erik. *The Northern Shawangunks. An Ecological Survey.* New Paltz, N.Y.: Mohonk Preserve, 1988.

Kudish, Michael. *The Catskill Forest: A History.* Fleischmanns, N.Y.: Purple Mountain Press, 2000.

Lenik, Edward J. *Iron Mine Trails.* New York–New Jersey Trail Conference. 1997.

Lewis, Cynthia C., and Thomas J. Lewis. *Best Hikes with Children in the Catskills and Hudson River Valley.* Seattle: Mountaineers Books, 1992.

Myles, William. *Harriman Trails: A Guide and History.* Mahwah, N.J.: New York-New Jersey Trail Conference, 1999.

Mylod, John. *Biography of a River: The People and Legends of the Hudson Valley.* Portland, Ore.: Hawthorne Books, 1969.

New York Walk Book: A Companion to the New Jersey Walk Book, 7th edition. Mahwah, N.J.: New York–New Jersey Trail Conference, 2001.

O'Brien, Raymond J. *American Sublime: Landscape and Scenery in the Lower Hudson Valley.* New York: Columbia University Press, 1981.

Perls, Jeffrey. *Paths along the Hudson: A Guide to Walking and Biking along the River.* Piscataway, N.J.: Rutgers University Press, 1999.

Podskoch, Martin. *Fire Towers of the Catskills: Their History and Lore.* Fleischmanns, N.Y.: Purple Mountain Press, 2000.

Quinn, George V. *The Catskills: A Cross-Country Skiing Guide.* Fleischmanns, N.Y.: Purple Mountain Press, 1997.

Ransom, James M. *Vanishing Ironworks of the Ramapos.* Piscataway, N.J.: Rutgers University Press, 1966.

Stalter, Elizabeth "Perk." *Doodletown: Hiking through History in a Vanished Hamlet on the Hudson.* Bear Mountain, N.Y.: Palisades Interstate Park Commission Press, 1996.

Turco, Peggy. *Walks and Rambles in Dutchess and Putnam Counties: A Guide to Ecology and History in Eastern Hudson Valley Parks.* Woodstock, Vt.: Countryman Press, 1990.

_____. *Walks and Rambles in Westchester and Fairfield Counties: A Nature Lover's Guide to 36 Parks and Sanctuaries.* Woodstock, Vt.: Countryman Press, 1993.

_____. *Walks and Rambles in the Western Hudson Valley: Landscape, Ecology, and Folklore in Orange and Ulster Counties.* Woodstock, Vt.: Countryman Press, 1996.

Van Valkenburgh, Norman J. *The Forest Preserve of New York State in the Adirondack and Catskill Mountains: A Short History,* revised edition. Fleischmanns, N.Y.: Purple Mountain Press, 1996.

Wadsworth, Bruce C. and Bill Rudge. *Guide to Catskill Trails, Volume 8,* revised edition. Lake George, N.Y.: Adirondack Mountain Club, 1998.

Waterman, Laura and Guy. *Forest and Crag: A History of Hiking, Trail Blazing, and Adventure in the Northeast Mountains.* Boston: Appalachian Mountain Club, 1989.

_____. *Backwoods Ethics. Environmental Issues for Hikers and Campers.* 2nd edition. Woodstock, Vt.: Countryman Press, 1993.

_____. *Wilderness Ethics: Preserving the Spirit of Wildness,* 2nd edition. Woodstock, Vt.: Countryman Press, 1993.

_____. *A Fine Kind of Madness: Mountain Adventures Tall and True.* Seattle: Mountaineers Books, 2000.

Weinman, Steve. *A Rock with a View: Trails of the Shawangunk Mountains.* New Paltz, NY: One Black Shoe Productions, 1997.

HIKING MAPS PUBLISHED BY THE NEW YORK–NEW JERSEY TRAIL CONFERENCE:

Catskill Trails, five-map set, 2001

East Hudson Trails, three-map set, 2001

Harriman/Bear Mountain Trails, two-map set, 2001

Hudson Palisades Trails, two-map set, 1991

Shawangunk Trails, four-map set, 2000

South Taconic Trails, 1998

Sterling Forest Trails, 2000

West Hudson Trails, two-map set, 2000

USEFUL ROAD MAPS:

Rand McNally/New York City, Metro Area Counties, Long Island

AAA New York State

Index

T

Taconic State Park Commission, 24, 62
talus, defined, 85
Teatown Lake Reservation (Westchester County), 40–44
Thatcher, John Boyd, 274
Thatcher Park (North Country), 274–277
Thiells (NY), 117, 126, 131
Thompson Pond Sanctuary, 249
timber harvesting, 97, 100
Timp Mountain (Harriman State Park), 56, 144–147
Tors, High and Low, The (Rockland County), 109–111
trail erosion, 20
Trapps Gateway Center, 199, 216
Trapps Gateway Center Loop, 222–225
Trapps to Gertrude's Nose, the, 216–221
trestles, railroad, 175–176

U

Undercliff Loop (East Hudson Highlands), 69–73

V

Van Cortlandt, Stephanus, 50
Van Leuven, James, 221
Vanderbilt Mansion, 235
Verkeerder Kill Falls Loop (Shawangunks, the), 205–209
vernal pools, 20, 30, 240
vertical rise, defined, 20
Vroman, Adam, 273
Vroman's Nose (North Country), 270–273

W

Wallace, DeWitt, 74, 155
Wappingers Falls (NY), 74
Ward, William Lukens, 31
Ward Pound Ridge Reservation (Westchester County), 31–35
Warren's Sugar House (Teatown Lake Reservation), 43
Washington, George, 64

water supply, 18–19, 96, 97, 205, 220, 255
waterfalls, 116, 163, 198, 208, 210, 245
Wayne, Gen. "Mad Anthony," 140
weather, hiking and, 17–18, 19
weirs, 48
Welch, Maj. William A., 103, 125, 138
West Hudson Hills
    about, 154–156
    Black Rock Forest–Northern Loop, 186–190
    Black Rock Forest–Southern Loop, 191–195
    Indian Hill Loop, 167–171
    Mount Peter to Arden on the Appalachian Trail, 161–166
    Schunemunk, summit of, 172–176
    Schunemunk Loop, 177–180
    Sterling Ridge to the Fire Tower, 157–160
    Storm King Mountain, 181–185
West Point Foundry, 62, 133
West Point (NY), 60, 64, 70, 74, 82
Westchester County
    about, 26
    Anthony's Nose, 55–59
    Blue Mountain Reservation, 50–54
    Camp Smith Trail, 55–59
    Leatherman's Cave, 31–35
    Mianus River Gorge, 27–30
    Old Croton Aqueduct State Historic Park, 45–49
    Rockefeller State Park Preserve, 36–38
    Teatown Lake Reservation, 40–44
    Ward Pound Ridge, 31–35
White Plains (NY), 36
Whittier, John Greenleaf, 228
Wiessner, Fritz, 198, 222
wildflowers, 40, 92, 108, 245, 271
wildlife, 90, 97, 138, 247
Willis, Nathaniel Parker, 182
woolly adelgid, 20, 29, 159
Wurtsboro (NY), 201

Z

zoos, 148